OXFORD AND ITS STO[

BY

CECIL HEADLAM

PREFACE

THE Story of Oxford touches the History of England, social and political, mental and architectural, at so many points, that it is impossible to deal with it fully even in so large a volume as the present.

Even as it is, I have been unavoidably compelled to save space by omitting much that I had written and practically all my references and acknowledgments. Yet, where one has gathered so much honey from other men's flowers not to acknowledge the debt in detail appears discourteous and ungrateful; and not to give chapter and verse jars also upon the historical conscience. I can only say that, very gratefully, *J'ai pris mon bien où je l'ai trouvé*, whether in the forty odd volumes of the Oxford Historical Society, the twenty volumes of the College Histories, the accurate and erudite monographs of Dr Rashdall ("Mediæval Universities") and Sir Henry Maxwell Lyte ("History of the University of Oxford to the year 1530") or innumerable other works. Where so much has been so well done by others in the way of dealing with periods and sections of my whole subject, my chief business has been to read, mark, digest, and then to arrange my story. But to do that thoroughly has been no light task. Whether it be well done or ill-done, the story now told has the great merit of providing an occasion, excuse was never needed, for the display of Mr Herbert Railton's art.

OXFORD & ITS STORY

CHAPTER I

S. FRIDESWIDE AND THE CATHEDRAL

"He that hath Oxford seen, for beauty, grace
And healthiness, ne'er saw a better place.
If God Himself on earth abode would make
He Oxford, sure, would for His dwelling take."
Dan Rogers,
Clerk to the Council of Queen Elizabeth.

"Vetera   majestas   quædam   et   (ut   sic   dixerim)   religio   commendat."
Quintilian.

IT is with cities as with men. The manner of our meeting some men, and the moment, impress them upon our minds beyond the ordinary. And the chance of our approach to a city is full also of significance. London approached by the Thames on an ocean-going steamer is resonant of the romance of commerce, and the smoke-haze from her factories hangs about her like folds of the imperial purple. But approach her by rail and it is a tale of mean streets that you read, a tale made yet more sad by the sight of the pale, drawn faces of her street-bred people. Calcutta is the London of the East, but Venice, whether you view her first from the sea, enthroned on the Adriatic, or step at dawn from the train into the silent gondola, is always different yet ever the same, the Enchanted City, Queen of the Seas. And many other ports there are which live in the memory by virtue of the beauty of the approach to them: Lisbon, with the scar of her earthquake across her face, looking upon the full broad tide of the Tagus, from the vantage ground of her seven hills; Cadiz, lying in the sea like a silver cup embossed with a thousand watch towers; Naples, the Siren City; Sidney and Constantinople; Hong-Kong and, above all, Rio de Janeiro. But among inland towns I know none that can surpass Oxford in the beauty of its approach.

Beautiful as youth and venerable as age, she lies in a purple cup of the low hills, and the water-meads of Isis and the gentle slopes beyond are besprent with her grey "steeple towers, and spires whose silent finger points to heaven." And all around her the country is a harmony in green—the deep, cool greens of the lush grass, the green of famous woods, the soft, juicy landscapes of the Thames Valley.

You may approach Oxford in summer by road, or rail, or river. Most wise and most fortunate perhaps is he who can obtain his first view of Oxford from Headington Hill, her Fiesole. From Headington has been quarried much of the stone of which the buildings of Oxford, and especially her colleges, have been constructed.

Oxford owes much of her beauty to the humidity of the atmosphere, for the Thames Valley is generally humid, and when the floods are out, and that is not seldom, Oxford rises from the flooded meadows like some superb Venice of the North, centred in a vast lagoon. And just as the beauty of Venice is the beauty of coloured marbles blending with the ever-changing colour of water and water-laden air, so, to a large extent, the beauty of Oxford is due to this soft stone of Headington, which blends with the soft humid atmosphere in ever fresh and tender harmonies, in ever-changing tones of purple and grey. By virtue of its fortunate softness this stone ages with remarkable rapidity, flakes off and grows discoloured, and soon lends to quite new buildings a deceptive but charming appearance of antiquity.

Arriving, then, at the top of Headington Hill, let the traveller turn aside, and, pausing awhile by "Joe Pullen's" tree, gaze down at the beautiful city which lies at his feet. Her sombre domes, her dreaming spires rise above the tinted haze, which hangs about her like a delicate drapery and hides from the traveller's gaze the grey walls and purple shadows, the groves and cloisters of Academe. For a moment he will summon up remembrance of things past; he will fancy that so, and from this spot, many a mediæval student, hurrying to learn from the lips of some famous scholar, first beheld the scene of his future studies; this, he will remember, is the Oxford of the Reformation, where, as has been said,[1] the old world and the new lingered longest in each other's arms, like mother and child, so much alike and yet so different; the Oxford also of the Catholic reaction, where the young Elizabethan Revivalists wandered by the Isis and Cherwell framing schemes for the restoration of religion and the deliverance of the fair Mary; the loyal and chivalrous Oxford of the Caroline period, the nursery of knights and gentlemen, when camp and court and cloister were combined within her walls; the Oxford of the eighteenth century, still mindful of the King over the water, and still keeping alive in an age of materialism and infidelity some sparks of that loftier and more generous sentiment which ever clings to a falling cause.

It is the Oxford, again, of the Tory and High Churchman of the old school; the home of the scholar and the gentleman, the Wellesleys, the Cannings, the Grenvilles and the Stanleys. But the Wesleys call her Alma Mater also, and, not less, Newman. Methodism equally with the High Church movement originated here. Old as the nation, yet ever new, with all the vitality of each generation's youth reacting on the sober wisdom of its predecessor, Oxford has passed through all these and many other stages of history, and the phases of her past existence have left their marks upon her, in thought, in architecture and in tradition. To connect events with the traces they have left, to illustrate the buildings of Oxford by her history, and her history by her buildings, has been the ideal which I have set before myself in this book. Let our traveller then at length descend the hill and passing over Magdalen Bridge, beneath the grey tower of ever-changing beauty, the bell-tower of Magdalen, enter upon the "stream-like windings of that glorious street," the High.

So, over Shotover, down a horse path through the thick forest the bands of mediæval scholars used to come at the beginning of each term, and wend their way across the moor to the east gate of the city. There is no gate to stop you now, no ford, no challenge of sentinels on the walls. The bell-towers of S. Frideswide and Osney have long been levelled to the dust, but the bells of Christ Church and Magdalen greet you.

But not altogether unfortunate, though perhaps with less time to ruminate, will he be who first approaches Oxford by means of the railway. If he is wise, he will choose at Paddington a seat on the off side of the carriage, facing the engine. After leaving Radley the train runs past low-lying water-meadows, willow-laden, yellow with buttercups, purple with clover and the exquisite fritillary, and passing the reservoir ere it runs into the station, which occupies the site of Osney Abbey, it gives the observant traveller a splendid view of the town; of Tom Tower, close at hand, and Merton Tower; of the spires of the Cathedral and S. Aldate's; of S. Mary's and All Saints'; of Radcliffe's Dome and the dainty Tower of Magdalen further away; of Lincoln Spire and S. Michael's Tower, and of S. Martin's at Carfax. And at last, very near at hand, the old fragment of the Castle:

"There, watching high the least alarms,
The rough, rude fortress gleams afar
Like some bold veteran, grey in arms
And marked with many a seamy scar."

Of the approaches to Oxford so much may be said; and as to the time when it is most fit to visit her, all times are good. But best of all are the summer months. In the spring or early summer, when the nightingales are singing in Magdalen walks and the wild flowers

spring in Bagley Woods, when the meadows are carpeted with purple and gold:

"The frail, white-leaved anemony,
Dark blue-bells drenched with dews of summer eves,
And purple orchises with spotted leaves;"

in June, in Eights' Week, when the University is bravely ploughing its way through a storm of gaiety and athleticism into the inevitable maelstrom of examinations, when the streets are crowded with cricketers, oarsmen, and their sisters, when the Schools and College quads are transformed into ball-rooms and many a boat lingers onward dreamily in the golden light of the setting sun beneath the willows that fringe the Cherwell—at these times Oxford seems an enchanted city, a land where it is always afternoon. But you will come to know her best, and to love her perhaps more dearly, if you choose the later summer months, the Long Vacation. Then all the rich meadow-lands that surround her are most tranquil, green and mellow, and seem to reflect the peace of the ancient city, freed for a while from the turmoil of University life. Then perhaps you will best realise the two-sided character of this Janus-City. For there are two Oxfords in one, as our story will show, upon the banks of the Isis—a great county town besides a great University. And as to the mood in which you shall visit her, who shall dictate a mood in a place so various? Something of the emotion that Wordsworth felt may be yours:

"I could not print
Ground where the grass had yielded to the steps
Of generations of illustrious men
Unmoved. I could not always pass
Through the same gateways, sleep where they had slept,
Wake where they waked, range that inclosure old,
That garden of great intellects, undisturbed;"

or something of the charming fancifulness of Charles Lamb which may lead you to play the student, or fetch up past opportunities, and so "pass for nothing short of a Seraphic Doctor." Or it may please you best to spend not all your time among the bricks and stone and mortar, ever-changing as they are in hue and aspect, or amid the College groves and gardens, rich as is their beauty, perfect as is their repose. The glories of the surrounding country may tempt you most. You may wander many happy miles through cool green country, full of dark-leaved elms and furzy dingles, with the calm, bright river ever peeping at you through gaps in woods and hedges, to Godstow, where Rosamund Clifford lived and died; to Cumnor, the warm green-muffled Cumnor Hills, and those oaks that grow thereby, on which the eyes of Amy Robsart may have rested. You may choose to track the shy Thames shore

"through the Wytham flats,
Red loosestrife and blond meadow-sweet among,
And darting swallows and light water-gnats—"

and, with the poet, learn to know the Fyfield tree, the wood which hides the daffodil:

"What white, what purple fritillaries
The grassy harvest of the river-fields,
Above by Ensham, down by Sandford, yields,
And what sedged brooks are Thames's tributaries."

Whichever way you choose you will turn now and again to look back upon the spires and towers of Oxford and Radcliffe's dome, clustering together among rich gardens and noble trees, watered by the winding, willow-fringed Cherwell and the silver stream of Isis, "rivulets," as

Wood quaintly phrases it, "which seem to the prying spectator as so many snakes sporting themselves therein." And so gazing you will let your fancy roam and think of her past history and her future influence on thought and the affairs of State.

Within fifty years of their first landing the Northern hordes had conquered the greater part of Britain. Mercia, the border kingdom of the marches, had been formed, embracing the site of Oxford; its heathen King Penda had lived and died, the Mercians had embraced Christianity, and Dorchester had become the seat of a Christian bishop. But it was not till the eighth century A.D. that the vill of Oxford, an unfortified border town on the confines of the kingdoms of Mercia and Wessex, came into existence; it was not till the year 727, one hundred and thirty years after S. Augustine's mission to England, that a religious community settled there. The history of that settlement is bound up with the story of S. Frideswide—Fritheswithe, "the Bond of Peace." For although the details of the legend are evidently in part due to the imagination of the monastic chroniclers, yet there is no reason to doubt the main facts of time and place.

That Frideswide, the daughter of an under-king named Didan, founded a nunnery at a spot where a bank of gravel ran up from what is now Christ Church Meadow, and offered a dry site, raised above the wandering, unbarred streams, set amid lush meadows untainted as yet by human dwellings, and fringed by the virgin forests that clad the surrounding hills, we need not hesitate to believe, or that here Didan presently built a little church, some traces of which yet remain in Christ Church Cathedral. For the rest, how Frideswide escaped by a miracle to Binsey and lived there in the woods, in dread of the hot courtship of a young and spritely prince; how that prince was miraculously deprived of his sight when about to assault the city in revenge for his disappointment, and how from that time forward disaster dogged the footsteps of any king who entered Oxford; how the virgin Frideswide returned at last to Oxford, and, after performing many miracles there, died and was buried in her church—are not all these things told at length in the charming prose of Anthony Wood? The Lady Chapel of the Cathedral, on the north side of the choir aisle, is the architectural illustration of this story in Oxford. It was enlarged in the thirteenth century, and has the early English pillars and vaulting of that period, but the eastern wall carries us back to S. Frideswide's day. And on the floor is a recent brass which marks the spot where the bones of the virgin Saint are now supposed to rest. Here too is the Shrine of S. Frideswide—that shrine which used to be visited twice a year by the Vice-Chancellor and the principal members of the University in solemn procession "to pray, preach and offer oblations at her shrine in the Mother Church of University and town." This is the site of S. Frideswide's first church. The Lady Chapel is in a line with what was the ancient nave, the central apse of that church, and there, at the east end of it and of the adjoining aisle, are the rough rag-stone arches which were built for her, and which led, according to the ancient Eastern plan, into three apses. And inseparably connected with S. Frideswide too is the adjacent Latin Chapel, by virtue of that window designed by Sir E. Burne-Jones, one of the earliest and one of the most beautiful of the artist's designs, so lovely in its conception that, if you take each picture separately, it seems like some perfect poem by Rossetti translated into colour by a mediæval craftsman. But take it as a whole and the effect is quite other than this. It is so full of subjects and dabs of bright colour that it is dazzling and almost unintelligible.

Burne-Jones had not grasped, even if he had studied the glazier's art. Apart from the fact that the great predominance of fiery reds offends the eye, the design is essentially one that has been made on paper and not in glass, drawn with pencil and brush and not in lead. Worked out on a flat, opaque surface the fussy effect of the window would not be foreseen; but the overcrowded and broken character of the design is painfully obvious when set up as a window. The scenes here depicted form an illustrated history of the story of S. Frideswide.

The splendid fourteenth-century glass of the Latin Chapel contains also, besides figures of S. Catherine, the patroness of students in divinity, two representations of S. Frideswide. This chapel was built on to the rest at two periods; the first bay from the west is part of the transept aisle, the second bay belongs to the thirteenth century, the third and fourth were added in the fourteenth, from which period the decorated vaulting, with its bosses of roses and water-lilies, dates. The chapel was used till recently as a lecture-room by the Regius Professor of Divinity. The carved wood-work of the stalls and desks should be noticed.

Didan's or S. Frideswide's Church was burnt on S. Brice's Day, 1002, when the general massacre of Danes, which Æthelred the Unready, in a fit of misguided energy, had ordered to take place on that day throughout the country, was carried out at Oxford. The Danes in their extremity rushed to S. Frideswide's Church, burst open the doors, and held the tower as a fortress against their assailants. The citizens failed to drive them out. As a last resource they set fire to the wooden roof and burned the church, "together with the ornaments and books thereof." The Danes perished in the burning.

Nothing now remains, save the parts that I have mentioned, of the church which was then gutted. But after the massacre the King made a vow that he would rebuild S. Frideswide's, and the church he then began to erect forms the main part of the Cathedral as we see it to-day.

Those arches, so plain and massive, over the western bays of the north choir aisle and Lady Chapel, were part of Æthelred's transept aisle; the south transept aisle, now S. Lucy's Chapel; the walls of the south choir aisle; the pillars of the choir and the open triforium of the south transept—these are the chief portions of the Cathedral which are thought to be unrestored parts of Æthelred's work.

It is now generally admitted that the Saxons, at the date of the Conquest, were more advanced than the Normans in the fine arts. Their sculpture was more highly finished and their masonry more finely jointed. We need not therefore be surprised at the excellence and ornamentation of the work in Oxford Cathedral, which is attributed to this date, nor, when we remember that Æthelred was the brother-in-law of Richard-le-bon, the great church-builder of Normandy, need we wonder at the unwonted magnificence of Æthelred's plans for this church.

The Danes soon took ample revenge for that treacherous massacre. They ravaged Berkshire and burned Oxford (1009). The climax came when Sweyn arrived. The town immediately submitted to him, and "he compelled the men of Oxford and Winchester to obey his laws" (Saxon Chronicle).

Æthelred's work was interrupted by the coming of Sweyn, and the King's flight to Richard's court in Normandy. In the south-east pier of the Cathedral tower there is a noticeable break in the masonry, which marks, it is supposed, the cessation of building that coincided with the close of Anglo-Saxon rule.

When Sweyn died Æthelred returned, and for three years held Cnut in check. The work at S. Frideswide's was probably resumed then. The richly carved, weather-beaten capitals of the choir, with their thick abaci and remarkable ornamentation, partly Saxon and partly Oriental in character, are eloquent of the exile of Æthelred and of the influence of the Eastern monks whom he met at the court of his brother in Normandy. And they speak not only of Byzantine influence, passing through Normandy into England, but also, through the existing traces of exposure to rain and wind, of the ruinous state into which the church had fallen when

"whether by the negligence of the Seculars or the continuall disturbance of the expelled Regulars, it was almost utterly forsaken and relinqueshed, and the more especially because of that troublesome warre betweene King Harold and William the Conqueror."

For the nunnery which S. Frideswide founded had soon ceased to be a nunnery. By the irony of fate, soon after her death, the nuns were removed, and the priory was handed over to a chapter of married men, the Secular Canons, whom S. Dunstan, in his turn, succeeded in suppressing. But the nuns never came back, for, after many vicissitudes, the priory was finally restored, under Henry I. (1111), as a house of the Canons Regular of S. Augustine. Some have thought that Guimond, the first prior (1122), was responsible for the building of the whole church, but he more probably found enough to do in re-establishing order and restoring the monastic buildings. His successor, Robert of Cricklade, perhaps it was who restored Æthelred's church on the old plan and inserted most of the later Norman work, especially the clerestory and presbytery.

The triforium and clerestory in the nave (roofed in with sixteenth-century wood-work) give us an interesting example of the latest Norman or Transitional style. The clerestory consists of a pointed arch enriched with shafts at the angles, and supported on either side by low circular arches which form the openings of a wall passage. The arrangement of the triforium is remarkable. The massive pillars of the nave are alternately circular and octagonal. From their capitals, which are large, with square abaci, spring circular arches with well-defined mouldings. These are, in fact, the arches of the triforium, which is here represented by a blind arcade of two arches set in the tympanum of the main arch. The true arches of the nave spring from half capitals, set against the pillars, and are plain, with a circular moulding towards the nave. The crown of these arches is considerably below the main capitals of the pillars, from which the upper or triforium arches spring. The half capitals assist in carrying the vaulting of the aisles.

The whole arrangement, rare on the Continent, is extremely unusual in England, but occurs, for instance, in the transept of Romsey Abbey. The pillars of the choir date, as has been said, from Æthelred's day; the rest is twelfth-century restoration, save the rich and graceful pendent roof, which accords so strangely well with the robust Norman work it crowns. The clerestory was converted into Perpendicular, and remodelled to carry this elaborate vaulting, which should be compared with that of the old Divinity School, or Henry VII.'s Chapel at Westminster, and attributed, not in accordance with tradition to the time of Wolsey, but to the close of the fifteenth century.

The very effective east end is a conjectural restoration of the old Norman design, and was the work of Sir Gilbert Scott, who also opened the lantern-story and made many other sweeping changes and restorations, necessitated by the previous restorations of seventeenth-century Dean Duppa, and the neglect of his successors.

When Cricklade's restoration was finished, or nearly so, it was decided, in order to revive the once so famous memory of S. Frideswide, to translate her relics from their obscure resting-place (probably the southernmost of the three Saxon apses) to some notable place in the church. The King, the Archbishop, many bishops, and many of the nobility and clergy gathered together to take part in this great ceremony. The bones of the Saint were taken up, set in a rich gilt coffin and placed on the north side of the choir. Miracles were wrought at the new shrine, and pilgrims crowded thither.

The money brought in by these means was badly needed, both for the purpose of the restoration which had been in process, and which was further necessitated by the great fire which destroyed a large part of Oxford in 1190, and, whilst damaging the church, much injured the monastic buildings. The fine old Norman doorway of the Chapter house, which is attributed to Prior Guimond (1122), still bears the red marks of that fire. The Chapter house itself is a very perfect chamber of the early English period. The rich and graceful carving of the capitals, the bosses of the roof, and the curious corbels, the superb glass in the side windows, the beautiful arcade of five arches, pierced for light, which fills the entire east end, complete and confirm, so pure are they in style, so excellent in detail, the just proportions of this noble room.

Early in the thirteenth century was built also the upper portion of the tower, and that lowly spire was added, which appears scarce peeping above the College buildings, modestly calling attention to the half-concealed site of the smallest cathedral in England. Oxford is a city of towers, and domes, and steeples, all of which possess their own peculiar character and beauty. As different as possible from the perfect proportions of Magdalen Tower or the ornate magnificence of the elaborate spire of the University Church, this spire is low and simple—squat almost in appearance. Its lowliness is easily explained. It was perhaps the very first spire built in England. The masons were cautious, afraid of their own daring in attempting to erect so lofty a construction, octagonal, upon the solid base of the Norman lower story. In this first effort they did not dream of the tapering elegance of the soaring spire of Salisbury, any more than of the rich ornamentation, the profusion of exuberant pinnacles, the statues and buttresses, gargoyles, crockets and arabesques, with which their successors bedecked S. Mary's or the Clocher Neuf of Chartres. Strength and security was their chief aim here, though the small turrets, terminating in pyramidal octagons, which surmount the angles of the tower, are the forerunners of that exuberant ornamentation.

In 1289 the bones of S. Frideswide were again translated. They were put in a new and more precious shrine, placed near where the old one stood. Fragments of the marble base of this shrine have been found, pieced together and set up in the easternmost arch between the Lady Chapel and the north choir aisle. These fragments of a beautiful work are themselves beautiful; they are adorned with finely carved foliage, intended to symbolise S. Frideswide's life when she took refuge in the woods.

The story of the destruction of the shrine is a strange one. Before the Reformation the Church of S. Frideswide and her shrine had enjoyed a high reputation as a place of sanctity. Privileges were conceded to it by royal authority. Miracles were believed to be wrought by a virtue attaching to it; pilgrims from all parts resorted to it—among them Queen Catherine of Aragon.

Such practices and privileges seemed to the zealous Reformers to call for summary interference. The famous shrine was doomed to destruction, and was actually destroyed. The fragments were used either at the time, or not long afterwards, to form part of the walls of a common well. The reliques of the Saint, however, were rescued by some zealous votaries, and carefully preserved in hope of better times. Meantime Catherine (the wife of Peter Martyr, a foreign Protestant theologian of high repute, who had been appointed Regius Professor of Theology) died, and was buried near the place lately occupied by the shrine. Over her grave sermons were preached, contrasting the pious zeal of the German Protestant with the superstitious practices that had tarnished the simplicity of the Saxon Saint. Then came another change. The Roman Church, under Mary Tudor, recovered a brief supremacy. The body of Peter Martyr's wife was, by order of Cardinal Pole, contemptuously cast out of the church, and the remains of S. Frideswide were restored to their former resting-place. But it does not appear that any attempt was made to restore the shrine. Party zeal still prevailed. Angry contests continued between the adherents of the two parties even after the accession of Elizabeth.

At length the authorities of Christ Church were commissioned to remove the scandal that had been caused by the inhuman treatment of Catherine Martyr's body. On January 11th, 1562, the bones of the Protestant Catherine and the Catholic S. Frideswide were put together, so intermingled that they could not be distinguished, and then placed together in the same tomb: "Iam coeunt pietas atque superstitio."

Under the easternmost arch, between the Lady Chapel and the Latin Chapel, is the fine chantry tomb, an elaborately wrought and very beautiful example of Perpendicular workmanship, which is supposed to have been the third and more splendid shrine of S. Frideswide, or else to have served as a "Watching Chamber," as it is commonly called, to protect the gold and jewels which hung about the earlier shrine.

Under the Prior Guimond there was certainly a school connected with the convent. Whatever the origin of the University may have been—and there are those who maintain that it sprang from the schools of S. Frideswide as naturally as that of Paris from the schools of Notre Dame—it is pleasant to remember, when you stand in the middle of Tom Quad, that you are on the site of this, the first educational institution of Oxford, just as when you stand in the Lady Chapel of the Cathedral you are on the site of the old priory, the mother church of the University and town.

Another faint echo of the priory days may be traced in the annual Cakestall in S. Olds, which is a survival of the Fair of S. Frideswide that used to last seven days. During that time the keys of the city passed from mayor to prior, and the town courts were closed in favour of the Pie-Powder Court,[2] held by the steward of the priory for the redress of all disorders committed during the fair.

The entrance to the Cathedral is through the two arches in the cloisters, directly opposite to you as you pass into Tom Quad beneath Tom Tower. This curious entrance reminds you at once of the peculiar position of the Cathedral as three parts College chapel. Tom Quad is the largest quadrangle in Oxford (264 by 261 feet), and was begun by Wolsey on a scale which is sufficient evidence of the extreme magnificence of his plans for "Cardinal's College." It was begun, but has never been finished. The shafts and marks of the arches, from which the vaults of the intended cloister were to spring, are, however, plainly visible. Of the old cloister of the monastery no trace remains save the windows and door of the chapter house; the fifteenth-century cloisters that do exist are not to be compared with those of New College or Magdalen. One side of them was destroyed by Wolsey to make room for the College Hall. On the south side of the cloister is the old library, which was formerly the refectory of the monastery. With the chapter house doorway it survives as a relic of the old conventual buildings, in quiet contrast to the splendour of the superb kitchen, and the still more magnificent hall, with its valuable collection of portraits. The vaulted chamber, which contains the staircase by which this hall is approached, is one of the most beautiful things in Oxford. The lovely fan-tracery of the vault and the central pillar were the work of "one Smith, an artificer from London," and were built as late as 1640, in the reign of Charles II. It affords a striking instance of the fact in architectural history, that good Gothic persisted in Oxford long after the influence of Italian work had destroyed it elsewhere.

To make room for this magnificent quadrangle of his the Cardinal also destroyed the three western bays of the Church of S. Frideswide. He had intended to build a new chapel along the north side of Tom Quad which should rival the chapel of King's College at Cambridge. But this work was interrupted by his fall. The foundations of the chapel have been traced, and they show that the west end ran in a line with the octagonal turrets in S. Aldate's Street, and the walls reached nearly to Fell's passage into Peckwater.

For its massive walls Wolsey used some of the stones from the demolished Osney Abbey. The building at the time of his fall had risen some feet above the ground. Dean Fell, it is supposed, used it as a quarry for the construction of his own quadrangle. Now, there had been constructed a new straight walk in the Meadows, and Fell, anxious to improve it, carted the chippings from his own work to lay on it. The chippings were white, so the walk got the name of White. This was corrupted at the end of the eighteenth century to Wide Walk, and hence to Broad Walk—its present name—which really describes it now better than the original phrase.

The destruction of the western bays of the church by Wolsey accounts for the shortened aspect of the nave, slightly relieved though it is by the new western bay which serves as a sort of ante-chapel to the nave and choir which now form the College Chapel of Christ Church. But the appearance of the Cathedral owes something of its strangeness to the fact that it represents, in general plan, the design of King Æthelred's Church reared upon the site of S. Frideswide's.

CHAPTER II

THE MOUND, THE CASTLE AND SOME CHURCHES

THE property of S. Frideswide's Nunnery formed one of the chief elements in the formation of the plan of Oxford. The houses of the population which would spring up in connection with it were probably grouped on the slope by the northern enclosure wall of the nunnery, and were themselves bounded on the north by the road which afterwards became the High Street, and on the west by that which was afterwards named Southgate Street, then Fish Street, and is now known as S. Aldate's. This road, giving access from Wessex to Mercia, was probably one of the direct lines from the north-west to London in the tenth century. It led down to the old fords over the shallows which once intersected the meadows of South Hincksey, and gave, as some suppose, its name to the town.[3] The fords were superseded by the old Grand Pont, and Grand Pont in turn by Folly Bridge.

Folly Bridge, as it now stands, was built a little south of Grand Pont, the old river-course to the north having been filled up by an embankment. The river now marks the Shire boundary which was once marked hereabouts by the Shire Ditch. Crossing the bridge to the Berkshire shore, the road, wherein you may still trace the piers of the old Grand Pont "linked with many a bridge," leads up to Hincksey. There the modern golf-links are, and the "lone, sky-pointing tree" that Clough and Arnold loved. And this road it was which, in the poetic imagination of Matthew Arnold, was haunted by the scholar gipsy.

The main road leads over the hill, which is crowned by Bagley Wood, to Abingdon. That charming village, where once the great monastery stood, was separated in early days from the city by a great oak forest. Wandering therein, book in hand, a certain student, so the story runs, was met by a ferocious wild boar, which he overcame by thrusting his Aristotle down the beast's throat. The boar, having no taste for such logic, was choked by it, and his head, borne home in triumph, was served up, no doubt, at table in the student's hall with a sprig of rosemary in its mouth. The custom of serving a boar's head on Christmas Day at Queen's College, whilst the tabarder sang:

"The Boar's Head in hand bear I
Bedecked with bays and rosemary,
And I pray you masters merry be—
Quotquot estis in convivio.

Chorus—*Caput apri defero*
Reddens laudes Domino," etc.,

is said to have originated in that incident.

S. Aldate's Road, after leaving the river, skirted the enclosure of S. Frideswide, and gradually ascended the sloping gravel bank in a northerly direction. Here it was met by another road which, coming from the east, connected Oxford with the Wallingford district. The crossing of these roads came to be known as the Four Ways, Quadrifurcus, corrupted into Carfax. And Carfax was the second of the chief elements in the formation of Oxford. For at this point, as if to mark its importance in the history of the town, was erected S. Martin's Church, which has always been the city church, and in the churchyard of which Town Councils (Portmannimotes) perhaps were held. It was founded under a Charter of Cnut (1034) by the wealthy and vigorous Abbey of Abingdon, which, together with the foundation at Eynsham, seems to have thrown the Monastery of S. Frideswide very much into the shade both as to energy and influence.

The tower, restored by Mr T. G. Jackson, is the only remaining fragment of the old church. A modern structure was wisely removed in 1896 to broaden the thoroughfare. Two quaint figures, which in bygone days struck the quarters on the old church, have been restored to a conspicuous position on the tower. Shakespeare, who on his way to Stratford used to stop at the Crown Inn, a house then situated near the Cross in the Cornmarket, is said to have stood sponsor in the old church to Sir William Davenant in 1606. John Davenant, father of the poet and landlord of the Inn, was Mayor of Oxford. His wife was a very beautiful woman. Scandal reported that Shakespeare was more than godfather to Sir William. But if the tower be all that remains of the original structure, "S. Martin's at Carfax" still commands the High Street, and, serene amidst the din of trams, of skurrying marketers and jostling undergraduates, recalls the days when the town was yet in the infancy of its eventful life.

The third element in the formation of the place was the Mound. Mediæval towns usually began by clustering thickly round a stronghold, and there is reason to believe that at the beginning of the tenth century Oxford was provided with a fortress. In the year 912 Oxford is mentioned for the first time in authentic history. For there is an entry in the Saxon Chronicle to the effect that

"This year died Æthelred, ealdorman of the Mercians, and King Edward took possession of London and Oxford and of all the lands which owed obedience thereto."

The Danes were ravaging the country. Mercia had been over-run by them the year before. The Chronicle for several years presents a record of the Danes attacking various places, and either Eadward or his sister Æthelflæd defending them and building fortresses for their defence. They fortified, for instance, Tamworth and Warwick and Runcorn, and at each of these places the common feature of fortification is a conical mound of earth. Take a tram from Carfax to the railway station, and stop at the County Courts and Gaol on your way. The County Gaol you need not visit, or admire its absurd battlements, but within the sham façade is the tower that remains from the Castle of Robert D'Oigli, and beside the tower is just such a conical mound of earth— the Castle Mound.

Against raids and incursions Oxford was naturally protected on three sides. For the Thames on the west and south and the Cherwell on the east cut her off from the attack of land forces, whilst even against Danes coming up the Thames from Reading, marsh lands and minor streams within the belt of these outer waters protected her. For in those early days, when Nature had things almost entirely her own way, there were many more branches of the river, many minor tributary streams flowing where now you see nothing but houses and streets. The Trill Mill stream, for instance, which left the main stream on the west of what is now Paradise Square, is now covered over for the greater part of its course; whilst the main stream, after passing beneath the road some seventy yards outside South Gate, gave off another stream running due south, parallel with the road to Folly Bridge, but itself evidently continued its own course across Merton Fields by the side of what is now Broad Walk, and finally found its way into the Cherwell. And besides this stream, which ran under S. Frideswide's enclosure, there were, on the east, the minor streams which now enclose the Magdalen Walks. But what Oxford needed to strengthen her was some wall or fosse along the line occupied afterwards by the northern wall of the city, along the line, that is, of George Street, Broad Street and Holywell, and also some *place d'armes*, some mound, according to the fashion of the times, with accompanying ditches. With these defences it seems probable that she was now provided. Thus fortified Oxford becomes the chief town of Oxfordshire, the district attached to it. And during the last terrible struggle of England with the Danes its position on the borders of the Mercian and West-Saxon realms seems for the moment to have given it a political importance under Æthelred and Cnut strikingly analogous to that which it acquired in the Great Rebellion.

After Sweyn's death Oxford was chosen as the meeting-place of the great gemot of the kingdom. The gemots, which were now and afterwards held at Oxford, were probably held about the Mound, where houses were erected for the royal residence. In one of these Æthelweard, the King's son, breathed his last; one was the scene of another dastardly murder of Danes, when Eadric (1015) ensnared Sigeferth and Morkere into his chamber, and there slew them. And here it was, according to Henry of Huntingdon, that King Edmund, who had been making so gallant a struggle against the conquering Cnut, was murdered by Eadric's son. Eadric, we know, was a traitor, and well-skilled in murders at Oxford. He, when his son had stabbed Edmund by his directions, came to Cnut and "saluted him, saying, 'Hail, thou art sole king.' When he had laid bare the deed done, the King answered, 'I will make thee on account of thy great deserts higher than all the tall men of England.' And he ordered him to be beheaded and his head to be fixed on a pole on the highest tower of London. Thus perished Edmund, a brave king."

And Cnut, the Dane, reigned in his stead. Beneath the shadow of the Mound, built to repel the Danish incursions, the Danish King now held an assembly of the people. At this gemot "Danes and Angles were unanimous, at Oxford, for Eadgar's law." The old laws of the country were, then, to be retained, and his new subjects were reconciled to the Danish King. But these subjects, the townsmen of those days, are but dim and shadowy beings to us. It is only by later records that we see them going on pilgrimage to the shrines of Winchester, or chaffering in their market-place, or judging and law-making in their husting, their merchant-guild regulating trade, their reeve gathering his King's dues of tax or honey, or marshalling his troop of burghers for the King's wars, their boats floating down the Thames towards London and paying the toll of a hundred herrings in Lent-tide to the Abbot of Abingdon by the way. For the river was the highway, and toll was levied on it. In Edward the Confessor's time, in return for the right of making a passage through the mead belonging to Abingdon, it was agreed that all barges that passed through carrying herrings during Lent should give to the cook of that monastery a hundred of them, and that when the servant of each barge brought them into the kitchen the cook should give him for his pains five of them, a loaf of bread and a measure of ale. In the seventeenth century the river had become so choked that no traffic was possible above Maidenhead till an Act was passed for the re-opening of it.

It was at Oxford that a great assembly of all the Witan was held to elect Cnut's successor Harold, and at Oxford, so pernicious a place for kings, that Harold died. At Oxford again when the Northumbrian rebels, slaying and burning, had reached it (1065), the gemot was held which, in renouncing Tostig, came to the decision, the direct result of which was to leave England open to the easy conquest of William of Normandy when he landed in the following year.

Five years later we find Robert D'Oigli in peaceful possession of Oxford, busy building one of those Norman castles, by which William made good his hold upon England, strongholds for his Norman friends, prisons for rebellious Englishmen. The river he held by such fortresses as this at Oxford, and the Castles of Wallingford and Windsor.

Oxford had submitted without resistance to the Conqueror. There is no evidence that she suffered siege like Exeter or York, but many historians, Freeman among them, state that she was besieged. They have been misled by the error of a transcriber. Savile printed *Urbem Oxoniam*, for *Exoniam*, in his edition of "William of Malmesbury," and the mischief was done. A siege at this time has been supposed to explain a remarkable fact which is recorded in the Domesday Survey. "In the time of King Edward," so runs the record of Domesday Book:

"Oxeneford paid for toll and gable and all other customs yearly—to the king twenty pounds, and six measures of honey, and to Earl Algar ten pounds, besides his mill within the [city]. When the king went out to war, twenty burgesses went with him in lieu of the rest, or they gave twenty pounds to the king that all might be free. Now Oxeneford pays sixty pounds at twenty-pence to the ounce. *In the town itself, as well within the wall as without, there are 243 houses that pay geld, and besides these there are 478 houses unoccupied and ruined (tam vastæ et destructæ) so that they can pay no geld.* The king has twenty wall mansions, which were Earl Algar's in the time of King Edward, paying both then and now fourteen shillings less twopence; and one mansion paying sixpence, belonging to Shipton; another paying fourpence, belonging to Bloxham; a third paying thirty pence, belonging to Risborough; and two others paying fourpence, belonging to Twyford in Buckinghamshire; one of these is unoccupied. They are called wall mansions because, if there is need and the king command it, they shall repair the wall.... All the burgesses of Oxeneford hold in common a pasture outside the wall that brings in six shillings and eightpence.... If any stranger who chooses to live in Oxeneford, and has a house, dies there without relatives, the king has all that he leaves."

The extraordinary proportion of ruined and uninhabited houses enumerated in this record, however, was probably due not to any siege by the Normans and not mainly to harsh treatment at their hands, but to the ravaging and burning of that rebellious band of Northumbrians who had come upon Oxford "like a whirlwind" in 1065. Robert D'Oigli himself is recorded to have had

"forty-two inhabited houses as well within as without the wall. Of these sixteen pay geld and gable, the rest pay neither, on account of poverty; and he has eight mansions unoccupied and thirty acres of meadow near the wall and a mill of ten shillings. The whole is worth three pounds and for one manor held he holds with the benefice of S. Peter...." (sentence incomplete).

These houses belonged wholly to Holywell Manor,[4] and the mill referred to is no doubt that known as *Holywell Mill*, supplied with water from the Cherwell.

Thus Domesday Book gives us a glimpse of a compact little town within a vallum, half a mile from east to west, and a quarter of a mile south to north. We may think of the gravel promontory as covered with houses and their gardens, and inhabited by some thousand souls.

A market-place there would have been at or near Carfax, and fairs must have been held there, though we have no mention of them till the reign of Henry I.

The "wall" of the enceinte, which, according to Domesday Book, the inhabitants of the mural mansions were compelled to repair, was probably a vallum of earth faced with stone, protected by a deep ditch in front, and surmounted by wood-work to save the soldiers from arrows.

D'Oigli, we may presume, put the existing fortifications of the town in order.

The fortifications, which were constructed in the reign of Henry III., followed in the main the line of the vallum repaired by D'Oigli. They consisted of a curtain wall and outer ditch, protected by a parapet and by round towers placed at regular intervals and advanced so as to command besiegers who might approach to attack the wall. There were staircases to the top of the towers. A good idea of them and the general scheme of the fortifications may be obtained by a visit to the fragment of the city wall which yet remains within the precincts of New College. The Slype, as it is called, forms a most picturesque approach to New College Gardens, and the old-bastioned wall forms part of the boundary between the New College property and Holywell Street. It is indeed owing to this fact that the wall still remains there intact, for the licence to found a College there was granted to William of Wykeham on condition of keeping the city wall in repair and of allowing access to the mayor and burgesses once in three years to see that this was done, and to defend the wall in time of war. From New College the city wall ran down to the High Street.[5]

The East Gate Hotel, facing the new schools, marks the site of the old entrance to the city hereabouts. It is a recent construction in excellent taste by Mr E. P. Warren. From this point the wall ran on to Merton, and thence to Christ Church. The south wall of the Cathedral chapter house is on the line of the old city wall. It is said that some of the old wall was taken down for the erection of the College Hall. Along the north side of Brewer Street (Lambard's Lane, Slaying Lane or King's Street) are here and there stones of the city wall, if not remnants of the walling. At the extreme end of Brewer Street the arch of Slaying Lane Well is just visible, once described as "under the wall."

The south gate spanned S. Aldate's, close to the south-west corner of Christ Church; Little Gate was at the end of Brewer Street, and the west gate was in Castle Street, beyond the old Church of S. Peter-le-Bailly. From the south gate faint traces in "The Friars" indicate its course, and the indications are clear enough by New Inn Hall Street, Ship Inn Yard and Bullock's Alley. Cornmarket Street was crossed by S. Michael's Church, where stood the north gate. The gate house of the north gate was used as the town prison. It rejoiced in the name of Bocardo, jestingly so called from a figure in logic; for a man once committed to that form of syllogism could not expect to extricate himself save by special processes.

Old bastions and the line of the ditch are found behind the houses opposite Balliol College. The site of Balliol College was then an open space, and Broad Street was Canditch. This name was derived by Wood from Candida Fossa, a ditch with a clear stream running along it. Wood's etymology is not convincing. Mr Hurst has suggested a more likely derivation in Camp Ditch. As a street name it reached from the angle of Balliol to Smith Gate. An indication of the old fosse, filled up, is to be found in the broad gravel walk north of the wall near New College.

From Bocardo the wall ran towards the Sheldonian Theatre. The outer line of the passage between Exeter Chapel and the house to the north of it was the line of the south face of the old city wall. A bastion was laid bare in 1852 in the north quad of Exeter. The wall passed in a diagonal line across the quadrangle south of the Clarendon Building, turned northwards in Cat's Street, and ran up to the octagonal Chapel of Our Lady by Smith Gate. The remains of this little chapel, with a beautiful little "Annunciation" in a panel over the south entrance, have recently been revealed to the passer-by by the new buildings of Hertford College, between which and the feeble mass of the Indian Institute it seems strangely out of place.

From Smith Gate the wall returned to New College, and so completed the circuit of the town. A reference to the map will elucidate this bare narration of mine.

But to return to Robert D'Oigli, the Conqueror's Castellan. From what little we know of him, he would appear to have been a typical Norman baron, ruthless, yet superstitious, strong to conquer and strong to hold. Very much the rough, marauding soldier, but gifted with an instinct for government and order, he came over to the conquest of England in the train of William the Bastard and in the company of Roger D'Ivry, his sworn brother, to whom, as the chronicler tells us, he was "iconfederyd and ibownde by faith and sacrament." Oxfordshire was committed to his charge by the Conqueror, to reduce to final subjection and order. He seems to have ruled it in rude soldierly fashion, enforcing order, tripling the taxation of the town and pillaging without scruple the religious houses of the neighbourhood. For it was only by such ruthless exaction that the work which William had set him to do could be done. He had indeed been amply provided for, so far as he himself was concerned, by the Conqueror, chiefly through a marriage with a daughter of Wiggod of Wallingford, who had been cupbearer to Edward the Confessor; but money was needed for the great fortress which was now to be built to hold the town, after the fashion of the Normans, and by holding the town to secure, as we have said, the river.

"In the year 1071," it is recorded in the Chronicle of Osney Abbey, "was built the Castle of Oxford by Robert D'Oigli." And by the Castle we must understand not the mound which was already there, nor such a castle as was afterwards built in the twelfth and thirteenth centuries, but at least the great tower of stone which still exists and was intended to guard the western approach to the Castle. S. George's tower, for so it was called because it was joined to the chapel of S. George's College within the precincts, was upon the line of the enceinte. The walls are eight feet four inches thick at the bottom, though not more than four feet at the top. The doorway, which is some twelve feet from the ground, was on the level of the vallum or wall of fortification, and gave access to the first floor. There are traces of six doorways above the lead roof, which gave access to the "hourdes." These were wooden hoardings or galleries that could be put up outside. They had holes for the crossbows, and holes for the pouring down of stones, boiling pitch or oil on to the heads of threatening sappers. They were probably stored in the top room of the tower, which is windowless.

The construction of the staircase of the tower is very peculiar. Ascend it and you will obtain a magnificent view of Oxford, of Iffley and Sandford Lock, Shotover and the Chiltern Hills, Hincksey, Portmeadow, Godstow, Woodstock and Wytham Woods.

On the mound close at hand there was, after D'Oigli's day, a ten-sided keep built in the style of Henry III. To reach the mound you go within the gaol, and pass by a pathetic little row of murderers' graves, sanded heaps, distinguished by initials. Under the mound is a very deep well, covered over by a groined chamber of Transitional design.

Five towers were added later to the Castle, as Agas' map (1568) shows us. After the Civil War, Colonel Draper, Governor of Oxford, "sleighted," as Wood expresses it, the work about the city, but greatly strengthened the Castle. But in the following year (1651), when the Scots invaded England, he, for some reason, "sleighted" the Castle works too. The five towers, shown in Agas' map, and other fortifications then disappeared. S. George's tower alone survives.

Stern and grim that one remaining fragment of the old Castle stands up against the sky, a landmark that recalls the good government of the Norman kings. But the most romantic episode connected with it occurred amidst the horrors of the time when the weakness and misrule of Stephen, and the endeavours of Matilda to supplant him, had plunged the country into that chaos of pillage and bloodshed from which the Norman rule had hitherto preserved it. After the death of his son, Henry I. had forced the barons to swear to elect his daughter Matilda as his successor. But they elected Stephen of Blois, grandson of the Conqueror, whose chief claim to the Crown, from their point of view, was his weak character. In a Parliament at Oxford (1135) he granted a charter with large liberties to the Church, but his weakness and prodigality soon gave the barons opportunities of revolt. Released from the stern control of Henry they began to fortify their castles; in self-defence the great ministers of the late King followed their example. Stephen seized the Bishops of Salisbury and Lincoln at Oxford, and forced them to surrender their strongholds. The King's misplaced violence broke up the whole system of government, turned the clergy against him and opened the way for the revolt of the adherents of Matilda. The West was for her; London and the East supported Stephen. Victory at Lincoln placed Stephen a captive in the hands of Matilda, and the land received her as its "Lady." But her contemptuous refusal to allow the claims of the Londoners to enjoy their old privileges, and her determination to hold Stephen a prisoner, strengthened the hand of her opponents. They were roused to renew their efforts. Matilda was forced to flee to Oxford, and there she was besieged by Stephen, who had obtained his release.

Stephen marched on Oxford, crossed the river at the head of his men, routed the Queen's supporters, and set fire to the city. Matilda shut herself up in the Castle and prepared to resist the attacks of the King. But Stephen prosecuted the siege with great vigour; every approach to the Castle was carefully guarded, and after three months the garrison was reduced to the greatest straits. Provisions were exhausted; the long-looked-for succour never came; without, Stephen pushed the siege harder than ever. It seemed certain that Matilda must fall into his hands. Her capture would be the signal for the collapse of the rebellion. But just as the end seemed inevitable, Matilda managed to escape in marvellous wise. There had been a heavy fall of snow; so far as the eye could see from the Castle towers the earth was hidden beneath a thick white pall. The river was frozen fast. The difficulty of distinguishing a white object on this white background, and the opportunity of crossing the frozen river by other means than that of the guarded bridge, suggested a last faint chance of escape. Matilda's courage rose to the occasion. She draped herself in white, and with but one companion stole out of the beleaguered Castle at dead of night, and made her way, unseen, unheard through the friendly snow. Dry-footed she stole across the river, and gradually the noise of the camp faded away into the distance behind her. For six weary miles she stumbled on through the heavy drifts of snow, until at last she arrived in safety at Wallingford.

The bird had flown, and the Castle shortly afterwards surrendered to the baffled King (*Gesta Stephani*).

During this siege the people were deprived of the use of the Church of S. George, and to supply their spiritual needs a new church sprang into existence. It was dedicated to S. Nicholas, and afterwards to S. Thomas a Becket. Of the original church, just opposite the L. & N.W. Railway Station, part of the chancel remains. The tower is fifteenth century.

The Castle mill is mentioned in the Domesday Survey. The present mill no doubt occupies the same site; its foundations may preserve some of the same masonry as that which is thus recorded to have existed hereabouts before the Conquest.

You will notice that the Castle occupies almost the lowest position in the town, and remembering all the other Norman castles you have seen, Windsor or Durham, Lincoln or William the Bastard's own birth-place at Falaise, the Oxford site may well give you pause, till you remember that the position of the old tenth-century fort had been chosen as the one which best commanded the streams against the Danes, whose incursions were mainly made by means of the rivers. If Carfax had been clear, D'Oigli would have built his castle at Carfax; but it was covered with houses and S. Martin's; and, shrinking from the expense that would have been involved, and the outcry that would have been raised, if he had cleared the high central point of the town, he was content to modify and strengthen the old fort. But as the descent of Queen Street from Carfax threatened the Castle, if the town were taken, there was no regular communication made between the Castle and the town. A wooden drawbridge across the deep ditches that defended the Castle led to the town, somewhere near Castle Street. This would be destroyed in time of danger. No other entrance to the town was allowed on this side. "All persons coming across the meadows from the West and all the goods disembarked at the Hythe from the barges and boats would have to be taken in at the North Gate of the town, the road passing along the North bank of the City ditch and following, probably, exactly the same course as that followed by George Street to-day" (Parker). And round about the Castle itself an open space was preserved by the policy of the Castellan, and known as the Bailly (ballium, outer court). The Church of S. Peter le Bailly recalls the fact.

Study the history of most cathedrals and you will discover that, like Chartres or Durham, "half house of God, half castle 'gainst the Scot," they have served and were intended to serve at some period of their career as fortresses as well as churches.

When Bishop Remigius removed the see from Dorchester to Lincoln, as he did at this time (1070), Henry of Huntingdon writes: "He built a church to the Virgin of Virgins, strong in a strong position, fair in a fair spot, which was agreeable to those who serve God and also, as was needful at the time, impregnable to an enemy." The tower of S. Michael's at North Gate is a good example of this mingling of the sacred with the profane, and the architectural feature of it is that it combines the qualities of a campanile with those of the tower of the Castle. It was a detached tower, and not part and parcel of the church which stood at the North Gate, as it is now. In the fifteenth century the city wall was extended northwards so as to include the church.

The tower is placed just where we should expect to find that the need of fortification was felt. South and East, Oxford was now protected by the Thames and the Cherwell as well as by her "vallum," and on the west was the Castle. But the North Gate needed protection, and D'Oigli built the tower of S. Michael's to give it, spiritual and temporal both. At a later date there was erected a chapel, also dedicated to S. Michael, near the South Gate, and with reference to this church and chapel and the Churches of S. Peter in the East and in the West, there is a mediæval couplet which runs as follows:

"Invigilat portæ australi boreæque Michael,
Exortum solem Petrus regit atque cadentem."

"At North Gate and at South Gate too S. Michael guards the way,
While o'er the East and o'er the West S. Peter holds his sway."

The military character of S. Michael's tower is marked by that round-headed doorway, which you may perceive some thirty feet from the ground on the north side. Just as the blocked-up archways at the top of the Castle tower once gave access to the wooden galleries which projected from the wall, so this doorway opened on to a lower gallery which guarded the approach to the adjoining gateway. On the south side of the tower you will find traces of another doorway, the base of which was about twelve feet from the level of the ground. It is reasonable to suppose that the tower projected from the north side of the rampart, and that this doorway was the means of communication between them. The other doorway, on the west side, level with the street, gave access from the road to the basement story of the tower.

Architecturally the tower may be said to be a connecting link between the romanesque and Norman styles. The system of rubble, with long-and-short work at the angles, has not yet given place to that of surface ashlar masonry throughout, and the eight pilaster windows, it should be observed, of rude stone-work carved with the axe, present the plain, pierced arches, with mid-wall shafts, which preceded the splayed Norman window and arches with orders duly recessed. The church itself adjoining the tower is of various periods, chiefly fourteenth century. It was, together with S. Mildred's, united (in 1429) to All Saint's Church, which then was made a collegiate parish church by the foundation of Lincoln College adjoining.

Not only was Robert D'Oigli a builder of walls and towers, but, in the end, of churches also. The Chronicle of Abingdon Abbey records the story of his conversion.

"In his greed for gain, says the Chronicler, he did everywhere harass the churches, and especially the Abbey of Abingdon. Amongst other evil deeds he appropriated for the use of the Castle garrison a meadow that lay outside the walls of Oxford and belonged to the Abbey. Touched to the quick the brethren assembled before their Altar and cried to Heaven for vengeance. Meantime, whilst day and night they were thus calling upon the Blessed Mary, Robert fell into a grievous sickness in which he continued many days impenitent, until one night he dreamed that he stood within the palace of a certain great King. And before a glorious lady who was seated upon a throne there knelt two of the monks whose names he knew and they said 'Lady, this is he who seizes the lands of your church.' After which words were uttered she turned herself with great indignation towards Robert and commanded him to be thrust out of doors and to be led to the meadow. And two youths made him sit down there, and a number of ruffianly lads piled burning hay round him and made sport of him. Some tossed haybands in his face and others singed his beard and the like. His wife, seeing that he was sleeping heavily, woke him up and on his narrating to her his dream she urged him to go to Abingdon and restore the meadow. To Abingdon therefore he caused his men to row him and there before the altar he made satisfaction."

There are two points to be noted in this story. First, that the meadow in question was doubtless that which bears the name of *King's Mead* to this day; second, that the river was a much used highway in those and in much later times, ere money and Macadam, and afterwards George Stephenson, had substituted roads and rails and made the water-way slow and no safer. To return to our Chronicler.

"And after the aforesaid vision which he had seen, how that he was tortured by evil demons at the command of the Mother of God, not only did he devote himself to the building of the Church of S. Mary of Abingdon but he also repaired at his own expense other parish churches that were in a ruined state both within and without the walls. A great bridge, also, was built by him on the North side of Oxford (High or Hythe (= Haven) Bridge). And he dying in the month of September was honourably buried within the Presbytery at Abingdon on the north side, and his wife lies in peace buried on his left."

Together with his sworn friend, Roger D'Ivry, he founded the "Church of S. George in the Castle of Oxenford." This church stood adjacent to the Castle tower, but it was removed in 1805 to make room for the prison buildings.[6]

Probably, also, D'Oigli founded a church, dedicated to S. Mary Magdalen, situated just without the North Gate, and intended to supply the spiritual wants of travellers and dwellers without the walls. The church was on the site of the present Church of S. Mary Magdalen; but no trace of the original work has been left by the early Victorian restorers. It passed with the Church of S. George to Osney Abbey, and then with its patron to the successors of the canons of S. Frideswide's, the prebends or canons of Christ Church.

D'Oigli probably built also the Church of S. Michael at the North Gate and S. Peter's within the East Gate; and as for his restorations, they may have included the parish church, S. Martin's, and also S. Mary's and S. Ebbe's, which latter may possibly have been built in the time of Edward the Confessor.

How very literally S. Peter's guarded the east may be gathered by inspecting the two turrets at the east end of the church. There were small openings in these whence a watch could be kept over the streams and the approach to East Gate.

Whether the crypt of this church, as we now have it, dates entirely from D'Oigli's time is a moot point. It may be that it does, but the actual masonry, it will be noticed, the ashlar work, capitals and arches, are superior to that of the Castle and S. Michael's. The plan of the original crypt of S. George's in the Castle shows that it had, in accordance with the general rule of eleventh-century work in this country, an apsidal termination. The crypt of S. Peter's, as built in D'Oigli's day, was, it is suggested, no exception. It had an apsidal termination which did not extend so far towards the east as the present construction. But, as happened again and again in the history of innumerable churches and cathedrals at home and abroad, of Chartres, Rochester, Canterbury, for instance, the crypt was presently extended eastwards. The extension in the present case would enable the small apse to be changed into a larger choir with a rectangular east end. The result is, that looking eastwards, and noticing that there is no apparent break between the wall of the crypt and the wall of the chancel above, which evidently belongs to the middle of the twelfth century, you would be inclined to attribute the whole crypt to that date, if you did not notice the small doorways on either side and at the western end. Looking westward, you see work which carries you back to the days when S. Michael's and the Castle tower were being built. For the three western arches, two of them doorways now blocked up and the central one open, indicate a type of crypt which is generally held not to have been used later than the beginning of the twelfth century. The essential features of this type were that the vault of the crypt was raised some feet above the level of the floor of the nave, and that both from the north and south side of the nave steps led down into the crypt. And in some cases there were central steps as well, or at least some opening from the nave. Here then, as at Repton, you have indications of this type, for behind each of the blocked-up doorways is a passage leading to some steps or clear traces of steps, and the central archway may have provided originally an opening to the nave, through which a shrine may have been visible, or else a communication by central steps.

The entrance to this remarkable crypt, with its vaulting of semi-circular arches of hewn stone, is from the outside. The crypt has capitals of a peculiar design to several of the shafts, and four of the bases ornamented with spurs formed by the heads of lizard-shaped animals. The chancel and the south doorway afford remarkably rich examples of the late Norman style. The fifteenth-century porch, with a room over it, somewhat hides, but has doubtless protected the latter. The early decorated tower, the exterior arcading of the chancel, the unique groining of the sanctuary

("S. Peter's Chain,") and the two beautiful decorated windows on the north, and the early English arcade of the nave, are all worthy of remark in this interesting church.

Of the old Church of S. Ebbe (S. Æbba was the sister of S. Oswald), which was rebuilt in 1814 and again partially in 1869, nothing now remains save the stone-work of a very rich late Norman doorway, which was taken down and built into the south wall of the modern building.

The other church which is mentioned at this period is S. Aldate's. Now, nothing is known of the Saint to whom this church is supposed to have been dedicated, and from whom, as we have seen, the street which runs from Carfax to Folly Bridge borrows its name. In no ancient martyrology or calendar does S. Aldate appear. It is quite possible that there was such a Saint, and if there was, he would not be the only one who survives in our memory solely by virtue of the churches dedicated to him. But the corruption—S. Told's—S. Old's is found in thirteenth-century chartularies and in popular parlance to-day. This corruption is curious, and may be significant. S. Aldate's Church at Oxford lies just within the old South Gate of the town; the only other church of the same name lies just within the old North Gate of Gloucester. In an old map of Gloucester this latter church is called S. Aldgate's; in an old map of Oxford the same spelling occurs. At Oxford the street now known as S. Aldate's was once called South Gate Street. It seems likely, therefore, that Aldate represents a corruption from Old Gate = Aldgate = Aldate, and that the name, when it had become so far corrupted, was supposed to be that of a Saint. But the true meaning, as so often happens, lived on, when men spoke with unconscious correctness of S. Old's.

The church itself, as it now stands, is chiefly the product of a restoration in 1863,[7] but the south aisle was built in 1335 by Sir John Docklington, a fishmonger who was several times mayor. Over it there used to be an upper story which served as a library for the use of students in Civil Law who frequented the neighbouring hall, Broadgates Hall, which became Pembroke College in 1624, when Thomas Tesdale endowed it and named it after Lord Pembroke the Chancellor, and King James assumed the honours of founder. In the library the refectory of the old hall survives. The rest of the front quadrangle was added in the seventeenth century and Gothicised in the eighteenth. It was in a room over the gateway that Dr Johnson lived, when Pembroke was "a nest of singing birds." The eighteenth-century chapel, decorated (1884) by Mr Kempe, and the new hall should tempt the visitor into the back quadrangle.

In the days of Robert D'Oigli, then, Oxford was provided with no less than eight churches, dedicated to S. Frideswide, S. Martin, S. George, S. Mary Magdalen, S. Mary the Virgin, S. Peter, S. Michael and S. Ebbe. By the end of the reign of Henry I. this number had been more than doubled. And seeing that much church building is and always was a sign of prosperity and security, the fact that eight new churches sprang up within so short a time after the Norman Conquest may be taken to prove that under her sheriffs and portreeves Oxford enjoyed good government and made rapid progress in population and wealth. Of these eight or ten new churches no trace remains of S. Mildred's, save the pathway across the old churchyard which survives in the modern Brasenose Lane; and the church dedicated to S. Eadward the martyr, which lay between S. Frideswide's and the High, has likewise disappeared; the exact sites of the church of S. Budoc, the Chapel of the Holy Trinity and of S. Michael at the South Gate, cannot be identified; the Chapel of S. Clement, on the other side of Magdalen Bridge, gave way to a fourteenth-century church, and was wholly cleared away at the beginning of the nineteenth century; All Saint's and S. Peter's, in the bailey of the Castle, were entirely rebuilt in the eighteenth century, and the latter re-erected on another site in the nineteenth. The old chancel arch in the Church of S. Cross (Holywell) dates from the end of the eleventh century, and this church was probably founded about this time by Robert D'Oigli or his successors for the benefit of the growing population on Holywell Manor.

The present Church of S. Clement, on the Marston Road, near the new Magdalen and Trinity Cricket Grounds, is an early Victorian imitation of Norman style, and well described as the "Boiled Rabbit."

The Castle tower, the tower of S. Michael's, the crypt of S. Peter's in the East, Holywell and the Castle mill, the chancel of S. Cross, these are all landmarks that recall the days when D'Oigli governed Oxford, and the servants of William surveyed England and registered for him his new estate. But there is one other item in the Domesday record which deserves to be noticed:

"All burgesses of Oxford hold in common a pasture without the wall which brings in 6s. 8d."

How many Oxford men realise, when they make their way to Port Meadow to sail their centre-boards on the upper river, that this ancient "Port" (or "Town") Meadow is still set apart for its ancient purpose, that the rights of the freemen of Oxford to have free pasture therein have been safeguarded for eight hundred years by the portreeve or shire-reeve (sheriff), annually appointed to fulfil this duty by the Portmannimot (or Town Council)?

Robert D'Oigli died childless. He was succeeded by his nephew, the second Robert, who had wedded Edith, a concubine of Henry I. She, dwelling in the Castle, was wont to walk in the direction of what is now the Great Western Railway Station and the cemetery, being attracted thither by the "chinking rivulets and shady groves."

And it is said that there one evening, "she saw a great company of pyes gathered together on a tree, making a hideous noise with their chattering, and seeming, as 'twere, to direct their chatterings to her." The experience was repeated, and the Lady sent for her confessor, one Radulphus, a canon of S. Frideswide's, and asked him what the reason of their chattering might be. Radulphus, "the wiliest pye of all," Wood calls him, explained that "these were no pyes, but so many poor souls in purgatory that do beg and make all this complaint for succour and relief;

and they do direct their clamours to you, hoping that by your charity you would bestow something both worthy of their relief, as also for the welfare of yours and your posterity's souls, as your husband's uncle did in founding the College and Church of S. George." These words being finisht, she replied, "And is it so indeed? now de pardieux, if old Robin my husband will concede to my request, I shall do my best endeavour to be a means to bring these wretched souls to rest." And her husband, as the result of her importunities, "founded the monastery of Osney, near or upon the place where these pyes chattered (1129), dedicating it to S. Mary, allotting it to be a receptacle of Canon Regulars of S. Augustine, and made Radulphus the first Prior thereof."

Osney was rebuilt in 1247. The Legate proclaimed forty days' indulgence to anyone who should contribute towards the building of it. The result was one of the most magnificent abbeys in the country. "The fabric of the church," says Wood, "was more than ordinary excelling." Its two stately towers and exquisite windows moved the envy and admiration of Englishmen and foreigners alike. When, in 1542, Oxford ceased to belong to the diocese of Lincoln, and the new see was created, Robert King, the last Abbot of Osney, was made first Bishop of Osney. But it was only for a few years that the bishop's stool was set up in the Church of S. Mary. In 1546 Henry the VIII. moved the see to S. Frideswide's, and converted the priory, which Wolsey had made a college, into both college and cathedral. And the Abbey of Osney was devoted to destruction. "Sir," said Dr Johnson when he saw the ruins of that great foundation, stirred by the memory of its splendid cloister and spacious quadrangle as large as Tom Quad, its magnificent church, its schools and libraries, the oriel windows and high-pitched roofs of its water-side buildings, and the abbot's lodgings, spacious and fair, "Sir! to look upon them fills me with indignation!" Agas' map (1568) represents the abbey as still standing, but roofless; the fortifications in 1644 accounted for the greater part of what then remained. The mean surroundings of the railway station mark the site of the first Cathedral of Oxford. The Cemetery Chapel is on the site of the old nave. A few tiles and fragments of masonry, the foundations of the gateway and a piece of a building attached to the mill, are the only remains that will reward you for an unpleasant afternoon's exploration in this direction. Better, instead of trying so to make these dead stones live, to go to the Cathedral and there look at the window in the south choir aisle, which was buried during the Civil War and, thus preserved from the destructive Puritans, put up again at the Restoration. This painted window, which is perhaps from the hand of the Dutchman Van Ling (1634), represents Bishop King in cope and mitre, and among the trees in the background is a picture of Osney Abbey already in ruins. The bishop's tomb, it should be added, of which a missing fragment has this year been discovered, lies in the bay between the south choir aisle and S. Lucy's Chapel. But there is one other survival of Osney Abbey of which you cannot long remain unaware. You will not have been many hours in the "sweet city of the dreaming spires" before you hear the "merry Christ Church bells" of Dean Aldrich's[8] well-known catch ring out, or the cracked B flat of Great Tom, booming his hundred and one strokes, tolling the hundred students of the scholastic establishment and the one "outcomer" of the Thurston foundation, and signalling at the same time to all "scholars to repair to their respective colleges and halls" and to all the Colleges to close their gates (9.5 P.M.).

And these bells, Hautclerc, Douce, Clement, Austin, Marie, Gabriel et John, as they are named in the hexameter, are the famous Osney bells, which were held to be the finest in England in the days when bell-founding was a serious art and a solemn rite, when bells were baptized and anointed, exorcised and blessed by the bishop, so that they might have power to drive the devil out of the air, to calm tempests, to extinguish fire, and to recreate even the dead. They are hung within the Bell-Tower (above the hall-staircase of Christ Church), which Mr Bodley has built about the wooden structure which contains them, and which he intended to surmount with a lofty and intricate wooden superstructure.

But Tom is placed in his own tower, over the entrance from S. Aldate's into the great Quad to which he has given his name.

The lower story of Tom Tower was built by Wolsey (the Faire Gate it was called, and the cardinal's statue is over the gateway), but the octagonal cupola which gives to it its characteristic appearance was added by Sir Christopher Wren. Tom weighed 17,000 pounds, and bore the inscription:—

In Thomæ laude resono Bim Bom sine fraude,

but he was re-cast in 1680 (7 ft. 1 in. in diameter, and weighing over 7 tons). The inscription records:—

Magnus Thomas Clusius Oxoniensis renatus, Ap. 8, 1680.

Translated here, he has rung out, since the anniversary of the Restoration on the 29th of May 1684, nightly without intermission, save on that night some years ago when the undergraduates of Christ Church cut the rope as a protest when they were not allowed to attend the ball given at Blenheim in honour of the coming of age of the Duke of Marlborough, and curfew did not ring that night.

There is one other monument in Oxford which is connected by popular tradition with the last Abbot of Osney, and that is the exceedingly picturesque old house[9] in S. Aldate's. Richly and quaintly carved, this old timber mansion is known as the Bishop's Palace, and is said to have been the residence of Bishop King, after the See was transferred from Osney to Christ Church.

The town, we have seen, had been ruined, and very many of the houses were "waste," when the Normans conquered England. But in the new era of prosperity and security which their coming gave to the land, in the sudden development of industry and wealth which the rule of the conquerors fostered, Oxford had her full share. The buildings of which remnants or records remain bear witness to the new order of things.

Such works as those which we have described could not then or now be done without money. The transformation of Oxford at this period, from a town of wooden houses, in great part uninhabited, to a town of stone houses, with a castle and many churches of stone, is an indication of wealth. And that wealth was a product not only of the new régime of order and security, but also of the new policy of the foreign kings.

The erection of stately castles and yet statelier Abbeys which followed the Conquest, says Mr Green, the rebuilding of almost every cathedral and conventual church, mark the advent of the Jewish capitalist. From this time forward till 1289 the Jew was protected in England and his commercial enterprise fostered. He was introduced and protected as a chattel of the King, and as such exempt from the common law and common taxation of Englishmen. In Oxford, as elsewhere, the Jews lived apart, using their own language, their own religion and laws, their own peculiar commerce and peculiar dress. Here the Great and Little Jewries extended along Fish Street (S. Old's) to the present Great Gate of Christ Church, and embraced a square of little streets, behind this line, which was isolated and exempt from the common responsibilities and obligations of the town. The church itself was powerless against the Synagogue, which rose in haughty rivalry beside the cloister of S. Frideswide. Little wonder if the Priory and Jewry were soon at deadly feud. In 1185 we find Prior Phillip complaining of a certain Deus-cum-crescat (Gedaliah) son of Mossey, who, presuming upon his exemption from the jurisdiction of any but the King, had dared to mock at the Procession of S. Frideswide. Standing at his door as the procession of the saint passed by, the mocking Jew halted and then walked firmly on his feet, showed his hands clenched as if with palsy and then flung open his fingers. Then he claimed gifts and oblations from the crowd who flocked to S. Frideswide's, on the ground that such recoveries of limb and strength were quite as real as any Frideswide had wrought. But no earthly power, ecclesiastic or civil, ventured to meddle with Deus-cum-crescat.

The feud between Jewry and Priory lasted long. It culminated in 1268 in a daring act of fanaticism, which incidentally provides a curious proof of the strong protection which the Jews enjoyed, and of the boldness with which they showed their contempt for the superstitions around them.

As the customary procession of scholars and citizens was returning on Ascension Day from S. Frideswide's, a Jew suddenly burst from the group of his friends in front of the synagogue, and snatching the crucifix from its bearer, trod it underfoot. But even in presence of such an outrage, the terror of the Crown shielded the Jewry from any burst of popular indignation. The King condemned the Jews of Oxford to make a heavy silver crucifix for the University to carry in the processions, and to erect a cross of marble where the crime was committed; but even this punishment was in part remitted, and a less offensive place was allotted for the cross in an open plot by Merton College.

But the time of the Jews had almost come. Their wealth and growing insolence had fanned the flames of popular prejudice against them. Protected by the kings whose policy it was to allow none to plunder them but their royal selves, they reaped a harvest greater than even the royal greed could reap.[10]

Their position as chattels of the King, outside the power of clergy or barons, and as citizens of little towns within towns in whose life they took no part except to profit by it, stirred the jealousy of the various classes. Wild stories were circulated then, as on the Continent still, of children carried off to be circumcised or crucified. The sack of Jewry after Jewry was the sign of popular hatred and envy during the Barons' war. Soon the persecution of the law fell upon these unhappy people. Statute after statute hemmed them in. They were forbidden to hold real property, to employ Christian servants, and to move through the streets without two tell-tale white tablets of wool on their breasts. Their trade, already crippled by the competition of bankers, was annihilated by the royal order which bade them renounce usury, under the pain of death. At last Edward, eager to obtain funds for his struggle with Scotland, yielded to the fanaticism of his subjects and bought the grant of a fifteenth from the clergy and laity at the price of driving the Jews from his realm. From the time of Edward to that of Cromwell no Jew touched English soil.

There is no reason to suppose with many historians that the Jews of Oxford contributed through their books, seized at this time, to the cultivation of physical and medical science, or that it was through the books of the Rabbis that Roger Bacon was enabled to penetrate to the older world of research. The traces which they have left in Oxford, save in the indirect manner I have suggested, are not many. The rising ground, now almost levelled, between the Castle and Broken Hayes, on the outer edge of the Castle ditch on the north side, was long known as the Mont de Juis, but being the place of execution, the name may more likely be derived from justice than from Jews. A more interesting reminiscence is provided by the Physic Garden opposite Magdalen College.

Henry II. had granted the Jews the right of burial outside of every city in which they dwelt. At Oxford their burial place was on the site where S. John's hospital was afterwards built, and was then transferred to the place where the Physic Garden now stands.

This garden, the first land publicly set apart for the scientific study of plants, was founded by Henry, Earl of Danby (1632), who gave the land for this purpose. Mr John Evelyn visiting it a few years later was shown the Sensitive Plant there for a great wonder. There also grew, he tells us, canes, olive trees, rhubarb, but no extraordinary curiosities, besides very good fruit. Curious, however, the shapes of the clipped trees were, if we may believe Tickell, who writes enthusiastically:

"How sweet the landskip! where in living trees,
Here frowns a vegetable Hercules;
There famed Achilles learns to live again
And looks yet angry in the mimic scene;
Here artful birds, which blooming arbours shew,
Seem to fly higher whilst they upwards grow."

The gateway was designed by Inigo Jones, and the figures of Charles I. and II. were added later, the expense being defrayed out of the fine levied upon Anthony Wood for his libel upon Clarendon.

About the same time that Osney Abbey was finished the palace which Henry Beauclerk had been building at Beaumont, outside the north gate of the city, was finished also. To satisfy his love of hunting he had already (1114) constructed a palace and park at Woodstock. Within the stone walls of the enclosure there he nourished and maintained, says John Rous, lions, leopards, strange spotted beasts, porcupines, camels, and such like animals, sent to him by divers outlandish lords.

The old palace at Beaumont lay to the north-east of Worcester College. Its site, chosen by the King "for the great pleasure of the seat and the sweetness and delectableness of the air," is indicated by Beaumont Street, a modern street which has revived the name of the palace on the hill,—Bellus mons.

When not occupied with his books or his menagerie, the Scholar-King found time to grant charters to the town, and he let to the city the collective dues or fee-farm rent of the place.

Henry II. held important councils at Beaumont. The one romance of his life is connected with Woodstock and Godstow.

One of the most charming of the many beautiful excursions by road or river from Oxford takes you to the little village of Godstow,

"Through those wide fields of breezy grass
Where black-winged swallows haunt the glittering Thames."

To sail here from Folly Bridge or the Upper River, to fish here, to play bowls or skittles here, to eat strawberries and cream here, has for centuries been the delight of Oxford students.

"So on thy banks, too, Isis, have I strayed
A tasselled student, witness you who shared
My morning walk, my ramble at high noon,
My evening voyage, an unskilful sail,
To Godstow bound, or some inferior port,
For strawberries and cream. What have we found
In life's austerer hours delectable
As the long day so loitered?"

Just opposite the picturesque old Trout Inn and the bridge which spans the river here you may see an old boundary wall, enclosing a paradise of ducks and geese, at one corner of which is a ruined chapel with a three-light perpendicular window. These are the only remaining fragments of the once flourishing Nunnery, which was the last home of Rosamund, Rosa Mundi, the Rose of the World.

During his residence at Oxford, Henry granted the growing city an important charter, confirming the liberties they had enjoyed under Henry I.,

"and specially their guild merchant, with all liberties and customs, in lands and in goods, pastures and other accessories, so that any one who is not of the guildhall shall not traffic in city or suburbs, except as he was wont at the time of King Henry, my grandfather. Besides I have granted them to be quit of toll and passenger tax, and every custom through all England and Normandy, by land, by water, by sea-coast, *by land and by strand*. And they are to have all other customs and liberties and laws of their own, which they have in common with my citizens of London. And that they serve me at my feast with those of my Butlery, and do their traffic with them, within London and without, and everywhere."

Oxford then (1161) enjoyed customs and liberties in common with London; her charter was copied from that of the Londoners, and on any doubtful matter she was bound to consult the parent town. She was soon provided with aldermen, bailiffs, and chamberlains, whose titles were borrowed from the merchant guild, and with councilmen who were elected from the citizens at large. The Mayor was formally admitted to his office by the Barons of the Exchequer at Westminster, and on his return thence, he was met always by the citizens in their liveries at Trinity Chapel, without Eastgate, where he stayed to return thanks to God for his safe return, and left an alms upon the altar.

The merchant guild was originally distinct from the municipal government, though finally the Guildhall became the common hall of the city. In practice the chief members of the merchant guild would usually be also the chief members of the Court-leet. The business of the merchant guild was to regulate trade. Its relation to the craft guilds is analogous to that which exists between the University and the Colleges.

The Crafts, to which, as to the freedom of the city, men obtained admission by birth, apprenticeship, or purchase, were numerous, flourishing and highly organised. Every trade from cordwainers to cooks, from tailors, weavers, and glovers to butchers and bakers, was a brotherhood, with arms and a warden, beadle, and steward of its own, and an annually elected headmaster.

The various Guilds had special chapels in the different churches where they burnt candles and celebrated mass, on particular days. The glovers held mass on Trinity Monday in All Saints' Church; the tailors in the same church, and they also founded a chantrey in S. Martin's. "A token of this foundation is a pair of tailor's shears painted in the upper south window of the south aisle" (Wood). The cooks celebrated their chief holiday in Whitsun week, when they showed themselves in their bravery on horseback.

The tailors had their shops in Wincheles Row, and they had a custom of revelling on the vigil of S. John the Baptist.

"Caressing themselves with all joviality in meats and drinks they would in the midst of the night dance and take a circuit throughout all the streets, accompanied by divers musical instruments, and using some certain sonnets in praise of their profession and patron."

But such customs led to disturbances and were finally prohibited. The barbers, a company which existed till fifty years ago, maintained a light in Our Lady's Chapel at S. Frideswide's. Some of the regulations by which they bound themselves when they were incorporated by order of the Chancellor in 1348 are typical. The barbers, it should be added, were the mediæval physicians too.

Their ordinances provided that no person of that craft should work on a Sunday or shave any but such as were to preach or do a religious act on Sundays. No servant or man of the craft should reveal any infirmity or secret disease he had to his customers or patients. A master of the craft was to be chosen every year, to whom every one of his craft should be obedient during his year of office. Every apprentice that was to set up shop after his time was expired should first give the master and wardens with the rest of the society a dinner and pay for one pound of wax, and that being done, the said master and wardens with three other seniors of the craft should bring him to the chancellor upon their shoulders, before whom he was to take his oath to keep all the ordinations and statutes of the craft, and pay to Our Lady's box eightpence and the like sum to the chancellor. The same procedure must be observed by any foreigner that had not been prenticed in Oxford but desired to set up a shop to occupy as barber, surgeon, or waferer or maker of singing bread. All such as were of the craft were to receive at least sixpence a quarter of each customer that desired to be shaved every week in his chamber or house. If any member of the craft should take upon him to teach any person not an apprentice, he should pay 6s. 8d., whereof 3s. 4d. should go to the craft, 1s. 8d. to the chancellor, and 1s. 8d. to the proctors. Rules are also given for the observance of the barbers' annual holiday and the election of their master.

Stimulated by the presence of the kings without its walls and the growth of the university within, trade flourished so greatly that it was soon necessary to regulate it by minute provisions. In the reign of Edward II. (1319) the mayor and bailiffs were commanded to "prevent confusion in the merchandising of strangers, and those who were not free of any guild from thrusting out those who were." All traders and sellers who came to Oxford on market days—Wednesdays and Saturdays—were to know each one their places.

"The sellers of straw, with their horses and cattle that bring it," so ran the regulation, "shall stand between East Gate and All Saints' Church, in the middle of the King's Highway. The sellers of wood in carts shall stand between Shidyard (Oriel) Street and the tenement of John Maidstone and the tenement on the east side of the Swan Inn (now King Edward's Street, the ugly row of smug, commonplace houses which has been erected on the site of Swan Yard). The sellers of bark shall stand between S. Thomas' Hall (Swan Inn) and S. Edward's Lane (Alfred Street). The sellers of hogs and pigs shall stand between the churches of S. Mary and All Saints; the ale sellers between S. Edward's Lane and the Chequer Inn; the sellers of earthen-pots and coals by the said lane of S. Edward on the north side of the High Street. The sellers of gloves and whitawyers (dresses of white leather) shall stand between All Saints' Church and the house on the west side of the Mitre Inn; the furriers, linen and woollen drapers by the two-faced pump (which perhaps stood on the site of the later conduit at Carfax. This conduit was erected in 1616 and water brought to it from the hill springs above North Hincksey. It was removed in 1787 and presented to Earl Harcourt, who re-erected it at Nuneham Park some five miles from Oxford, where it may still be seen, on a slope commanding an extensive view of the Thames Valley between Abingdon and Oxford.)

"The bakers," the regulation continued, "shall stand between Carfax and North Gate, and behind them the foreign sellers of fish and those that are not free or of the guild. The tanners shall stand between Somner's Inn and Carfax; the sellers of cheese, milk, eggs, beans, new peas and butter from the corner of Carfax towards the Bailly; the sellers of hay and grass at the Pillory; the cornsellers between North Gate and Mauger Hall (the Cross Inn)."

Besides these market-stands the permanent trades and resident guilds had distinct spheres allotted to them. The cutlers, drapers, cooks and cordwainers had their special districts; the goldsmiths had their shops in All Saints' parish, the Spicery and Vintnery[11] lay to the south of S. Martin's; Fish Street extended to Folly Bridge, the Corn Market stretched away to North

Gate, the stalls of the butchers ranged in their Butchers' Row along the road to the Castle (Queen's Street). As for the great guild of weavers, there was a wool market in Holywell Green. Part of the ground since included in Magdalen College Grove was known as Parry's Mead, and here twenty-three looms were working at once, and barges came up to it on the Cherwell.

Thus then Oxford had attained to complete municipal self-government. She stood now in the first rank of municipalities. Her political importance is indicated by the many great assemblies that were held there. The great assembly under Cnut had closed the struggle between Englishman and Dane; that under Stephen ended the conquest of the Norman, whilst that under Henry III. begins the regular progress of constitutional liberty. In 1265, Simon de Montfort issued writs from Woodstock summoning the famous parliament to which towns sent members for the first time. Oxford no doubt was among the number, but the sheriff's returns are lost and it is not till 1295 that the names of two burgesses elected to represent her in the national council are recorded. The University did not obtain members until the first Parliament of James I. (1609), although her advice had often been consulted by kings and parliaments before.[12] So far, then, we have followed the growth of a town of increasing political and commercial importance. We have now to trace the growth within its borders of a new and rival body, which was destined, after a century or more of faction and disorder, to humble her municipal freedom to the dust.

CHAPTER III

THE ORIGIN OF THE UNIVERSITY

THE chroniclers of every mediæval town like to begin from Jove—or Genesis. The Oxford historians are no exception.

Famous antiquaries of ancient days carried back the date of the city to fabulous years. Wood gives the year 1009 B.C. as the authentic date, when Memphric, King of the Britons, built it and called it Caer Memphric. But these famous antiquaries, as we shall see, had an axe to grind.

Whatever the origin of Oxford may have been, a few bronze weapons and some pottery, preserved in the Museum, are the only remains of the British period that have been discovered. Great as were the natural advantages of the place, lying as it does on the banks of the chief river of the country at a point where a tributary opens up a district to the north, it would yet seem that there was no British settlement of importance at Oxford, for it was dangerous borderland between the provinces into which Britain was divided, liable to frequent hostile incursions, and therefore left uninhabited. And this would seem to be the reason why, when the road-making

Romans were driving their great streets through the neighbourhood, they left this seductive ford severely alone.

The first chronicler to associate Oxford with the name of King Memphric was John Rous, an imaginative historian, no respecter of facts, who died, full of years and inventions, in 1491. Hear him discourse in his fluent, pleasantly circumstantial style:

"About this time Samuel the servant of God was Judge in Judea, and King Magdan had two sons, that is to say Mempricius and Malun. The younger of the two having been treacherously slain by the elder, the fratricide inherited the kingdom. In the twentieth year of his reign, he was surrounded by a large pack of very savage wolves, and being torn and devoured by them, ended his existence in a horrible manner. Nothing good is related of him except that he begot an honest son and heir, Ebrancus by name, and built one noble city which he called from his own name Caer-Memre, but which afterwards in course of time was called Bellisitum, then Caerbossa, at length Ridohen, and last of all Oxonia, or by the Saxons Oxenfordia, from a certain egress out of a neighbouring ford. There arose here in after years an universal and noble seat of learning, derived from the renowned University of Grek-lade.

"It is situated between the rivers Thames and Cherwell which meet there. The city, just as Jerusalem, has to all appearance been changed; for as Mount Calvary, when Christ was crucified, was just outside the walls of the city, and now is contained within the circuit of the walls, so also there is now a large level space outside Oxford, contiguous to the walls of the town, which is called Belmount, which means beautiful mount, and this in a certain way agrees with one of the older names of the city before named and recited; that is to say Bellisitum; whence many are of opinion that the University from Greklade was transferred to this very Bellus Mons or Bellesitum before the coming of the Saxons and while the Britons ruled the island, and the Church of S. Giles, which was dedicated under the name of some other saint, was the place for the creation of graduates, as now is the Church of S. Mary, which is within the walls...."

The origin of the city is, of course, not the same thing as the origin of the University, and John Rous, it will be observed, has adopted the story according to which the University was said to have been transplanted to Oxford from "Grekelade." This story is found in its earliest form in the Oxford *Historiola*, the account of the University prefixed to the official registers of the chancellor and proctors. It was probably written towards the end of the reign of Edward III., somewhere in the third quarter of the fourteenth century. The sound of Greek in the name Cricklade is quite enough, in the minds of those who have studied mediæval chronicles— histories "farct with merry tales and frivolous poetry"—to account for the origin of the myth as to the Greek philosophers. Do you not find for instance, the name of Lechelade suggesting Latin schools (Latinelade) at that place by an analogous etymological conceit?

Saith the *Historiola*, then, after premising that the University is the most ancient, the most comprehensive, the most orthodox and the most richly endowed with privileges:—

"Very ancient British histories imply the priority of its foundation, for it is related that amongst the warlike Trojans, when with their leader Brutus they triumphantly seized the island, then called Albion, next Britain, and lastly England, certain philosophers came and chose a suitable place of habitation upon this island, on which the philosophers who had been Greek bestowed the name which they have left behind them as a record of their presence, and which exists to the present day, that is to say Grekelade...."

The grounds of the other statements quoted from John Rous are yet more fanciful. The assertion that the University was transferred from without to within the city walls is a vague echo of a worthless story, and the name given to the town Bellesitum is obviously a confusion arising from the latinised form of Beaumont, the palace which Henry I. built on the slope towards S. Giles. The names of Caer-bossa and Ridochen (Rhyd-y-chen) are equally unhistorical, and are based upon the fantastic Welsh equivalents of Oxenford, invented by the fertile genius of Geoffrey of Monmouth for the purposes of his romance (twelfth century).

It would scarcely have been worth while to mention even so briefly the ingenious myths of the early chroniclers if it had not been for the fact that they have swamped more scientific history and that they were used with immense gusto by the champions in that extraordinary controversy which broke out in the days of Elizabeth, and lasted, an inky warfare of wordy combatants, almost for centuries. It was a controversy in which innumerable authorities were quoted, and resort was had even to the desperate device of forgery.

It arose from the boast of the Cambridge orator, who on the occasion of a visit of Elizabeth to Cambridge, declared:

"To our great glory all histories with one voice testify that the Oxford University borrowed from Cambridge its most learned men, who in its schools provided the earliest cradle of the *ingenuæ artes*, and that Paris also and Cologne were derived from our University."

With that assertion the fat was in the fire. Assertions were issued, and counter-assertions, commentaries and counter-commentaries.

It is impossible to follow the course of the controversy here. Suffice it to say that when the war had been waged for some years, it seemed evident that the victory would lie with the Oxonians, who claimed Alfred as their founder, if they could prove their claim. And the claim appeared to be proved by a passage attributed to Asser, the contemporary historian of Alfred's deeds, and surreptitiously inserted into his edition of that author by the great Camden. But that passage occurs in none of the manuscripts of Asser, and certainly not in the one which Camden copied. It was probably adopted by him on the authority of an unscrupulous but interested partisan who, having invented it, attributed it to a "superior manuscript of Asser."

The University cannot, then, claim Alfred the Great either as her founder or restorer. All the known facts and indications point the other way. It was not till 912, some years after Alfred's death, that Edward the Elder obtained possession of Oxford, which was outside Alfred's kingdom; Asser knew nothing of this foundation. It was not till the days of Edward III., that Ralph Higden's *Polychronicon* apparently gave birth to the myth with the statement that Alfred

——

"By the counsel of S. Neot the Abbot, was the first to establish schools for the various arts at Oxford; to which city he granted privileges of many kinds."

And from that time the myth was repeated and grew.

But if King Alfred did not found the University who did? or how did it come into existence?

Briefly the case stands thus. Before the second half of the twelfth century—the age of Universities—there are no discoverable traces of such a thing at Oxford, but in the last twenty years of that century references to it are frequent and decided. The University was evidently established, and its reputation was widely spread.

There abounded there, contemporaries inform us, "men skilled in mystic eloquence, weighing the words of the law, bringing forth from their treasures things new and old." And the University was dubbed by the proud title "The Second School of the Church."

She was second, that is, to Paris, as a school of Theology, and to Paris, the researches of modern experts like Dr Rashdall lead us to believe, she owed her origin.

The Universities, the greatest and perhaps the most permanent of Mediæval Institutions, were a gradual and almost secret growth. For long centuries Europe had been sunk in the gloom of the Dark Ages. The light of learning shone in the cloister alone, and there burned with but a dim and flickering flame. In Spain not one priest in a thousand about the age of Charlemagne could address a common letter of salutation to another. Scarcely a single person could be found in Rome who knew the first elements of letters; in England, Alfred declared that he could not recollect one priest at the time of his accession who understood the ordinary prayers. Learning lay buried in the grave of Bede. At Court, emperors could not write, and in the country contracts were made verbally for lack of notaries who could draw up charters.

But towards the end of the eleventh century Europe began to recover from this state of poverty and degradation. Christendom had gained a new impulse from the Crusades. Trade revived and began to develop, some degree of tranquillity was restored, and the growing wealth of the world soon found expression in an increasing refinement of manners, in the sublime and beautiful buildings of the age of Cathedrals, and in a greater ardour for intellectual pursuits.

A new fervour of study arose in the West from its contact with the more cultured East. Everywhere throughout Europe great schools which bore the name of Universities were established.

The long mental inactivity of Europe broke up like ice before a summer's sun. Wandering teachers, such as Lanfranc or Anselm, crossed sea and land to spread the new power of knowledge. The same spirit of restlessness, of inquiry, of impatience with the older traditions of mankind, either local or intellectual, that had hurried half Christendom to the tomb of its Lord, crowded the roads with thousands of young scholars, hurrying to the chosen seats where teachers were gathered together. A new power, says an eloquent historian, had sprung up in the midst of a world as yet under the rule of sheer brute force. Poor as they were, sometimes even of a servile race, the wandering scholars, who lectured in every cloister, were hailed as "Masters" by the crowds at their feet.

This title of "Master" suggests, of course, the nomenclature of the Guilds. A University, in fact, was a Guild of Study. The word implies[13] a community of individuals bound together for any purpose, in this case for the purpose of teaching. It was applied to the whole body of students frequenting the "studium," and hence the term came to be used as synonymous with "studium" to denote the institution itself. The system of academical degrees dates from the second half of the twelfth century. After the manner of mediæval craftsmen in other trades, the profession of teaching was limited to those who had served an apprenticeship in a University or Guild of Study and were qualified as Masters of their Art. Nobody was allowed to teach without a licence from such a Guild, just as no butcher or tailor was allowed to ply his trade without having served his proper term and having been approved by the Masters of his Guild. A University degree, therefore, was originally simply a diploma of teaching, which afterwards came to be regarded as a title, when retained by men who had ceased to lecture or teach. "Bachelor" was the term applied to students who had ceased to be pupils but had not yet become teachers. The word was generally used to denote an apprentice or aspirant to Knighthood, but in the Universities came to have this technical signification. The degree of Bachelor was in fact an important step on the way to the higher degree of Master or Doctor.

One of the first symptoms of the twelfth century renaissance may be traced in the revival in Italy of the study of jurisprudence as derived from the laws of Justinian. For early in the twelfth century a professor named Irnerius opened a school of civil law at Bologna, and Lombardy was soon full of lawyers. Teachers of that profitable art soon spread from Bologna throughout

Europe, and their University was the first to receive from Frederic Barbarossa the privileges of legal incorporation. It presently became known as the special University of young archdeacons, whose mode of life gave rise to the favourite subject of debate "Can an archdeacon be saved?" But it was the school of philosophy at Paris which chiefly attracted the newly-kindled enthusiasm of the studious. The tradition of the schools of Charlemagne may have lingered there, although no direct connection between them and the University which now sprang into being can be proved. As early as 1109 William of Champeaux opened a school of logic, and it was to his brilliant and combative pupil, Peter Abelard, that the University owed its rapid advancement in the estimation of mankind. The multitude of disciples who flocked to his lectures, and listened with delight to his bold theories and his assertion of the rights of reason against authority, showed that a new spirit of enquiry and speculation was abroad. The poets and orators of antiquity were, indeed, beginning to be studied with genuine admiration, and the introduction into Europe of some of the Arabian writings on geometry and physics was opening the door to the development of mathematical science. But the flower of intellectual and scientific enquiry was destined to be nipped in the bud by the blighting influence of scholasticism. Already among the pupils of Abelard was numbered Peter Lombard, the future author of "The Sentences," a system of the doctrines of the Church, round which the dogmatic theology of the schoolmen, trammelled by a rigid network of dialectics, was to grow up.

It was the light before a dawn which never broke into day. But as yet the period was one of awakening and promise. Students from all parts crowded to Paris, and the Faculty[14] of Arts in the University was divided into four "nations"—those of France, Picardy, Normandy and England. John of Salisbury became famous as one of the Parisian teachers. Becket wandered to Paris from his school at Merton. After spending twelve years at Paris, John of Salisbury, the central figure of English learning in his time, finally returned to England. S. Bernard recommended him to Archbishop Theobald, and in the archbishop's household at Canterbury he found in existence a very School of Literature, where scholars like Vacarius came to lecture on civil law, where lectures and disputations were regularly held, and men like Becket and John of Poictiers were trained.

"In the house of my Lord the Archbishop," writes Peter of Blois, "are most scholarly men, with whom is found all the uprightness of justice, all the caution of providence, every form of learning. They after prayers and before meals, in reading, in disputing, in the decision of causes constantly exercise themselves. All the knotty questions of the realms are referred to us...."

This archiepiscopal school was in fact a substitute for the as yet undeveloped Universities. Besides this school there were, in England, schools in connection with all the great Cathedral establishments and with many of the monasteries as well as the houses of the nobles. There were, for instance, great schools at S. Alban's and at Oxford. But these *studia* were not *studia generalia*; they were schools merely, not Universities. It was perhaps to the school which had sprung up in connection with S. Frideswide's monastery that Vacarius lectured, if he lectured at Oxford at all.

It was in such a monastic school, in connection with S. Frideswide's, Osney, or S. George's in the Castle, that Robert Pullen of Paris lectured on the Bible for five years (1133), and Theobaldus Stampensis taught. Henry Beauclerc endeavoured to retain the services of the former by offering him a bishopric, but he refused it and left England; Stephen, on the other hand, bade Vacarius cease from lecturing, since the new system of law, which he taught and which had converted the Continent, was inconsistent with the old laws of the English realm. As to Theobaldus Stampensis, he styles himself Magister Oxenefordiæ, and letters from him exist which show that he, a Norman ecclesiastic who had taught at Caen, taught at Oxford before 1117. An anonymous reply to a tractate in which he attacked the monks, is responsible for the statement that this former Doctor of Caen had at Oxford "sixty or a hundred clerks, more or less." But one school or one lecturer does not make a University.

It has, however, been held, that just as the University of Paris developed from the schools of Notre Dame, so the University of Oxford grew out of the monastic schools of S. Frideswide's. Such a growth would have been natural. But if this had been the real origin of the University, it may be regarded as certain that the members of it would have been subjected to some such authority as that exercised by the Chancellor of Notre Dame over the masters and scholars of Paris. But at Oxford, the masters and scholars were never under the jurisdiction of the Prior or Abbot of S. Frideswide's or Osney. If they had been, some trace or record of their struggle for emancipation must have survived. The Chancellor, moreover, when he is first mentioned, proves to be elected by the masters and scholars and to derive his authority, not from any capitular or monastic body in Oxford, but from the Bishop of Lincoln. And the University buildings themselves, in their primitive form, bear silent witness to the same fact, that the schools or studium in connection with which the University grew up were in no way connected with conventual churches and monasteries. For the schools were not near S. Frideswide's but S. Mary's.

The independence of the Oxford masters from any local ecclesiastical authority is a significant fact. Combined with another it seems to admit of but one explanation. That other fact is the suddenness with which the reputation of Oxford sprang up. Before 1167 there is, as we have shown, no evidence of the existence of a *studium generale* there, but there are indications enough that in the next few years students began to come, clerks from all parts of England.

The account of the visit of Giraldus Cambrensis (1184-5) reveals the existence of a Studium on a large scale, with a number of Masters and Faculties. It is a Studium Generale by that time without a doubt. And in 1192 Richard of Devizes speaks of the clerks of Oxford as so numerous that the city could hardly feed them.

What, then, is the explanation of this so sudden development? Probably it lies in a migration of scholars to Oxford at this time. The migratory habits of mediæval masters and scholars are familiar to everyone who has the smallest acquaintance with the history of the Universities. The Universities of Leipzig, Reggio, Vicenza, Vercelli, and Padua, for instance, were founded by migrations from one University or another. The story of Oxford itself will furnish instances in plenty of the readiness of the University to threaten to migrate and, when hard pressed, to fulfil their threat. Migrations to Cambridge, Stamford, and Northampton are among the undoubted facts of our history. Such a migration then would be in the natural course of things, though it would not satisfy the pride of the inventors of the Alfred myth. But a migration of this kind did not take place without a cause. A cause however is not to seek. At this very period the quarrel of Henry II. with Thomas a Becket was the occasion for a migration from Paris, the ordinary seat of higher education for English ecclesiastics.

A letter from John of Salisbury to Peter the Writer in 1167 contains this remark: "France, the most polite and civilised of all nations, has expelled the foreign students from her borders."

This, as Dr Rashdall suggests, may possibly have been a measure of hostility aimed by the French King against the oppressor of Holy Church and against the English ecclesiastics, who as a body sided with their King against their not yet canonised primate.

Henry II., on the other hand, took the same measures to punish the partisans of Becket. All clerks were forbidden to go to or from the Continent without leave of the King, and all clerks who possessed revenues in England were summoned to return to England within three months, "as they love their revenues." This would produce an exodus from Paris. A large number of English masters and scholars must have been compelled to return home. According to the usual procedure of mediæval students they were likely to collect in some one town and set up under their old masters something of their old organisation. These ordinances were promulgated between the years 1165 and 1169. The ports were strictly watched in order to enforce this edict.

The migrating scholars would land at Dover and lodge, perhaps, for a night or two at the Benedictine Priory there, before going on to Canterbury. Here, if they had been so minded, they might have stayed, and swelled the great literary circle, with its teachers and libraries, which had been formed there. But they left Gervase at Canterbury to write his history, and Nigel to compose his verses and polish his satires. Passing northwards, they might, had they come a little later, have been absorbed at Lambeth, and the scheme of Archbishop Baldwin for setting up a College there, which should be a centre of ecclesiastical learning, emancipated from monastic restrictions, might then have been realised. Or, if they had wished to attach themselves to any existing establishment, the monastic schools of St Alban's might have welcomed them.

But they chose otherwise. It may be that their experience of Paris led them to choose a place which was neither a capital nor a See-town. At any rate the peculiar position of Oxford, which was neither of these and yet an important commercial and political centre, made it admirably suited for the free development of a University, unharassed by bishops and unmolested by lord mayors.

At Oxford, too, was the Palace of the King, and Henry II. was a champion of literary culture by his very descent. His grandfather had earned the title of Henry Beauclerk, the scholar King; and Fulk the Good, who had told King Lothar that an unlearned king is a crowned ass, was a lineal ancestor of his. And apart from his own hereditary tastes, the position of Henry as the most powerful king of the West, and the international correspondence which that position involved, tended to make the Court a centre of literary activity. Learning was sought not for itself only, but as a part of the equipment of a man of the world. For whatever reason, whether they were influenced by a desire, springing from experience of Paris, to establish themselves where they might be most independent, or by the physical advantages of Oxford, or the hope of favour from the King who had recalled them, and who at his Court and about his Palace of Beaumont had gathered round him all that was enlightened and refined in English and Norman society, or whether they were directed by mere chance, settling for a session and staying for centuries, it was to Oxford they came.

Here ready to receive them they would find a town which stood in the front rank of municipalities, commanding the river valley along which the commerce of Southern England mainly flowed. The mitred Abbey of Austin Canons, the Priory of S. Frideswide, the Castle of the D'Oiglis, and the Royal Palace without the Vallum marked the ecclesiastical and political importance of the place; the settlement of one of the wealthiest of the English Jewries in the very heart of the town indicated, as it promoted, the activity of its trade. It was still surrounded on all sides by a wild forest country. The moors of Cowley and Bullingdon fringed the course of the Thames; the great woods of Shotover and Bagley closed the horizon on south and east. But Oxford was easy of access, for there were the great roads that crossed at Carfax and there was the thoroughfare of the Thames. And facility of communication meant regularity of supplies, a matter of great importance to a floating population of poor students.

Here, then, the migrating masters and scholars set up their schools, and within a very short time the reputation of the University was established throughout the length and breadth of the land.

Giraldus Cambrensis, a Welshman, who had achieved fame as a lecturer at Paris, has given us an interesting account of his visit to Oxford in 1187. He came there with the purpose of reading aloud portions of his new work, as Herodotus read his history at the Panathenaic festival at Athens or at the National Games of Greece. Giraldus had written a book on Ireland— Topographia—and he chose this method of publishing and advertising it. He writes of himself in the third person, without any excessive modesty. You might almost think he was a modern author, asking his critics to dinner and writing his own "Press notices."

"In course of time, when the work was finished and revised, not wishing to hide his candle under a bushel, but wishing to place it in a candlestick so that it might give light, he resolved to read it before a vast audience at Oxford, where the clergy in England chiefly flourished and excelled in clerkly lore. And as there were three distinctions or divisions in the work, and each division occupied a day, the readings lasted three successive days. On the first day he received and entertained at his lodgings all the poor people of the whole town; on the second all the doctors of the different faculties, and such of their pupils as were of fame and note; on the third the rest of the scholars with the milites of the town, and many burghers. It was a costly and noble act, for the authentic and ancient times of the poets were thus in some measure renewed; and neither present nor past time can furnish any record of such a solemnity having ever taken place in England."

It is evident from this passage that the Schools at Oxford were by this time of considerable note and size. There was a University here now in fact if not in name or by charter. A few years later the records reveal to us the first known student in it. He was a clerk from Hungary named Nicholas, to whom Richard I. who had been born in the Palace of Beaumont, made an allowance of half a mark weekly for his support during his stay at Oxford for the purpose of study.

Thus, then, by the beginning of the reign of King John, we may be sure that there was established at Oxford a University, or place of general study, and this University had attracted to itself an academic population, which was estimated by contemporaries at no less than three thousand souls. And now, just as the country won its Great Charter of Liberties from that oppressive and intolerable Angevin monarch, so documentary evidence of the independent powers of the University was first obtained, as the result of a series of events, in which the citizens of Oxford had been encouraged to commit an act of unjust revenge by their reliance on John's quarrel with the pope and the clergy. The pope had laid the whole country under an interdict; the people were forbidden to worship their God and the priests to administer the sacraments; the church-bells were silent and the dead lay unburied on the ground. The King retaliated by confiscating the land of the clergy who observed the interdict, by subjecting them in spite of their privileges to the Royal Courts, and often by leaving outrages on them unpunished. "Let him go," he said, when a Welshman was brought before him for the murder of a priest, "he has killed my enemy." Such were the political conditions, when at Oxford a woman of the town was found murdered in circumstances which pointed to the guilt of a student. The citizens were eager for vengeance, and they took the matter into their own hands (1209).

The offender had fled, but the mayor and burgesses invading his hostel arrested two innocent students who lodged in the same house. They hurried them outside the walls of Oxford, and, with the ready assent of John, who was then at Woodstock, hung them forthwith. This was a defiance of ecclesiastical liberty. For it was a chief principle of the Church that all clerks and scholars, as well as all higher officials in the hierarchy, should be subject to ecclesiastical jurisdiction alone. For this principle Becket had died, and in defence of this principle a quarrel now arose between the University and the town which bade fair to end in the withdrawal of the former altogether from Oxford. In protest the masters and scholars migrated from the town, and transferred their schools to Paris, to Reading and to Cambridge. It is, indeed, to this migration that the Studium Generale on the banks of the Cam may owe its existence.

The halls of Oxford were now deserted, the schools were empty. So they remained as long as John's quarrel with the pope endured. But when the King had knelt before the Papal Legate, Pandulf (1213), and sworn fealty to the pope, the Church succeeded in bringing the citizens, who had no doubt found their pockets severely affected in the meantime, to their senses. A Legatine ordinance of the following year is the University's first charter of privilege. The citizens performed public penance; stripped and barefooted they went daily to the churches, carrying scourges in their hands and chaunting penitential psalms. When they had thus obtained absolution, and the University had returned, the Legate issued a decree by which the townsmen were bound in future, if they arrested a clerk, to deliver him up on demand to the Bishop of Lincoln, the Archdeacon of Oxford or his official, to the Chancellor set over the scholars by the bishop, or some other authorised representative of the episcopal power. And thus was established that immunity from lay jurisdiction which, under slightly different conditions, is still enjoyed by every resident member of the University.

This is the first allusion in any authentic document to the existence of the chancellorship.

Among the minor penalities to which the townsmen were now subjected was the provision that for ten years one-half the rent of existing hostels and schools was to be altogether remitted, and for ten years more rents were to remain as already taxed before the secession by the joint authority of the town and the masters. Further, the town was forever to pay an annual sum of fifty-two shillings to be distributed among poor scholars on the feast of S. Nicholas, the patron of scholars, and at the same time to feast a hundred poor scholars on bread and beer, pottage and flesh or fish. Victuals were to be sold at a reasonable rate, and an oath to the observance of these provisions was to be taken by fifty of the chief burgesses, and to be annually renewed at the discretion of the bishop. The payment of the fine was transferred by an agreement with the town to the Abbey of Eynsham in 1219, and by an ordinance of Bishop Grossetete the money was applied to the foundation of a "chest."

The size and importance of the University was shortly afterwards increased by a somewhat similar disturbance which took place in Paris (1229). A brawl developed into a serious riot, in which several scholars, innocent or otherwise, were killed by the Provost of Paris and his archers. The masters and students failing to obtain redress departed from Paris in anger. Henry seized this opportunity of humiliating the French Monarchy by fomenting the quarrel and at the same time inviting "the masters and the University of scholars at Paris" to come to study in England, where they should receive ample liberty and privileges. A migration to Oxford was the result of this royal invitation, which was highly appreciated not only by the English students at Paris but also by many foreigners. Two years later the King was able to boast that Oxford was frequented by a vast number of students, coming from various places over the sea, as well as from all parts of Britain.

The University remained till well towards the end of the thirteenth century a customary rather than a legal or statutory corporation. And in its customs it was a reproduction of the Society of Masters at Paris.

The privileges and customs of Paris were, in fact, the type from which the customs and privileges of all the Universities which were now being founded in Europe were reproduced, and according to which they were confirmed by bulls and charters. Thus in 1246 Innocent V. enjoined Grossetete to see that in Oxford nobody exercised the office of teaching except after he had qualified according to the custom of the Parisians. Whilst then the idea of a University was undoubtedly borrowed from the Continent, and Oxford, so far as her organisation was concerned, was framed on the Continental models, yet the establishment of a University in England was an event of no small importance. Teaching was thereby centralised, competition promoted, and intellectual speculation stimulated. At a University there was more chance of intellectual freedom than in a monastic school.

If such was the origin of the University, Alfred did not found it, still less did he found University College.

University College, "the Hall of the University," may undoubtedly claim with justice to be the earliest University endowment. But it was at one time convenient to that College, in the course of a lawsuit in which their case was a losing one, to claim, when forgeries failed them, to be a royal foundation. The Alfred myth was to hand, and they used it with unblushing effrontery and a confident disregard of historical facts and dates. Their impudence for the time being fulfilled its purpose, and it also left its mark on the minds of men. The tradition still lingers. The College Chapel was dedicated at the end of the fourteenth century to S. Cuthbert, Durham's Saint, but the seventeenth-century Bidding Prayer still perpetuates the venerable fiction, and first among the benefactors of the "College of the great Hall of the University," the name of King Alfred is cited. In 1872 the College even celebrated, by the English method of a dinner, the supposed thousandth anniversary of its existence. At that dinner the Chancellor of the Exchequer, Robert Lowe (Lord Sherbrooke), wittily upheld the tradition of his College. For, he argued, if Oxford was in the hands of the Danes at the time when Alfred founded the University, that fact only strengthened their case. For King Alfred was a man so much in advance of his age that it is not surprising to find that he had anticipated the modern political doctrine, which teaches us that the surest way to earn popularity, is to give away the property of our opponents.

The story of the lawsuit will be found to be instructive if discreditable.

In 1363 the College by two purchases obtained possession of considerable property in land and houses which had been the estate of Philip Gonwardy and Joan his wife. After the College had been in possession some fourteen years, however, a certain Edmund Francis and Idonea his wife came forward to dispute the right to it. They maintained that Philip Gonwardy and his wife had had no true title to the estate, for it, or part of it, had been bequeathed to them by one John Goldsmith in 1307. And he, they asserted, had by a later document settled the same property upon them. The case was tried at Westminster; transferred to Oxford, where the College obtained a verdict in their favour, and then taken back on appeal to Westminster.

It was at this point that the document known as the French petition—it is written in the Court French of the day—was filed. Finding, apparently, that the case was going against them, the College determined to use the myth about Alfred, claim to be a royal foundation and thus throw the matter, and their liberties along with it, into the King's hands, leaving the case to be decided by the Privy Council.

"To their most excellent and most dread and most sovereign Lord the King," so ran the petition, "and to his most sage council, shew his poor orators, the master and scholars of his College, called Mickle University Hall in Oxenford, which College was first founded by your noble progenitor, King Alfred, whom may God assoil, for the maintenance of twenty-six divines for ever; that whereas one Edmund Francis, citizen of London, hath in virtue of his great power commenced a suit in the King's Bench, against some of the tenants of the said masters and scholars, for certain lands and tenements, with which the College was endowed ... and from time to time doth endeavour to destroy and utterly disinherit your said College of the rest of its endowment.... That it may please your most sovereign and gracious Lord King, since you are our true founder and advocate, to make the aforesaid parties appear before your very sage council, to show in evidences upon the rights of the aforesaid matter, so that upon account of the poverty of your said orators your said College be not disinherited, having regard, most gracious Lord, that the noble saints, John of Beverley, Bede, and Richard Armacan (Fitzralph, Archbishop of Armagh), and many other famous doctors and clerks, were formerly scholars in your said College, and commenced divines therein, and this for God's sake, and as a deed of charity."

This deed, then, and others, these mere children in litigation did deliberately forge, attaching the Chancellor's seal thereto, in order to substantiate their absurd, but profitable, pretension.

The device was successful for a time, although the very petition contains within itself glaring historical contradictions, which either show supreme ignorance on the part of the masters and scholars or a cynical assumption of the historical ignorance of lawyers. If the College was founded by King Alfred who came to the throne in 872, it would seem a little unwise to instance as famous scholars of that foundation "noble Saints" like John of Beverley, who was Archbishop of York in 705, and the venerable Bede who died in 735.

As to the real founder of University College all the evidence points to William, Archdeacon of Durham, who is mentioned as one of the five distinguished English scholars who left Paris in 1229, in consequence of the riots between the townsfolk and the University. Henry's invitation to the Paris masters to come and settle at Oxford was immediately accepted by the other four. Their example was probably soon followed by William, after a sojourn at Angers. He was appointed Rector of Wearmouth, and is said to have "abounded in great revenues, but was gaping after greater." Some litigation with the Bishop of Durham led him to appeal to the Papal Court. His appeal was successful, but it availed him little, for on his journey home he died at Rouen (1249). His bones are said by Skelton to lie in the Chapel of the Virgin in the Cathedral there. He left 310 marks in trust to the University to invest for the benefit and support of a certain number of masters. It was actually the first endowment of its kind, but it is to Alan Basset, who died about 1243, that the credit of providing the first permanent endowment for an Oxford scholar is due. For he conceived the idea of combining a scholarship with a Chantry. He left instructions in his will in accordance with which his executors arranged with the Convent of Bicester for the payment of eight marks a year to two chaplains, who should say mass daily for the souls of the founder and his wife, and at the same time study in the schools of Oxford or elsewhere.

This was a step in the direction of founding a College, and indeed the original plan of William was hardly more imposing.

The University placed Durham's money in a "Chest," and used it partly on their own business and partly in loans to others, barons in the Barons' War for instance. Such loans were seldom repaid, and only 210 marks remained. This sum was expended in purchasing houses. The first house bought (1253) by the University was at the corner of School Street and St Mildred's Lane (*tenementum angulare in vico scholarum*).

The site of this the first property held by the University for educational purposes[15] is now included in the front, the noisy, over-decorated front, of Brasenose College. It was called, naturally enough, first the Hall of the University and afterwards the little Hall of the University. A second purchase was made in 1255, when a tenement called Drogheda Hall, the then first house in the High Street on the north side, was bought. It stands almost opposite to the present Western Gate of the College. Brasenose Hall was the next purchase under William's bequest (1262), and (1270) a quit rent of fifteen shillings, charged on two houses in S. Peter's parish, was the last. William of Durham had not founded a College. There is nothing to show that the purchase of houses by the University was originally made with any other object than that of securing a sound investment of the trust money. There is nothing to show, that is, either that the houses were bought originally and specifically as habitations for the pensioned masters (though they *may* have lodged there), or that it was originally intended, either by the University or the founder, that they should form a community.

Statutes were not granted to the masters admitted to the benefits of this foundation until the year 1280, and by that time a precedent had been created. From the year 1280, then, may be dated the incorporation of what is now known as University College. A very small society of poor masters were, according to the revised plan, to live together on the bounty of William of Durham and devote themselves to the study of theology. And this idea of association was evidently adopted from the rule for Merton Hall laid down by Merton six years before. The revenue from the fund increased rapidly, so that by 1292, the society was increased from "four poor masters" to one consisting of two classes of scholars, the seniors receiving six and eightpence a year more than the juniors, and having authority over them. Other clerks of good character, not on the foundation, were permitted to hire lodgings in the Hall, prototypes of the modern commoner. Funds and benefactions accrued to the Hall. A library was built, and the society gradually enlarged. Members of it were enjoined to live like Saints and to speak Latin. In the election of new Fellows a preference was given to those "born nearest to the parts of Durham." And a graduated fine was imposed, according to which a scholar who insulted another in private was to pay a shilling, before his fellows two shillings, and if in the street, in church or recreation ground, six and eightpence. For the administration of the College funds a bursar was annually appointed, whose accounts were subsequently approved and signed by the Chancellor. This practice of University supervision was maintained till 1722.

Yet another body of statutes was promulgated in 1311. The study of theology and the preference given to those who hailed from Durham were emphasised in accordance with the founder's wishes. The Senior Fellow was required to be ordained, but any Fellow who was appointed to a benefice of five marks a year now forfeited his election. This latter regulation, which occurs in substance in most of the fourteenth century foundations—by the Statutes of Queens, indeed, a Fellow who refused a benefice forfeited his fellowship—shows that fellowships were intended not as mere endowments of learning but as stepping-stones to preferment. It does not, on the other hand, show that the founders did not contemplate the existence of life-fellows. I think that it is tolerably clear Walter de Merton did. The office of Master of the College grew out of the position of the Senior Fellow; his authority was asserted by new statutes given in 1476.

It was in 1332 that the scholars of William of Durham moved from the corner house on the north side of the High Street, if that was where they abode, to the site of their present College, bounded by Logic Lane and Grove Street, and forming in the southern curve of the High Street, one of the most effective and noble features in that splendid sweep which embraces, on the other side, Queen's, All Souls', St Mary's, Brasenose, and All Saints'.

The society had received large benefactions from a generous donor, Philip Ingleberd of Beverley, and they now purchased Spicer's (formerly Durham's) Hall, the first house in St Mary's parish, which stood near the present western gateway of University College. Further benefactions made further purchases possible. White Hall and Rose Hall in Kybald Street were bought, and Lodelowe Hall, on the east of Spicer's Hall (1336). Spicer's Hall soon came to be known as the University Hall; the hall next to it, when acquired, was distinguished as Great University Hall. The reversion to the remainder of the High Street frontage, between Lodelowe Hall and the present Logic Lane, was not secured till 1402, when the munificence of Walter Skirlaw, Bishop of Durham, enabled the society to extend their property and their numbers. The tenements thus acquired were called Little University Hall and the Cock on the Hoop. The next purchase of the College involved them in that lawsuit which has had so curious a result upon the imaginations of its subsequent members.

Thus, then, the foundation of William had become a College, "the first daughter of Alma Mater." Being the first "Hall" acquired by the University it came to be spoken of as "The Hall of the University," and the members of the foundation, as "Scholars of University Hall." Their proper title, "Scholars of the Hall of William of Durham," gradually fell out of use. Strangers to the University system usually find themselves confused by the relations of the University and the Colleges. The University, then, let it be said, is a corporation existing apart from the Colleges; the Colleges are separate incorporated foundations, independent though practically subordinate to it.

The old thatched halls of wood and clay were used till it became necessary to rebuild in 1632. A smaller version of the seventeenth century quadrangle then constructed was finished in 1719.

For in 1714 had died Dr John Radcliffe, a famous and witty doctor, whose skill had secured him the post of court physician and whose wit had deprived him of it. For he offended William III. by remarking to that dropsical monarch, that he would not have his two legs for his two kingdoms. It had long been known that the worthy doctor intended to make his College and his University his heirs. His munificence was rewarded by a public funeral of unexampled splendour and a grave in the nave of St Mary's. The bulk of his fortune he devoted to specific purposes benefiting the University, but he left a large sum to University College "for the building of the front down to Logic Lane, answerable to the front already built, and for building the master's lodging therein, and chambers for his two travelling Fellows," whom he endowed. The Radcliffe Quadrangle commemorates his benefaction to his College; the Radcliffe Infirmary (Woodstock Road, 1770), the Radcliffe Observatory, built 1772-1795, on a site given by George, Duke of Marlborough; and last, but not least the Radcliffe Library, or as it is more usually termed the Camera Bodleiana (James Gibbs, architect, 1737-1749) stand forth in the city as the noble monuments of his intelligent munificence.

The magnificent dome of the latter forms one of the most striking features among Oxford buildings.[16]

Neither the University of Oxford nor University College can justly claim to be connected with the name of Alfred the Great. But there are relics of Alfred and Alfred's time preserved at Oxford which should be of interest to the visitor. In the Bodleian may be seen certain coins which have led historians to assume that Alfred set up a mint at Oxford, and to argue from this supposed fact that his rule was firmly established over Mercia. The coins in question, which were all found in Lancashire, are variations of the type bearing these letters;—

Obverse. ORSNA, then in another line ELFRED, and in the third line FORDA. *Reverse* BERNV + + + ALDN°

It is assumed that these words indicate that Bernwald was a moneyer who was authorised by Alfred to strike coins at Oxford. But why Oxford should be written Orsnaforda and why, instead of the usual practice of abbreviation, the name of the place of the mint should have been written wrongly and at excessive length is not explained. I do not think there is any sufficient reason to connect the Orsnaforda coins with Oxford at all.

Whether Alfred's sceptre held sway over Mercia so that it can be stated definitely that "Wessex and Mercia were now united as Wessex and Kent had long been united by their allegiance to the same ruler" (Green) or not, the fact is not to be deduced from an imaginary mint at Oxford, any more than from the forged documents in the archives of University College or from the presence of what is known as King Alfred's jewel in the University galleries, (Beaumont Street).

This beautiful specimen of gold enamelled work was found in Somersetshire in 1693 and added to the Ashmolean collections a little later. The inscription "Aelfred mee heht gevvrcan" (Alfred ordered me to be made) which it bears has earned it its title.

The promotion of Edmund Rich, the Abingdon lad who was first made an archbishop and then a saint, to the degree of Master of Arts, is the earliest mention of that degree in Oxford. The story of his life there gives the best illustration we have of the early years and growth of the University.

In the ardour of knowledge and the passionate purity of youth he vowed himself to a life of study and chastity. In the spirit of mystical piety which was ever characteristic of him, secretly as a boy he took Mary for his bride. Perhaps at eventide, when the shadows were gathering in the Church of S. Mary and the crowd of teachers and students were breaking up from the rough schools which stood near the western doors of the church in the cemetery without, he approached the image of the Virgin and slipped on Mary's finger a gold ring. On that ring was engraved "that sweet Ave with which the Angel at the Annunciation had hailed the Virgin."

Devout and studious, the future saint was not without boyish tastes. He paid more attention to the music and singing at S. Mary's, we are told, than to the prayers. On one occasion he was slipping out of the church before the service was finished in order to join the other students at their games. But at the north door a divine apparition bade him return, and from that time his devotion grew more fervent. It is recorded with astonishment by his biographers as a mark of his singular piety, that when he had taken his degree as Master he would attend mass each day before lecturing, contrary to the custom of the scholars of that time, and although he was not yet in orders. For this purpose he built a chapel to the Virgin in the parish where he then lived. His example was followed by his pupils. "So study," such was the maxim he loved to impress upon them, "as if you were to live for ever; so live as if you were to die to-morrow." How little the young scholar, to whom Oxford owes her first introduction to the Logic of Aristotle, cared for the things of this world is shown by his contemptuous treatment of the fees which the students paid to the most popular of their teachers. He would throw down the money on the window-sill, and there burying it in the dust which had accumulated, "dust to dust, ashes to ashes," he would cry, celebrating its obsequies. And there the fee would lie till a student in joke or earnest theft ran off with it. So for six years he lectured in Arts. But even knowledge brought its troubles. The Old Testament, which with the copy of the Decretals long formed his sole library, frowned down upon a love of secular learning, from which Edmund found it hard to wean himself. The call came at last. He was lecturing one day in Mathematics, when the form of his dead mother appeared to him. "My son," she seemed to say, "what art thou studying? What are these strange diagrams over which thou porest so intently?"

She seized Edmund's right hand, and in the palm drew three circles, within which she wrote the names of the Father, Son and the Holy Ghost. "Be these thy diagrams henceforth, my son," she cried. And so directed, the student devoted himself henceforth to Theology.

This story, Green observes, admirably illustrates the latent opposition between the spirit of the University and the spirit of the Church. The feudal and ecclesiastical order of the old mediæval world were both alike threatened by the new training. Feudalism rested on local isolation. The University was a protest against this isolation of man from man. What the Church and Empire had both aimed at and both failed in, the knitting of Christian nations together into a vast commonwealth, the Universities of the time actually did.

On the other hand, the spirit of intellectual inquiry promoted by the Universities, ecclesiastical bodies though they were, threatened the supremacy of the Church. The sudden expansion of the field of education diminished the importance of those purely ecclesiastical and theological studies, which had hitherto absorbed the whole intellectual energies of mankind. For, according to the monastic ideal, theology was confined to mere interpretation of the text of Scripture and the dicta of the Fathers or Church. To this narrow science all the sciences were the handmaids. They were regarded as permissible only so far as they contributed to this end. But the great outburst of intellectual enthusiasm in the twelfth and thirteenth centuries created a momentary revolution in these matters. The whole range of science as revealed by the newly discovered treasures of Greek thinkers and Roman Jurists was now thrown open to the student. And this faint revival of physical science, this temporary restoration of classical literature, a re-discovery as it were of an older and a greater world, and contact with a larger, freer life, whether in mind, in society or politics, introduced a spirit of scepticism, of doubt, of denial, into the realms of unquestionable belief.

But the Church was alive to the danger. Fiercely she fought the tide of opposition, and at last won back the allegiance of the Universities. Through the Schoolmen ecclesiasticism once more triumphed, and the reign of Theology was resumed. Soon scholasticism absorbed the whole mental energy of the student world. The old enthusiasm for knowledge died down; science was discredited, and literature in its purer forms became extinct.

The scholastic philosophy, so famous for several ages, has passed away and been forgotten. We cannot deny that Roscelin, Anselm, Abelard, Peter Lombard, Albertus Magnus, Thomas Aquinas, Duns Scotus and Ockham were men of acute and even profound understanding, the giants of their own generation. But all their inquiries after truth were vitiated by two insurmountable obstacles—the authority of Aristotle and the authority of the Church. For Aristotle, whom the scholastics did not understand, and who had been so long held at bay as the most dangerous foe of mediæval faith, whom none but Anti-Christ could comprehend, was now turned, by the adoption of his logical method in the discussion and definition of theological dogma, into its unexpected ally. It was this very method which led to that "unprofitable subtlety and curiosity" which Lord Bacon notes as the vice of the scholastic philosophy.

Yet the scholastic mode of dispute, admitting of no termination and producing no conviction, was sure in the end to cause scepticism, just as the triviality of the questions on which the schoolmen wasted their amazing ingenuity was sure at last to produce disgust. What could be more trifling than a disquisition about the nature of angels, their means of conversing, and the morning and evening states of their understanding, unless perhaps it were a subtle and learned dispute as to whether a chimæra, buzzing in a vacuum, can devour second intentions? John of Salisbury observed of the Parisian dialecticians in his own time, that after several years absence he found them not a step advanced, and still employed in urging and parrying the same arguments. His observation was applicable to the succeeding centuries. After three or four hundred years the scholastics had not untied a single knot or added one equivocal truth to the domain of philosophy. Then men discovered at last that they had given their time for the promise of wisdom, and had been cheated in the bargain. At the revival of letters the pretended science had few advocates left, save among the prejudiced or ignorant adherents of established systems.

And yet, in the history of education and of the historical events which education directs, the discussions of the schoolmen hold a place not altogether contemptible. Their disputes did at least teach men to discuss and to define, to reason and to inquire. And thus was promoted the critical spirit which was boldly to challenge the rights of the Pope, and to receive and profit by the great disclosures of knowledge in a future age.

Of the early schools and the buildings which sprang into existence to mark the first beginnings of the University, no trace remains.

The church of S. Giles in north Oxford, which, as we have seen, is the church claimed by Rous as the S. Mary's of his imaginary University in Beaumont Fields, is the only architectural illustration of this period. It was consecrated by S. Hugh, the great Bishop of Lincoln, and is of interest as affording one of the earliest examples of lancet work in England (1180-1210?). The high placed windows in the north wall of the nave are Norman; the tower is in the Transition style.

CHAPTER IV

THE COMING OF THE FRIARS

SCARCELY had the University established itself in Oxford, when an immigration into that city took place, which was destined to have no inconsiderable influence on its history. Bands of men began to arrive and to settle there, members of new orders vowed to poverty and ignorance, whose luxury in after years was to prove a scandal, and whose learning was to control the whole development of thought.

In the thirteenth century the power of the priesthood over Christendom was at its height, but it was losing its religious hold over the people. The whole energy of the Church seemed to be absorbed in politics; spiritually the disuse of preaching, the decline of the monastic orders into rich landowners, the non-residence and ignorance of parish priests combined to rob her of her proper influence. Grossetete issued ordinances which exhorted the clergy, but in vain, not to haunt taverns, gamble or share in drinking bouts, and in the rioting and debauchery of the barons.

It was in these circumstances that Dominic and Francis, men so strangely different in other ways, were moved to found orders of New Brethren, who should meet false sanctity by real sanctity; preaching friars who should subsist on the alms of the poor and carry the Gospel to them. The older monasticism was reversed; the solitary of the cloister was exchanged for the preacher, the monk for the friar. Everywhere the itinerant preachers, whose fervid appeal, coarse wit and familiar stories brought religion into the market-place, were met with an outburst of enthusiasm. On their first coming to Oxford, the Dominicans or Black Friars were received with no less enthusiasm than elsewhere.

Lands were given to them in Jewry; buildings and a large school were erected for them by benefactors like Walter Malclerk, Bishop of Carlisle, and Isabel de Boulbec, Countess of Oxford, or the friendly Canons of St Frideswide. So greatly did they flourish that they soon outgrew their accommodation. They sold their land and buildings, and with the proceeds built themselves a house and schools and church "on a pleasant isle in the south suburbs," which was granted them by Henry III. (1259). The site of their new habitation at the end of Speedwell Street (Preachers' Lane) is indicated by the Blackfriars Road and Blackfriars Street in the parish of St Ebbe. Their library was large and full of books; the church was dedicated to S. Nicholas. It was situated near Preachers' Bridge, which spanned the Trill Mill Stream.

The Grey Friars followed hard on the heels of the Black. For in the year 1224 nine Franciscans arrived at Dover. Five of them went to Canterbury, four to London, whence two of them made their way to Oxford—Richard of Ingeworth and Richard of Devon. Their journey was eventful. Night drew on as they approached Oxford. The waters were high and they were fain to seek shelter in a grange belonging to the monks of Abingdon "in a most vast and solitary wood" (Culham?).

"Humbly knocking at the door, they desired the monks for God's love to give them entertainment for that night. The porter who came to the door looked upon them (having dirty faces, ragged vestments, and uncouth speech) to be a couple of jesters or counterfeits. The Prior caused them to be brought in that they might quaff it and show sport to the monks. But the friars said they were mistaken in them; for they were not such kind of people, but the servants of God, and the professors of an apostolic life. Whereupon the expectation of the monks being thus frustrated, they vilely spurned at them and caused them to be thrust out of the gate. But one of the young monks had compassion on them and said to the porter: 'I desire thee for the love thou bearest me that when the Prior and monks are gone to rest thou wouldest conduct those poor people into the hayloft, and there I shall administer to them food.' Which being according to his desire performed, he carried to them bread and drink, and remaining some time with them, bade them at length a good night, and devoutly commended himself to their prayers.

"No sooner had he left them, solacing their raging stomachs with refreshment, but he retired to his rest. But no sooner had sleep seized on him, than he had a dreadful dream which troubled him much. He saw in his sleep Christ sitting upon His throne calling all to judgment; at length with a terrible voice He said: 'Let the patrons of this place be called to me.' When they and their monks appeared, came a despised poor man in the habit of a minor friar, and stood opposite them saying to Christ these words: 'O just Judge, the blood of the minor friars cryeth to thee, which was the last night by those monks standing there endangered to be spilt; for they, when they were in great fear of perishing by the fury of hunger and wild beasts, did deny them lodging and sustenance—those, O Lord, who have leaved all for thy sake and are come hither to win souls for which thou dying hast redeemed—have denied that which they would not to jesters.'

These words being delivered, Christ with a dreadful voice said to the Prior: 'Of what order art thou?' He answered that he was of the order of S. Benedict. Then Christ, turning to S. Benedict said, 'Is it true that he speaks?' S. Benedict answered, 'Lord, he and his companions are overthrowers of my religion, for I have given charge in my rule that the Abbot's table should be free for guests, and now these have denied those things that were but necessary for them.' Then Christ, upon this complaint, commanded that the Prior before mentioned should immediately be hanged on the elm-tree before the cloister. Afterwards the sacrist and cellarer being examined did undergo the same death also. These things being done, Christ turned Himself to the young monk that had compassion on the said friars, asking him of what order he was. Who thereupon, making a pause and considering how his brethren were handled, said at length, 'I am of the order that this poor man is.' Then Christ said to the poor man, whose name was as yet concealed, 'Francis, is it true that he saith, that he is of your order?' Francis answered, 'He is mine, O Lord, he is mine; and from henceforth I receive him as one of my order.' At which very time as those words were speaking, Francis embraced the young monk so close that, being thereupon awakened from his sleep, he suddenly rose up as an amazed man; and running with his garments loose about him to the Prior to tell him all the passages of his dream found him in his chamber almost suffocated in his sleep. To whom crying out with fear, and finding no answer from him, ran to the other monks, whom also he found in the same case. Afterwards the said young monk thought to have gone to the friars in the hayloft; but they fearing the Prior should discover them, had departed thence very early. Then speeding to the Abbot of Abingdon, told him all whatsoever had happened. Which story possessing him for a long time after with no small horror, as the aforesaid dream did the said young monk, did both (I am sure the last) with great humility and condescension come afterwards to Oxon, when the said friars had got a mansion there, and took upon them the habit of S. Francis."

This quaint story of the first coming of the Grey Friars to Oxford illustrates very plainly the hostility between the old orders of the friars and the new; the opposition of the parochial priesthood to the spiritual energy of the mendicant preachers, who, clad in their coarse frock of grey serge, with a girdle of rope round their waist, wandered barefooted as missionaries over Asia, battled with heresies in Italy and Gaul, lectured in the Universities and preached and toiled among the poor.

The Grey Friars were hospitably received by the Black, till Richard le Mercer, a wealthy burgess, let them a house in St Ebbe's parish, "between the church and water-gate (South-gate), in which many honest bachelors and noble persons entered and lived with them." Perhaps it was this increase in their numbers which compelled them to leave their first abode somewhere by the east end of Beef Lane, and to hire a house with ground attached from Richard the Miller. This house lay between the wall and Freren Street (Church Street). All sorts and conditions of men flocked to hear them. Being well satisfied, it is said, as to their honest and simple carriage and well-meaning as also with their doctrine, they began to load them with gifts and to make donations to the city for their use. One of their benefactors, Agnes, the wife of Guy, for instance, gave them "most part of that ground which was afterwards called Paradise" (*cf.* Paradise Square). A small church was built, and bishops and abbots relinquishing their dignities and preferments became Minorites. They scorned not "the roughness of the penance and the robe," but "did with incomparable humility carry upon their shoulders the coul and the hod, for the speedier finishing this structure." The site chosen by the Grey Friars for their settlement is not without significance. The work of the friars was physical as well as moral. Rapid increase of the population huddled within the narrow circle of the walls had resulted here as elsewhere in overcrowding, which accentuated the insanitary conditions of life. A gutter running down the centre of unpaved streets was supposed to drain the mess of the town as well as the slops thrown from the windows of the houses. Garbage of all sorts collected and rotted there. Within the houses the rush-strewn floors collected a foul heritage of scraps and droppings. Personal uncleanliness, encouraged by the ascetic prohibitions and directions of a morbid monasticism, which, revolting from the luxury of the Roman baths and much believing in the necessity of mortifying the flesh, regarded washing as a vice and held that a dirty shirt might cover a multitude of sins, was accentuated by errors of diet, and had become the habit of high and low. Little wonder that fever or plague, or the more terrible scourge of leprosy, festered in the wretched hovels of the suburbs of Oxford as of every town. Well, it was to haunts such as these that S. Francis had pointed his disciples. At London they settled in the shambles of Newgate; at Oxford they chose the swampy suburb of S. Ebbe's. Huts of mud and timber, as mean as the huts around them, rose within the rough fence and ditch that bounded the Friary; for the Order of St Francis fought hard, at first, against the desire for fine buildings and the craving for knowledge which were the natural tendencies of many of the brethren. In neither case did the will of their founder finally carry the day.

"Three things," said Friar Albert, Minister General, "tended to the exaltation of the Order—bare feet, coarse garments, and the rejecting of money." At first the Oxford Franciscans were zealous in all those respects. We hear of Adam Marsh refusing bags of gold that were sent him; we hear of two of the brethren returning from a Chapter held at Oxford at Christmas-time, singing as they picked their way along the rugged path, over the frozen mud and rigid snow, whilst the blood lay in the track of their naked feet, without their being conscious of it. Even from the robbers and murderers who infested the woods near Oxford the barefoot friars were safe.

But it was not long before they began to fall away from "the Rule," and to accumulate both wealth and learning. Under the ministry of Agnellus and his successor the tendency to acquire property was rigorously suppressed, but under Haymo of Faversham (1238) a different spirit began to prevail. Haymo preferred that "the friars should have ample areas and should cultivate them, that they might have the fruits of the earth at home, rather than beg them from others." And under his successor they gained a large increase of territory. By a deed dated Nov. 22, 1244, Henry III. granted them "that they might enclose the street that lies under the wall from the Watergate in S. Ebbe's to the little postern in the wall towards the castle, but so that a wall with battlements, like to the rest of the wall of Oxford, be made about the dwelling, beginning at the west side of Watergate, and reaching southward to the bank of the Thames, and extending along the bank westward as far as the land of the Abbot of Bec in the parish of S. Bodhoc, and then turning again to the northward till it joins with the old wall of the borough, by the east side of the small postern." In 1245 he made a further grant. "We have given the Friars Minor our island in the Thames, which we bought of Henry, son of Henry Simeon, granting them power to build a bridge over the arm of the Thames (Trill stream) which runs between the island and their houses, and enclose the island with a wall."

When it was completed, then, the Convent of the Grey Friars could compare favourably with any convent or college in Oxford, except perhaps S. Frideswide's or Osney. On the east side of it, where the main entrance lay, at the junction of the present Littlegate Street and Charles Street, was the road leading from Watergate to Preacher's Bridge; on the South side, Trill Mill stream; on the West, the groves and gardens of Paradise; on the North, as far as West-gate, ran the City wall.

"Their buildings were stately and magnificent; their church large and decent; and their refectory, cloister and libraries all proportionable thereunto."

The traditional site of this church is indicated by Church Place as it is called to-day. The cloisters probably lay to the south of the church, round "Penson's Gardens."

As the Franciscans fell away by degrees from the ideal of poverty, so also they succumbed to the desire of knowledge. "I am your breviary, I am your breviary," S. Francis had cried to a novice who had asked for a Psalter. The true Doctors, he held, were those who with the meekness of wisdom show forth good works for the edification of their neighbours. But the very popularity of their preaching drove his disciples to the study of theology. Their desire not only to obtain converts but also to gain a hold on the thought of the age had led the friars to fasten on the Universities. The same purpose soon led them to establish at Oxford a centre of learning and teaching.

Their first school at Oxford was built by Agnellus of Pisa, and there he persuaded Robert Grossetete, the great reforming bishop of Lincoln, to lecture. Agnellus himself was a true follower of S. Francis and no great scholar. "He never smelt of an Academy or scarce tasted of humane learning." He was indeed much concerned at the results of Grossetete's lectures. For one day when he entered this school to see what progress his scholars were making in literature, he found them disputing eagerly and making enquiries whether there was a God. The scandalised Provincial cried out aloud in anger, "Hei mihi! Hei mihi! Fratres! Simplices cœlos penetrant, et literati disputant utrum sit Deus!" The miracles which were afterwards reputed to be performed at the grave of this same excellent friar caused the church of the Grey Friars to be much frequented.

The friars now began to accumulate books and we soon find mention of two libraries belonging to them. The nucleus of them was formed by the books and writings of Grossetete, which he bequeathed to the brethren. And they collected with great industry from abroad Greek, Hebrew and mathematical writings, at that time unknown in England. The fate of this priceless collection of books was enough to make Wood "burst out with grief." For, when the monasteries had begun to decay, and the monks had fallen into ways of sloth and ignorance and were become "no better than a gang of lazy, fat-headed friars," they began to sell their books for what they would fetch and allowed the remainder to rot in neglect.

Meanwhile the teaching of such scholars as Grossetete and Adam Marsh (de Marisco), the first of the Order to lecture at Oxford, was not without result. From the school of the Franciscans came forth men who earned for the University great fame throughout Europe. Friars were sent thither to study, not only from Scotland and Ireland, but from France and Acquitaine, Italy, Spain, Portugal, and Germany; while many of the Franciscan schools on the Continent drew their teachers from Oxford. Duns Scotus and William Ockham were trained by these teachers; Roger Bacon, the founder of modern scientific enquiry, ended his days as one of the Order. His life, which stretched over the greater portion of the thirteenth century, was passed for the most part at Oxford; his aspirations and difficulties, his failures and achievements form an epitome, as it were, of the mental history of his age.

It was only when he had spent forty years and all his fortune in teaching and scientific research that, having gained the usual reward of scholarship, and being bankrupt in purse, bankrupt in hope, he took the advice of Grossetete, and became a Friar of the Order of S. Francis. "Unheard, buried and forgotten," as a member of an Order which looked askance on all intellectual labour not theological, he was forbidden to publish any work under pain of forfeiture, and the penance of bread and water. Even when he was commanded by the Pope to write, the friars were so much afraid of the purport of his researches that they kept him in solitude on bread and water, and would not allow him to have access even to the few books and writings available in those days. Science, they maintained, had already reached its perfection; the world enjoyed too much light; why should he trouble himself about matters of which enough was known already? For as an enquirer Bacon was as solitary as that lone sentinel of science, the Tuscan artist in Valdarno. From the moment that the friars settled on the Universities, scholasticism had absorbed the whole mental energy of the student world. Theology found her only efficient rivals in practical studies such as medicine and law.

Yet, in spite of all difficulties and hindrances, so superhuman was Bacon's energy, and so undaunted his courage, that within fifteen months the three great works, the Opus Majus, the

Opus Minus, and the Opus Tertium were written. If this had been true of the Opus Majus alone, and if that work had not been remarkable for the boldness and originality of its views, yet as a mere feat of industry and application it would have stood almost if not quite unparalleled. For the Opus Majus was at once the Encyclopædia and the Novum Organum of the thirteenth century.

Of the Opus Minus the only MS. of the work yet known is a fragment preserved in the Bodleian Library (Digby, No. 218).

The amazing friar met with no reward for his labours. According to one story, indeed, his writings only gained for him a prison from his Order. His works were sold, allowed to rot, or nailed to the desks that they might do no harm. For Bacon's method of study exposed him to the charge of magic. It was said that he was in alliance with the Evil One, and the tradition arose that through spiritual agency he made a brazen head and imparted to it the gift of speech, and that these magical operations were wrought by him while he was a student at Brazen Nose Hall.

Necromancy, you see, *was* practised by the more daring students, for was there not a certain clerk in Billyng Hall who, when he had summoned the Devil into his presence by his art, observed with astonishment that he did reverence when a priest carrying the sacrament passed without. "Thereupon the student was much disturbed and came to the conclusion that God was much the greater and that Christ should be his Lord...."

And later, was not Dr Thomas Allen of Gloucester Hall, the astrologer and mathematician to whom Bodley left his second best gown and cloak—a common sort of bequest in those days—suspected by reason of his figuring and conjuring, so that his servitor found a ready audience when, wishing to impose upon Freshmen and simple people, he used to say that sometimes he would meet the spirits coming up his master's stairs like bees?

Apart from the tradition of the Brazen Nose, Bacon's long residence in Oxford left other marks on the nomenclature of the place. Wood tells us that in his day a fragment of the ruined Friary was pointed out as the room where the great wizard had been wont to pursue his studies. And at a later time tradition said that Friar Bacon was wont to use as an observatory the story built over the semi-circular archway of the gate on the south bridge, and it was therefore known as Friar Bacon's Study. The little "gate-house" must have resembled Bocardo. It was leased to a citizen named Welcome, who added a story to it, which earned it the name of "Welcome's Folly." So the bridge came to be called Folly Bridge, and though gate and house have disappeared, the new bridge still retains the name.

The Black and the Grey Friars were followed to Oxford some years later by the White or Carmelite Friars. Nicholas de Meules or Molis, sometime governor of the castle, gave them a house on the west side of Stockwell Street,[17] now part of Worcester College. They would

OXFORD AND ITS STORY

seem, like the other Orders, soon to have forgotten their traditional austerity. Lands accrued to them; they erected suitable buildings with planted groves and walks upon a large and pleasant site. But not content with this, they presently obtained from Edward II. the royal Palace of Beaumont. Thus they presented the curious paradox of an Order of monks who derived their pedigree in regular succession from Elijah, and trod in theory in the footsteps of the prophets who had retired into the desert, living at Oxford in the palace of a king.

"When King Edward I. waged war with the Scots (1304) he took with him out of England a Carmelite friar, named Robert Baston, accounted in his time the most famous poet of this nation, purposely that he should write poetically of his victories. Again, when King Edward II. maintained the same war after the death of his father, he entertained the same Baston for the same purpose. At length the said king encountering Robert Bruce, was forced with his bishops to fly. In which flight Baston telling the king that if he would call upon the Mother of God for mercy he should find favour, he did so accordingly, with a promise then made to her that if he should get from the hands of his enemies and find safety, he would erect some house in England to receive the poor Carmelites.... Soon after, Baston and some others were not wanting to persuade him to give to the Carmelites his palace at Oxford" (1317),

where Richard Cœur de Lion had been born. Beaumont Palace, whilst it remained in the hands of the Carmelites, was used not merely as a convent for the habitation of twenty-four monks, but also as a place of education for members of this Order throughout England; as well as for seculars who lived there as "commoners." Cardinal Pole is said to have been educated in this seminary.

The library and the church of the White Friars were unusually fine.

The Austin Friars (or Friars eremite of S. Augustine) came also to Oxford and gradually acquired property and settled "without Smith Gate, having Holywell Street on the south side of it and the chief part of the ground on which Wadham College now stands on the north."

The Austin Friars were famous for their disputations in grammar, and soon drew to themselves much of the grammatical training of the place. They engaged also in violent philosophical controversies with the other Orders, so that at last they were even threatened with excommunication if they did not desist from their quarrelling. It was in their convent that the weekly general disputations of Bachelors, known for centuries after as "Austins," were held.

In 1262 the Penitentiarian Friars or Brothers of the Sack, so called because they wore sackcloth, obtained from Henry III. a grant of land which formed the parish of S. Budoc and lay to the west of the property of the Franciscans. The Order was soon afterwards suppressed and the Franciscans acquired their house and lands.

The brethren of the Holy Trinity also made a settlement in Oxford (1291). Their house, afterwards known as Trinity Hall, was situated outside the East Gate (opposite Magdalen Hall). They also acquired the old Trinity Chapel adjoining and the surrounding land.

The Trinitarians had, besides, a chapel within the East Gate, which was purchased by Wykeham to make room for New College.

The Crossed or Cruched Friars, after one or two moves, settled themselves in the parish of S. Peter's in the East.

The older religious Orders were presently stimulated by the example and the success of the friars to make some provision for the education of their monks. But they never aimed at producing great scholars or learned theologians. Historians of their Order and canonists who could transact their legal business were the products which the monastic houses desired.

A Chapter-General held at Abingdon in 1279 imposed a tax on the revenues of all the Benedictine monasteries in the province of Canterbury with a view to establishing a house at Oxford where students of their Order might live and study together. John Giffard, Lord of Brimsfield, helped them to achieve their object.

Gloucester Hall, adjoining the Palace of Beaumont, had been the private house of Gilbert Clare, Earl of Gloucester, who built it in the year 1260. It passed to Sir John Giffard, who instituted it a "nursery and mansion-place solely for the Benedictines of S. Peter's Abbey at Gloucester." The buildings were afterwards enlarged to provide room for student-monks from other Benedictine abbeys. Of the lodgings thus erected by the various abbeys for their novices, indications may still be traced in the old monastic buildings which form the picturesque south side of the large quadrangle of Worcester College. For over the doorways of these hostels the half-defaced arms of different monasteries, the griffin of Malmesbury or the Cross of Norwich, still denote their original purpose.

At the dissolution, the college was for a short while made the residence of the first bishop of Oxford. After his death it was purchased by Sir Thomas White, and by him converted into a hall for the use of his College of S. John. Gloucester Hall, now become S. John Baptist Hall, after a chequered career, was refounded and endowed in 1714 as Worcester College out of the benefaction of Sir Thomas Cookes. In the latter half of the eighteenth century the hall, library and chapel were built and the beautiful gardens of "Botany Bay" were acquired.

The Benedictines also held Durham Hall, on the site of the present Trinity College, having secured a property of about ten acres with a frontage of about 50 feet (including Kettell Hall) on Broad Street, and 500 feet on the "Kingis hye waye of Bewmounte." It was here that Richard de

Bury, Bishop of Durham, founded the first public library in Oxford. Bury had studied at Oxford and was the tutor of Edward III.; statesman and churchman, he was above all

Gateway in Garden of Worcester College things a book-lover. He had more books, it is recorded, than all the other bishops put together and, wherever he was residing, so many books lay about his bed-chamber that it was hardly possible to stand or move without treading upon them. In the *Philobiblon* the bishop describes his means and methods of collecting books. In the course of his visitations he dug into the disused treasures of the monasteries, and his agents scoured the Continent for those "sacred vessels of learning." The collection of books so made he intended for the use of scholars, not merely for himself alone.

"We have long cherished in our heart of hearts," he writes, "the fixed resolve to found in perpetual charity a hall in the reverend University of Oxford, and to endow it with the necessary revenues, for the maintenance of a number of scholars; and, moreover, to enrich the hall with the treasures of our books, that all and every one of them should be in common as regards their use and study, not only to the scholars of the said hall, but by their means to all the students of the aforesaid University for ever."

And he proceeds to lay down strict regulations based on those of the Sorbonne, for the use and preservation of his beloved books and the catalogue he had made of them.

Richard of Hoton, prior of Durham Monastery, had begun in 1289 the erection of a college building to receive the young brethren from that monastery, whom his predecessor, Hugh of Darlington, had already begun to send to Oxford to be educated. This colony of Durham students it was apparently Richard de Bury's intention to convert into a body corporate, consisting of a prior and twelve brethren. And in gratitude for the signal defeat of the Scots at Halidon Hill, Edward III. took the proposed college under his special protection. Bury, however, died, and died in debt, so that he himself never succeeded in founding the hall he intended. His successor, Bishop Hatfield, took up the scheme, and entered into an agreement with the prior and convent of Durham for the joint endowment of a college for eight monks and eight secular scholars. This project was completed, by agreement with his executors, after his death (1381).

But what became of the books of the bishop and bibliophile, Richard de Bury? Some of them, indeed, his executors were obliged to sell, but we need not distrust the tradition which asserts that some of them at least did come to Oxford. There, it is supposed, they remained till Durham Hall was dissolved by Henry VIII., when they were dispersed, some going to Duke Humphrey's library, others to Balliol College, and the remainder passing into the hands of Dr George Owen, who purchased the site of the dissolved college.

Whatever happened to Bury's books, it is certain that the room which still serves as a library was built in 1417, and it may be taken to form, happily enough, the connecting link between the old monastic house and the modern Trinity College. Some fragments of the original "Domus et clausura" may also survive in the Old Bursary and Common Room.

The stimulating effect of the friars upon the old Orders is shown also by the foundation of Rewley Abbey, of which the main entrance was once north-west of Hythe Bridge Street. Rewley (*Locus Regalis* in North Osney) was built for the Cistercians.

Richard, Earl of Cornwall, brother of Henry III., who like the King had often been at Oxford, directed in his will that a foundation should be endowed for three secular priests to pray for his soul. His son Edmund, however, founded an Abbey of regulars instead, Cistercian monks from Thame. He gave sixteen acres to the west of the Abbey for walks and for private use. To represent the twenty-one monks of the foundation, twenty-one elm-trees were planted within the gates, and at the upper end a tree by itself to represent the abbot. It was to this Abbey, then, that the Cistercian monks came up to study, till Archbishop Chichele founded S. Bernard's for them (1437). The college which Chichele founded for the Bernardines, the "Black" Cistercians who followed the reformed rule of S. Bernard, was built on the east side of S. Giles', "after the same mode and fashion for matters of workmanship as his college of All Souls." It is the modern college of S. John Baptist. But a large part of the buildings date from Chichele's foundation, and the statue of S. Bernard still stands in its original niche to recall to the modern student the Bernardines whom he has succeeded.

The Abbey was dissolved by Henry VIII., who gave the site to the Cathedral of Christ Church. The ruins were still standing in Wood's day, "seated within pleasant groves and environed with clear streams." Only a fragment of a wall and doorway now remain. A memorial stone, purchased from the site of Rewley by Hearne the Antiquarian for half a crown, is preserved in the Ashmolean. It bears the name of Ella Longepée, the benevolent Countess of Warwick, "who made this chapel."

In addition to the numerous parish churches and convents and colleges, there were now innumerable smaller religious foundations in Oxford. There was the House of Converts; there were several hospitals and hermitages and "Ancherholds"—solitary little cells and cabins standing in the fields and adjoining abbeys or parish churches.

The House of Converts was founded by Henry III. (1234), and here "all Jews and infidels converted to the Christian faith were ordained to have sufficient maintenance." After the expulsion of the Jews and when the number of converts began to fail, it was used as a Hall for scholars and known as Cary's Inn. Later it was the magnificent old Inn, the Blue Boar, which spanned the old south boundary of Little Jewry, Blue Boar, Bear or Tresham Lane. The whole of its site is occupied by the modern Town Hall.

The hospital of S. Bartholomew, which lay about half a mile to the east of the city, was founded by Henry I. for leprous folk. It consisted of one master, two healthful brethren, six lepers and a clerk. The chapel and buildings were given in 1328 by Edward III. to Oriel College. In the fourteenth century forty days' indulgence or pardon of sins was granted by the Bishop of Lincoln to all who would pay their devotions at the chapel of S. Bartholomew, on the feast of that saint, and give of their charity to the leprous alms-folk. The result was that multitudes resorted there, and the priests and poor people benefited considerably. But after the Reformation the custom died out. Later, it was revived, for charitable reasons, by the Fellows of New College. They changed the day to May-day, and then

"after their grave and wonted manner, early in the morning, they used to walk towards this place. They entered the chapel, which was ready decked and adorned with the seasonable fruits of the year. A lesson was read, and then the fellows sung a hymn or anthem of five or six parts. Thereafter one by one they went up to the altar where stood a certain vessel decked with Tuttyes, and therein offered a piece of silver; which was afterwards divided among the poor men. After leaving the chapel by paths strewn with flowers, they in the open space, like the ancient Druids, the Apollinian offspring, echoed and warbled out from the shady arbours harmonious melody, consisting of several parts then most in fashion." And Wood adds that "the youth of the city would come here every May-day with their lords and ladies, garlands, fifes, flutes, and drums, to acknowledge the coming in of the fruits of the year, or, as we may say, to salute the great goddess Flora, and to attribute her all praise with dancing and music."

The income of the hospital had previously been much augmented by the relics which it was fortunate enough to possess. S. Edmund the Confessor's comb, S. Bartholomew's skin, as well as his much revered image, the bones of S. Stephen and one of the ribs of S. Andrew the apostle, all helped to draw to this shrine without the walls the worship and the offerings of the sick and the devout. It is difficult to realise with what reverential awe men regarded the jaw-bone of an ancient cenobite, the tooth or even the toe-nail of a saint or martyr. Charms, in those days, were considered more efficacious than drugs, and the bones of saints were the favourite remedies prescribed by the monkish physicians. Comb your hair with this comb of Saint Edmund, then, and you would surely be cured of frenzy or headache; apply the bones of S. Stephen to your rheumatic joints, and your pains would disappear. So it was most firmly believed; and faith will remove mountains. There was a saint for every disease. To touch the keys of S. Peter or to handle a relic of S. Hubert was deemed an effectual mode of curing madness. S. Clare, according to monkish leechcraft, cured sore eyes; S. Sebastian the plague, and S. Apollonia the toothache. The teeth of S. Apollonia, by the way, were by a fortunate dispensation almost as numerous as the complaint which she took under her charge was common.

It is said that Henry VI., disgusted at the excess of this superstition, ordered all who possessed teeth of that illustrious saint to deliver them to an officer appointed to receive them. Obedient crowds came to display their saintly treasures, and lo! a ton of the veritable teeth of S. Apollonia were thus collected together. Were her stomach, says Fuller, proportionate to her teeth, a country would scarce afford her a meal.

The relics at S. Bartholomew's were so highly prized that Oriel College thought it desirable to remove them to their church of S. Mary—where more people might have the benefit of them. S. Bartholomew's hospital was used as a common pest-house for the plague in 1643, and shortly after was completely demolished. The chapel fared no better, for it was put to base uses by the Parliamentarians, and the roof, which was of lead, was melted down to provide bullets for "the true Church Militant."

The buildings and chapel were, however, restored by the patrons, Oriel College. If you follow the Cowley Road towards Cowley Marsh, you will find on your left, opposite the College cricket grounds, and just short of the Military College and barracks, a ruined building which is the old chapel of S. Bartholomew, and contains the screen put up in the time of the Commonwealth. The letters O. C., 1651, mark it. They stand for Oriel College, not Oliver Cromwell, we must suppose.

There was a hospital in Stockwell Street, at the back of Beaumont Palace; there was a hospital of Bethlehem at the north end of S. Giles' Church and Alms-house Place in Holywell. Of hermitages we may mention that known as S. Nicholas Chapel on the west side of South Bridge. The hermits who lived there successively were called the hermits of Grand Pont. They passed their lives, we are told, in continual prayer and bodily labour—"in prayer against the vanities of the world, for poor pilgrims and passengers that steered their course that way, receiving of them something of benevolence for that purpose; in bodily labour by digging their own graves and filling them up again, as also in delving and making highways and bridges."

"Our Lady in the wall" was the name of another hermitage near S. Frideswide's Grange, which was in great repute at one time for the entertainment of poor pilgrims who came to be cured by the waters of S. Edmund's well (Cowley Place).

The hospital of S. John Baptist was founded some time before the end of the thirteenth century for the relief of poor scholars and other miserable persons. Among the property granted or confirmed to it by Henry III. in a very liberal charter, was the mill known as King's Mill at the Headington end of the path now called Mesopotamia, because it runs between the two branches of the river.

As a site for rebuilding the hospital the brethren were given (1231) the Jews' Garden, outside the East Gate of Oxford, but it was provided that a space should be reserved for a burial-ground for the Jews. This ground formed part of the present site of Magdalen College, and part of the site of the Physic Garden, which lies on the other side of the High Street, facing the modern entrance to that college. The latter site was that reserved for the Jews' cemetery; the hospital buildings were erected on the other portion. When Waynflete began to enlarge and remodel his foundation of Magdalen Hall (1456), he obtained a grant from the king whereby the hospital (which had ceased to fulfil its purpose) and its possessions were assigned to the President and Fellows of the Hall.

Two years later a commission was appointed by the Pope, which confirmed the suppression of the hospital and its incorporation in the college which Waynflete had been licensed to found,

"whereby he proposed to change earthly things to heavenly, and things transitory to things eternal, by providing in place of the Hospital a College of a President, secular scholars and other ministers for the service of God and the study of theology and philosophy; of whom some are to teach these sciences without fee at the cost of the College."

Of the buildings which were once part of the old hospital very little remains. In the line of the present college, facing the street, a blocked-up doorway to the west of the tower marks one of the entrances to the hospital. And Wood was probably correct in saying that the college kitchen was also part of the original fabric. There is a little statue of a saint over a doorway inside the kitchen which appears to bear out this statement.

The various religious Orders were, then, well represented at Oxford. Their influence on the University was considerable; their relations with it not always amicable. At first, doubtless, they did much to stimulate mental activity, whilst the friendship which Grossetete, who as Bishop of Lincoln exercised a sort of paternal authority over the University, manifested towards his "faithful counsellor," Adam Marsh, and the Franciscans in general, helped to reconcile their claims with the interests of the University. But the University was always inclined to be jealous of them; to regard them bitterly, and not without reason, as grasping bodies, who were never tired of seeking for peculiar favours and privileges and always ready to appeal to the Pope on the least provocation. Before long, indeed, it became evident that their object was to gain control of the University altogether. And this endeavour was met by a very strenuous and bitter campaign against them. For, as at Paris, the friars soon outlived their welcome, and as at Paris, it was deemed advisable to set a limit to the number of friar doctors and to secure the control of the University to the regular graduates.[18]

The friars who were sent up to Oxford had usually completed their eight years' study of Arts in the Friars' schools, and were probably chosen for the promise they had shown in the course of their earlier studies. Their academic studies were confined to the Faculty of Theology, in its wide mediæval sense, and of Canon Law, the hand-maid of theology. But though the regulars were for the most part subject to the same regulations as the secular students in these faculties, yet the Orders were bound before long to find themselves in antagonism with the customs of the University. The rules of the Preaching Friars forbade them to take a degree in Arts; the University required that the student of theology should have graduated in Arts. The issue was definitely raised in 1253, and became the occasion of a statute, providing that for the future no one should incept in Theology unless he had previously ruled in Arts in some University and read one book of the Canon, or of the Sentences, and publicly preached in the University. This statute was challenged some fifty years later by the Dominicans, and gave rise to a bitter controversy which involved the Mendicant Orders in much odium. The Dominicans appealed first to the King and then to the Pope, but the award of the arbitrators appointed upheld the statute. The right of granting dispensations, however, or graces to incept in Theology, to those who had not ruled in Arts, was reserved to the Chancellor and Masters. A clause which prohibited the extortion of such "graces" by means of the letters of influential persons was inserted, but was not altogether effective. Certain friars who had used letters of this kind are named in a proclamation of the year 1358. "These are the names of the wax-doctors who seek to extort graces from the University by means of letters of lords sealed with wax, or because they run from hard study as wax runs from the face of fire. Be it known that such wax-doctors are always of the Mendicant Orders, the cause whereof we have found; for by apples and drink, as the people fables, they draw boys to their religion, and do not instruct them after their profession, as their age demands, but let them wander about begging, and waste the time when they could learn in currying favour with lords and ladies."

From an educational point of view no doubt the University was right in insisting on the preliminary training in Arts.

Roger Bacon speaks with contempt of the class that was springing up in his day—people who studied theology and nothing but theology, "and had never learnt anything of real value. Ignorant of all parts and sciences of mundane philosophy, they venture on the study of philosophy which demands all human wisdom. So they have become masters in theology and philosophy before they were disciples."

The tendency and the danger of our modern educational system is to specialise, not in theology but in science, without any proper previous training in the humanities.

Whilst the University was engaged in desperate combat with the friars in defence of its system, the regulars had succeeded in securing almost a monopoly of learning. The same fight and the same state of affairs prevailed at Paris. And just as at Paris in order to save the class of secular theologians from extinction, Robert de Sorbonne established his college (1257) for secular clerks, so now at Oxford, Walter de Merton took the most momentous step in the history of our national education by founding a college for twenty students of Theology or Canon Law, who not only were not friars or monks, but who forfeited their claims to his bounty if they entered any of the regular Orders. And that his object was achieved the names of Walter Burley, the Doctor Perspicuus, Thomas Bradwardine, the profound doctor, and perhaps John Wycliffe stand forth to prove.

As an institution for the promotion of academical education under a collegiate discipline but secular guidance, the foundation of Merton College was the expression of a conception entirely new in England. It deserves special consideration, for it became the model of all other collegiate foundations, and determined the future constitution of both the English Universities.

Walter de Merton was born at Merton in Surrey. He studied at Oxford and won such high honour with the King that he was made Chancellor of the kingdom. Ranged on the side opposite to that of Simon de Montford, he was enabled perhaps by the very success of his opponent and the leisure that so came to him, to perfect the scheme which he had early begun to develop. At first he set aside his estates of Malden, Farleigh and Chessington to support eight of his young kinsmen in study at the University.

But in 1263 he made over his manor-house and estate of Malden to a "house of Scholars of Merton," with the object of supporting twenty students preferably at Oxford.

The first statutes were granted in the following year. The scholars in whom the property of this house was vested were not allowed to reside within its walls for more than one week in the year, at the annual audit. The house was to be occupied by a Warden and certain brethren or Stewards. It was their business to administer the estate and pay their allowances to the scholars. The scholars themselves were all originally nephews of the founder. Their number was to be filled up from the descendants of his parents, or failing them, other honest and capable young men, with a preference for the diocese of Winchester. They were to study in some University where they were to hire a hall and live together as a community. It was in the very year of the secession to Northampton that the statutes were issued, and it would have been obviously inexpedient to bind the students to one University or one town. The Studium might be removed from Oxford or the scholar might find it desirable to migrate from that University, to Stamford, Cambridge, or even Paris. The founder, indeed, in view of such a possibility did acquire a house at Cambridge for his college (Pythagoras Hall).

The little community thus established at Oxford was to live simply and frugally, without murmuring, satisfied with bread and beer, and with one course of flesh or fish a day.

A second body of statutes given to the community in 1270 fixed their abode definitely at Oxford and regulated their corporate life more in detail. A sub-warden was now appointed to preside over the students in Oxford, as well as one to administer at Malden.

Strict rules of discipline were laid down. At meals all scholars were to keep silence save one, who was to read aloud some edifying work. All noisy study was forbidden. If a student had need to talk, he must use Latin. In every room one Socius, older and wiser than the others, was to act as Præpositus, control the manners and studies of the rest and report on them. To every twenty scholars a monitor was chosen to enforce discipline. One among so many was not found to suffice, and by the final statutes of Merton one monitor to ten was appointed. Thus originated the office of Decanus (Dean).

A new class of poor students—"secondary scholars"—was also now provided for. They were to receive sixpence a week each from Michaelmas to Midsummer, and live with the rest at Oxford. In these secondary scholars may be seen the germ of the distinction, so characteristic of English colleges, between the full members of the society, afterwards known as Fellows or Socii, and the scholars or temporary foundationers. Socii originally meant those who boarded together in the same hall. It was the founder of Queen's who first used the word to distinguish full members of the society from foundationers, who were still later distinguished as "scholares." Wykeham followed his example, distinguishing the *verus et perpetuus socius* from the probationer.

And from these secondary scholars it is probable that a century later Willyot derived his idea of the institution of a separate class of *Portionistae*, the Merton Postmasters. They originally received a "stinted portion," compared with the scholars.

Merton became Chancellor once more on the death of Henry. He was practically Regent of the Kingdom till the return of Edward from the Crusades. As soon as he resigned the seals of office in 1274, he set himself to revise the statutes of his college at Oxford, before taking up his duties as Bishop of Rochester.

The wardens, bailiffs and ministers of the altar were now transferred from Malden to Oxford, which was designated as the exclusive and permanent home of the scholars. The statutes now given remained in force till 1856, and are, to quote the verdict of the late warden,

"a marvellous repertory of minute and elaborate provisions governing every detail of college life. The number and allowances of the scholars; their studies, diet, costume, and discipline; the qualifications, election and functions of the warden; the distribution of powers among various college officers; the management of the college estates and the conduct of the college business are here regulated with remarkable sagacity. The policy which dictates and underlies them is easy to discern. Fully appreciating the intellectual movement of his age, and unwilling to see the paramount control of it in the hands of the religious Orders—the zealous apostles of papal supremacy—Walter de Merton resolved to establish within the precincts of the University a great seminary of secular clergy, which should educate a succession of men capable of doing good service in Church and State.

"The employment of his scholars was to be study—not the *claustralis religio* of the older religious Orders, nor the more practical and more popular self-devotion of the Dominicans and Franciscans. He forbade them ever to take vows; he enjoined them to maintain their corporate independence against foreign encroachments; he ordained that all should apply themselves to studying the liberal arts and philosophy before entering on a course of theology; and he provided special chaplains to relieve them of ritual and ceremonial duties. He contemplated and even encouraged their going forth into the great world. No ascetic obligations were laid on them, but residence and continual study were strictly prescribed, and if any scholar retired from the college with the intention of giving up study, or even ceased to study diligently, his salary was no longer to be paid. If the scale of these salaries and statutable allowances was humble, it was chiefly because the founder intended the number of scholars to be constantly increased as the revenues of the house might be enlarged."

In this foundation Walter De Merton was the first to express the only true idea of a college. Once expressed, it was followed by every succeeding founder. The collegiate system revolutionised University life in England. Merton was never tired of insisting upon the one great claim which his community should have to the loyalty, affection and service of its members.

It was this idea which has produced all that is good in the system. To individual study in the University schools was added common life; to private aims the idea of a common good. "The individual is called to other activities besides those of his own sole gain. Diversities of thought and training, of taste, ability, strength and character, brought into daily contact, bound fast together by ties of common interest, give birth to sympathy, broaden thought, and force enquiry, that haply in the issue may be formed that reasoned conviction and knowledge, that power of independent thought, to produce which is the great primary aim of our English University education" (Henderson).

The founder, who had long been busy acquiring property in Oxford, had impropriated the Church of S. John the Baptist for the benefit of the college, and several houses in its immediate neighbourhood were made over to the scholars. The site thus acquired (1265-8) became their permanent home and was known henceforth as Merton Hall.

Of the buildings which were now erected and on which the eyes of the founder may have rested in pride and hope, little now remains. The antique stone carving over the college gate, the great north door of the vestibule of the Hall, with its fantastic tracery of iron, perhaps the Treasury and Outer Sacristy are relics of the earliest past. But Chapel, Hall, Library and Quadrangle are later than the Founder.

As if to emphasise the ecclesiastical character of the English college, he had begun at once to rebuild the parish church as a collegiate church. The high altar was dedicated in the year of his death, 1277; the rest of the chapel is of later dates.

The choir belongs to the end of the thirteenth century (1297), (Pure Decorated); the transepts (Early Decorated, with later Perpendicular windows and doors) were finished in 1424, but begun perhaps as early as the choir; and the massive tower, with its soaring pinnacles, a fine specimen of Perpendicular work, was completed in 1451.

It will be noticed that the chapel has no nave, but that, probably in imitation of William of Wykeham's then recently finished naveless chapel at New College, the nave which had evidently been intended was omitted at Merton (after 1386). Two arches blocked with masonry in the western wall and the construction of the west window indicate this original intention of adding a nave.

The old thirteenth century glass in the Geometrical windows of the chancel is of great interest. The arms of Castile and the portrait of Elinor of Castile (d. 1290) will be noticed. Merton Chapel is very rich both in glass and brasses.

On entering the college you are struck at once by the fact that Merton is not as other colleges arranged on a preconceived plan. But the irregular and disconnected arrangement of the buildings of the quadrangle are themselves suggestive of the fact that it was from Merton and the plans of its founder that the college quadrangles may trace their origin; as it is from Merton that they derive their constitution. The hall, the chapel, the libraries and the living rooms, as essentials for college life, were first adopted here, and these buildings were disposed in an unconnected manner about a quadrangular court after the fashion of the outer Curia of a monastery. The regular disposition of college quadrangles was first completed by Wykeham, and whilst other colleges have conformed to the perfected shape, Merton remains in its very irregularity proudly the prototype, the mother of colleges.

Of the college buildings the most noteworthy is the library, the oldest example of the mediæval library in England. It was the gift of William Rede, Bishop of Chichester (1377). The dormer and east windows and the ceiling are later, but the library as it is, though enriched by the improvements of succeeding centuries, beautiful plaster-work and panelling, noble glass and a sixteenth century ceiling, is not very different from that in which the mediæval student pored over the precious manuscripts chained to the rough sloping oaken desks which project from the bookcases. These bookcases stand out towards the centre of the room and form, with a reader's bench opposite to each of the narrow lancet windows, a series of reader's compartments. How the books were fastened and used in those days, you may gain a good idea by examining the half case numbered forty-five.

It was in this library that the visitors of Edward VI. took their revenge on the schoolmen and the popish commentators by destroying in their stupid fanaticism not only innumerable works of theology, but also of astronomy and mathematical science. "A cart-load," says Thomas Allen, an eye-witness, "of such books were sold or given away, if not burnt, for inconsiderable nothings."

In this library Anthony Wood was employed in the congenial occupation of "setting the books to rights," and here is preserved, according to tradition, the very astrolabe which Chaucer studied. And, for a fact, a beautiful copy of the first Caxton edition of his works is stored in the sacristy —a building which up till 1878 was used as a brew-house.

The charming inner quadrangle, in which the library is, rejoices in the name "Mob" Quad—a name of which the derivation has been lost. Like the Treasury, it probably dates from about 1300. The high-pitched roof of the latter, made of solid blocks of ashlar, is one of the most remarkable features of Merton. The outer sacristy is on the right of the main entrance passage to Mob Quad, and thence an old stone staircase leads to the Treasury or Muniment room. Another passage from the front quadrangle leads to Patey's Quad. The Fellows' Quadrangle was begun in 1608, and the large gateway with columns of the four orders (Roman-Doric, Ionic, Corinthian, and Composite) is typical of the architectural taste of the times. The quadrangle itself, very similar to that of Wadham, is one of the most beautiful and charming examples of late Gothic imaginable. It would have been a fortunate thing if this had been the last building added to Merton. But it was destined that the taste of the Victorian era should be painfully illustrated by the new buildings which were erected in 1864 by Mr Butterfield. The architect was eager and the college not disinclined at that time to destroy part of the library and the Mob Quad. The abominable building which replaced the beautiful enclosure known as the Grove, combines with the new buildings of Christ Church to spoil what might have been one of the most beautiful effects of water, wood and architecture in the world—the view of Oxford from the Christ Church and Broad Walks.

Inspired by the example of Merton and a similar dislike of monks and friars, Walter de Stapeldon, the great Bishop of Exeter, ordained that the twelve scholars whom he originally endowed (1314) should not study theology or be in orders. The society, afterwards known as Exeter College, was housed at first in Hart Hall and Arthur Hall, in the parish of S. Peter in the East, and was intended by the founder to be called Stapeldon Hall. In the following year he moved his scholars, eight of whom, he stipulated, must be drawn from Devonshire and four from Cornwall, to tenements which he had bought between the Turl and Smith Gate, just within the walls. The founder added a rector to their number and gave them statutes, based on those of Merton, which clearly indicated that his object was to give a good education to young laymen. The college was practically refounded in 1566 by Sir William Petre, a successful servant of the Tudors. Of the pre-reformation buildings, nothing unhappily remains save a fragment of the tower. The rest is seventeenth century or nineteenth, the front on Turl Street dating from 1834, and the unlovely "modern Gothic" front on Broad Street from 1854. Sir Gilbert Scott, who designed the latter, destroyed the old chapel and replaced it with a copy of the Sainte Chapelle.

Ten years later another daughter of Merton was born. For in 1324 Adam de Brome, Almoner of Edward II. and Rector of S. Mary's, obtained the royal licence to found a college of scholars, Bachelor Fellows, who should study theology and the Ars Dialectica. The statutes of this "Hall of the Blessed Mary at Oxford," afterwards known as King's Hall and Oriel College, were copied almost verbatim from those of Merton. Tackley's Inn, on the south side of High Street (No. 106), and Perilous Hall, on the north side of Horsemonger, now Broad Street, were purchased for the College. But in 1326 it was refounded by the King, endowed with the advowson and rectory of the Church of S. Mary, and ordered to be governed by a Provost, chosen by the scholars from their own number. The first Provost was the founder, who was also Rector of S. Mary's, and the society now established itself in the Rectory House on the south side of the High Street (St Mary Hall), at the north end of Schidyard (Oriel) Street. The college gradually acquired property stretching up to St John's (now Merton) Street, and in so doing became possessed of the tenement at the angle of Merton and Oriel Street called /p, or, for some uncertain reason, but probably on account of its possessing one of the architectural features indicated by that word, La Oriole. It was here, then, that the society fixed its abode and from this hall it took its name. The present front quadrangle, resembling the contemporary front quadrangles of Wadham and University, and endowed with a peculiar charm by the weather-stained and crumbling stone, stands on the site of La Oriole and other tenements. It was completed in the year of the outbreak of the Civil War, *Regnante Carolo*, as the legend on the parapet between the hall and chapel records, and the statue of Charles I. above it indicates. The Garden Quadrangle was added in the eighteenth century.

The monks and friars have gone their way and the place of their habitation knows them no more. But they have left their mark upon Oxford in many ways. Though their brotherhoods were disbanded by Henry VIII. and most of their buildings demolished, the quadrangles and cloisters of many colleges recall directly the monastic habit, and the college halls the refectory of a convent. Whilst the College of S. John dates back from the scholastic needs of the Cistercians, and the Canterbury Quad and gate at Christ Church keep alive by their names the recollection of the Canterbury college founded by Archbishop Islip (1363) for the Benedictines of Canterbury, the old hostels, which were once erected to receive the Benedictine students from other convents, survive in those old parts of Worcester which lie on your left as you approach the famous gardens of that college. Trinity College occupies the place of Durham, and Wadham has risen amid the ruins of a foundation of Augustines, whose disputative powers were kept in memory in the exercises of the University schools down to 1800. The monks of S. Frideswide's Priory, S. George's Church, the Abbey of Osney, have all disappeared with the friaries. But Christ Church is a magnificent monument to the memory of the abbots and canons regular whom it has succeeded. The very conception of an academical college was no doubt largely drawn from the colleges of the regular religious Orders, which, unlike those of the Mendicants, were entirely designed as places of study.

We have seen how the foundation of Merton, and therefore of Exeter and Oriel, was directly due to the coming of the friars. And it is to their influence that yet another great and once beautiful college, beautiful no longer, but greater now and more famous than ever by virtue of the services in politics and letters of its successful alumni, owes its origin. For it was under the guidance of a

Franciscan friar, one Richard de Slikeburne, that the widow of Sir John de Balliol carried out her husband's intention of placing upon a thoroughly organised footing his house for poor scholars.

He, the Lord of Barnard Castle, father of the illustrious rival of the Bruce, having about the year 1260 "unjustly vexed and enormously damnified" the Church of Tynemouth and the Church of Durham, was compelled by the militant bishop whose hard task it was to keep peace on the Border, to do penance. He knelt, in expiation of his crime, at the door of Durham Abbey, and was there publicly scourged by the bishop. He also undertook to provide a perpetual maintenance for certain poor scholars in the University.

Balliol's original scheme of benefaction had little in common with the peculiarly English college-system inaugurated by Walter de Merton. It was drawn up on the lines of the earlier foundations of Paris.

For the Hall of Balliol was originally a college for Artists only who lost their places when they took a degree in Arts. Their scholarships meanwhile supplied them only with food and lodging of a moderate quality. But these youthful students, according to the democratic principles on which the halls were carried on, made their own statutes and customs, and it was in accordance with this code that the Principal was required to govern them.

Balliol's scholars were established in Oxford by June 1266, and were at first supported by an annual allowance from him. He granted them a commons of eightpence a week. The hostel in which he lodged them was a house he hired in Horsemonger Street (Broad Street), facing the moat and city wall. But before he had made any provision for the permanent endowment of his scholars Balliol died. A close connection had apparently from the first been established between the hall and the Franciscans. One of the agents by whom Balliol's dole had been distributed was a Franciscan friar. Now, under the guidance and probably at the instigation of the friar Richard of Slikeburne, whom she appointed her attorney in the business, Lady Dervorguilla of Galloway, the widow of John of Balliol, set herself to secure the welfare of her husband's scholars. Since his death the very existence of the newly formed society had been in jeopardy. The Lady Dervorguilla, then, addressed a letter to the procurators or agents of Balliol's dole, instructing them to put in force a code of statutes which was no doubt in great part merely a formal statement of customs already established at the Old Balliol Hall. She next fitted up the north aisle of the parish church (S. Mary Magdalen) for the use of her scholars; she endowed them with lands in Northumberland, and purchased for their dwelling-place three tenements east of Old Balliol Hall. These tenements, which were south-west of the present front quadrangle, and faced the street, were soon known as New Balliol Hall or Mary Hall. The whole of the site of the front quadrangle was acquired by the Society as early as 1310.

A few years later (1327) the scholars built themselves a chapel, part of which, said to be preserved in the dining-room of the Master's House, forms an interesting link between the original scholars of Balliol and the modern Society which is connected with the name of Dr Jowett. The statutes, which had been much tinkered by subsequent benefactors and bishops, were finally revised by Bishop Fox, the enlightened and broad-minded founder of C.C.C.

Fox gave Balliol a constitution, not altogether in harmony with his own ideals as expressed in the statutes of Corpus, but such as he thought best fitted to fulfil the intentions of the founders. He divided the Society into two halves:—ten juniors, *Scholastici*, and ten Fellows, *Socii*, each of whom had a definite duty. In their hands the whole government of the College was placed.

According to the new regulations the scholars or servitors of Balliol were to occupy a position humbler than that of the younger students at any other College. They were to wait upon the Master and the graduate Fellows and to be fed with the crumbs that should fall from the table of their superiors. They were to be nominated by the Fellow whom they were to serve, to be from eighteen to twenty-two years of age, and if they proved themselves industrious and well-behaved they were to be eligible to Fellowships even though they had not taken the degree of B.A. Commoners, as in most other Colleges, were to be allowed to lodge within the walls of the College, and to take their meals with the members of the Society.

The Fellowships, which entitled the holder to a "commons" of 1s. 8d. a week, were thrown open to competition, candidates being required, however, to be Bachelors of Arts, of legitimate birth, good character, proficient in their studies, and in need of assistance, for any cure of souls, or a private income of more than 40s. a year, was accounted a reason for disqualification.

Fox had a weakness for metaphors. In the statutes of Corpus he "spoke horticulturally; his metaphor was drawn from bees." On the present occasion he uses a metaphor as elaborate and appropriate. The College is described as a human body. The Master was the head, endued with the five senses of seeing clearly, hearing discreetly, smelling sagaciously, tasting moderately, and touching fitly; the senior Fellow was the neck; the Deans were the shoulders; the two priests the sides; the Bursars the arms and hands; the Fellows the stomach; the scholars the legs; and the servants the feet, whose function it is to go whithersoever they are bidden. Just as the body when sick would require a physician, so it was said would the College sometimes require a visitor. The Master and Fellows were given the unusual privilege of choosing their own visitor.

In the fifteenth century the whole quadrangle was rebuilt; the Old Hall, the Old Library, the Master's House, and the block of buildings and gateway facing Broad Street being then erected. Of these the shell of the Master's House, the Old Hall, now converted into an undergraduates' library, and the Old Library, much defaced by Wyatt, survive. The east wall of the library was used to form the west end of the chapel, which was built in 1529 to replace the old oratory. The sixteenth century chapel was removed and the present building erected as a memorial to Dr Jenkins, under whom Balliol had begun to develop into a College of almost national importance.

Mr Butterfield, the architect who had done his best to ruin Merton, and who perpetrated Keble, was entrusted with this unfortunate method of perpetuating the worthy Master's memory.

Mr Waterhouse is responsible for the present front of the College, the east side of the first quadrangle, the north side of the Garden Quadrangle and the new Hall therein (1867-1877).

Not content with fighting the University, the Oxford Friars soon began to fight each other. Rivalries sprang up between the Orders; enormous scandals of discord, as Matthew Paris phrases it. Jealousy found its natural vent in politics as in the schools. Politically, the Oxford Franciscans supported Simon de Montfort; the Dominicans sided with the King. The Mad Parliament met in the Convent of the Black Friars. In philosophy the Franciscans attacked the doctrine of the Dominican, S. Thomas Aquinas, who had made an elaborate attempt to show that natural and revealed truth were complementary the one of the other. In order to establish this thesis and to reconcile human philosophy and the Christian faith, the Angelic Doctor, for so he was commonly termed, had written an encyclopædia of philosophy and theology, in which he advanced arguments on both sides of every question and decided judicially on each in strict accordance with the tenets of the Church.

The light of this "sparkling jewel of the clergy, this very clear mirror of the University of Paris, this noble and illuminating candlestick," was somewhat dimmed, however, when the great Franciscan hero, the "subtle doctor," Duns Scotus, took up the argument, and clearly proved that the reasoning of this champion of orthodoxy was itself unorthodox. The world of letters was divided for generations into the rival camps of Scotists and Thomists. But the two doctors have fared very differently at the hands of posterity. Thomas was made a Saint, judged to be a "candlestick," and awarded by Dante a place high in the realms of Paradise. Duns Scotus, on the other hand, whose learning and industry were as great and his merit probably not much inferior, survives chiefly in the English language as a "dunce." The name of the great Oxford scholar stands to the world chiefly as a synonym for a fool and a blockhead. For when the Humanists, and afterwards the Reformers, attacked his system as a farrago of needless entities and useless distinctions, the Duns men, or Dunses, on their side railed against the new learning. The name of Dunce, therefore, already synonymous with cavilling sophist or hair-splitter, soon passed into the sense of dull, obstinate person, impervious to the new learning, and of blockhead, incapable of learning or scholarship. Such is the justice of history.

Duns Scotus had carried the day and the Church rallied to the side of the Franciscans. But such a successful attack involved the Orders in extreme bitterness. The Dominicans retorted that these Franciscans, who claimed and received such credit throughout Europe for humility and Christlike poverty, were really accumulating wealth by alms or bequests. The charge was true enough.

The pride and luxury of the Friars, their splendid buildings, their laxity in the Confessional, their artifices for securing proselytes, their continual strife with the University and their endeavours to obtain peculiar privileges therein had long undermined their popularity. They were regarded as "locusts" who had settled on the land and stripped the trees of learning and of life.

Duns Scotus held almost undisputed sway for a while. His works on logic, theology and philosophy were text-books in the University. But presently there arose a new light, a pupil of his own, to supplant him.

William of Ockham, the "singular" or "invincible" doctor, revived the doctrine of Nominalism. At once the glory and reproach of his Order, he used the weapons of Scholasticism to destroy it.

But if in Philosophy the "invincible doctor" was a sceptic, in Theology he was a fanatical supporter of the extreme Franciscan view that the ministers of Christ were bound to follow the example of their Master, and to impose upon themselves absolute poverty. It was a view which found no favour with popes or councils. But undeterred by the thunders of the Church, Ockham did not shrink from thus attacking the foundations of the papal supremacy or from asserting the rights of the civil power.

Paris had been, as we have seen, the first home of Scholasticism, but with the beginning of the fourteenth century, Oxford had taken its place as the centre of intellectual activity in Europe. The most important schoolmen of the age were all Oxonians, and nearly all the later schoolmen of note were Englishmen or Germans educated in the traditions of the English "nation" at Paris.

And when the old battle between Nominalism and Realism was renewed, it was fought with more unphilosophical virulence than before. "It was at this time that Philosophy literally descended from the schools into the street, and that the *odium metaphysicum* gave fresh zest to the unending faction fight between north and south at Oxford, between Czech and German at Prague" (Rashdall).

Yet this was not without good results. For Scholasticism began now to come in contact with practical life. The disputants were led on to deal with the burning questions of the day, the questions, that is, as to the foundations of property, the respective rights of king and pope, of king and subject, of priest and people.

The day was now at hand when the trend of political events, stimulated by the influence of the daring philosophical speculations of the Oxford schoolmen, was to issue in a crisis. The crisis was a conflict between the claims of papal supremacy and the rights of the civil power, and for this crisis Oxford produced the man—John Wycliffe.

Born on the banks of the Tees, he, the last of the great schoolmen, was educated at Balliol, where he probably resided till he was elected master of that College in 1356. In 1361 he accepted a College living and left Oxford for a while, but was back again in 1363, and resided in Queen's College. He combined his residence there and his studies for a degree in theology with the holding of a living at Ludgershall in Bucks. Some suppose that he was then appointed Warden of Canterbury Hall,[19] but this supposition is probably incorrect. At any rate he was already a person of importance, not only at Oxford, but at the Court.

When Parliament decided to repudiate the annual tribute to the Pope which John had undertaken to pay, Wycliffe officially defended this repudiation. He continued to study at Oxford, developing his views. That he was in high favour at Court is shown by the fact that he was nominated (1374) by the Crown to the Rectory of Lutterworth and appointed one of the Royal Commissioners to confer with the papal representatives at Bruges. But he continued lecturing at Oxford and preaching in London.

Politically he threw in his lot with the Lancastrian party. For he had been led in the footsteps of his Italian and English predecessors, Marsiglio and Ockham, to proclaim that the Church suffered by being involved in secular affairs, and that endowments were a hindrance to the proper spiritual purpose of the Church. So it came about that the "Flower of Oxford," as he was called, the priest who desired to reform the clergy, found himself in alliance with John of Gaunt, the worldly statesman, who merely desired to rob them. He soon found himself in need of the Duke's protection. The wealthy and worldly churchmen of the day were not likely to listen tamely to his lectures. He was summoned before Bishop Courtenay of London to answer charges of erroneous teaching concerning the wealth of the Church (1377). The Duke of Lancaster accepted the challenge as given to himself. He stood by Wycliffe in the Consistory Court at S. Paul's, and a rude brawl between his supporters and those of Courtenay, in which the Duke himself is said to have threatened to drag the Bishop out of the church by the hair of his head, put an end to the trial. Papal bulls were now promulgated against Wycliffe. The University was directed to condemn and arrest him, if he were found guilty of maintaining certain "conclusions" extracted from his writings. The Oxford masters, however, were annoyed at the attack made upon a distinguished member of their body, and they resented, as a threatened infringement of their privileges, the order of the Archbishop and Bishop of London, which commanded the Oxford divines to hold an enquiry and to send Wycliffe to London to be heard in person. What they did, therefore, was simply to enjoin Wycliffe to remain within the walls of Black Hall, whilst they, after considering his opinions, declared them orthodox, but liable to misinterpretation. But Wycliffe could not disobey the Archbishop's summons to appear at Lambeth. There he proved the value of a Schoolman's training. The subtlety of "the most learned clerk of his time" reduced his opponents to silence.

The prelates were at a loss how to proceed. They were relieved from their dilemma by the arrival of a Knight from the Court, who brought a peremptory message from the Princess of Wales, mother of Richard II., forbidding them to issue any decree against Wycliffe.

The session was dissolved by an invasion of the London crowd. Wycliffe escaped scot-free. Then followed the scandal of the Great Schism, when two, or even three, candidates each claimed to be the one and only Vicar of Christ.

It is the Great Schism which would appear to have converted Wycliffe into a declared opponent of the papacy. Pondering on the problems of Church and State which had hitherto occupied his energies, he was now forced to the conclusion that the papal, and therefore the sacerdotal power in general must be assailed. It was a logical deduction from his central thesis, the doctrine of "dominion founded on grace." He organised a band of preachers who should instruct the laity in the mother tongue and supply them with a Bible translated into English. Thus under his auspices Oxford became the centre of a widespread religious movement. There the poor or simple priests, as they were called, had a common abode, whence, barefooted and clad in russet or grey gowns which reached to their ankles, they went forth to propagate his doctrines. And since the Friars, who owed their independence of the bishops and clergy to the privilege conferred upon them by the popes, were strong supporters of the papal autocracy, Wycliffe attacked them, by his own eloquence and that of his preachers, and that at a time when their luxurious and degenerate lives laid them open to popular resentment.

Already (1356) Richard Fitzralph, Archbishop of Armagh, who like Wycliffe had been a scholar of Balliol and in 1333 had held the office of Vice-Chancellor, had attacked the Friars for their encroachments upon the domain of the parish priests; their power, their wealth, their mendicancy, he maintained, were all contrary to the example and precepts of Christ and therefore of their founder. He charged them also with encroaching upon the rights of parents by making use of the confessional to induce children to enter their convents and become Friars. This was the reason, he asserted, why the University had fallen to one-fifth of its former numbers, for parents were unwilling to send their sons thither and preferred to bring them up as farmers.

This attack furnished Wycliffe with a model for his onslaught. In his earlier days he had treated the Friars with respect and even as allies—"a Franciscan" he had said, "is very near to God"— for then he had been attacking the endowments of the Church, and it was the monks or "possessioners" and the rich secular clergy to whom he was opposed. In theory the Mendicant Orders were opposed to these by their poverty and in practice by their interests.

But the Friars were the close allies and chief defenders of the Pope. Now, therefore, when Wycliffe passed from political to doctrinal reform, his attitude towards the Mendicant Orders becomes one of uncompromising hostility.

He and his followers denounced them with all the vehemence of religious partisanship and all the vigour of the vernacular. Iscariot's children, they called them, and irregular Procurators of the Fiend, adversaries of Christ and Disciples of Satan.

Wycliffe indeed went so far as to attribute an outbreak of disease in Oxford to the idleness and intellectual stagnation of the Friars.

"Being inordinately idle and commonly gathered together in towns they cause a whole sublunary unseasonableness."

Finally, Wycliffe aimed at undermining the power of the priesthood by challenging the doctrine of Transubstantiation. According to this doctrine the priest had the power of working a daily miracle by "making the body of Christ." Wycliffe, in the summer of 1381, first publicly denied that the elements of the sacrament underwent any material change by virtue of the words uttered by the priest. The real presence of the body and blood of Christ he maintained, but that there was any change of substance he denied.

The heresy was promulgated at Oxford. An enquiry was immediately held by the Chancellor (William Berton) and twelve doctors, half of them Friars, and the new "pestiferous" doctrines were condemned. The condemnation and injunction forbidding any man in future to teach or defend them in the University was announced to Wycliffe as he was sitting in the Augustinian Schools, disputing the subject. He was taken aback, but at once challenged chancellor or doctor to disprove his conclusions. The "pertinacious heretic," in fact, continued to maintain his thesis, and made a direct appeal, not to the Pope, but to the King. The University rallied to his side and tacitly supported his cause by replacing Berton with Robert Rygge in the office of Vice-Chancellor. Rygge was more than a little inclined to be a Wycliffite. And Wycliffe meanwhile appealed also to the people by means of those innumerable tracts in the English tongue, which make the last of the schoolmen the first of the English pamphleteers. Whilst he was thus entering on his most serious encounter with the Church, suddenly there broke out the Peasant Revolt. The insurrection blazed forth suddenly, furiously, simultaneously and died away, having spent its force in a fortnight. It was a sporadic revolt with no unity of purpose or action except to express the general social discontent. But the upper classes were seriously frightened and some of the odium was reflected on the subversive doctrines of Wycliffe, whose Lollard preachers had doubtless dabbled not a little in the socialism which honey-combed the Middle Ages.

When order was again restored, Courtenay, now become Archbishop, began to take active measures to repress the opinions of Wycliffe. He summoned a synod at the Blackfriars in London to examine them. The first session was interrupted by an earthquake, which was differently interpreted as a sign of the divine approval or anger. The Earthquake Council had no choice but to condemn such doctrines as those they were asked to consider, that God ought to obey the devil, for instance, or that no one ought to be recognised as Pope after Urban VI.

When these doctrines were condemned, Wycliffe does not appear to have been present, nor was any action at all taken against him personally. It is supposed that his popularity at Oxford rendered him too formidable a person to attack. He was left at peace and the storm fell upon his disciples. The attack was made on "certain children of perdition," who had publicly taught the condemned doctrines, and "who went about the country preaching to the people, without proper authority." All such preachers were to be visited with the greater excommunication.

As Oxford, however, was the centre of the movement a separate mandate was sent thither.

The Archbishop sent down a commissary, Peter Stokes, a Carmelite friar, to Oxford, to prohibit the teaching of incorrect doctrines, but avoiding any mention of the teacher's name. The University authorities were by no means pleased at this invasion, so they held it, of their ancient privileges. The Chancellor Rygge had just appointed Nicholas Hereford, a devoted follower of Wycliffe, to preach before the University; he now appointed a no less loyal follower, Philip Repyngdon to the same office. His sermon was an outspoken defence of the Lollards. Stokes reported that he dared not publish the Archbishop's mandate, that he went about in the fear of his life; for scholars with arms concealed beneath their gowns accompanied the preachers and it appeared that not the Chancellor only, but both the Proctors were Wycliffites, or at least preferred to support the Wycliffites to abating one jot of what they considered the privileges of the University. And for once the Mayor was of the same opinion as the rulers of the University. Still, when the Chancellor was summoned before the Archbishop in London, he did not venture to disobey, and promptly cleared himself of any suspicion of heresy. The council met again at the Blackfriars, and Rygge submissively took his seat in it. On his bended knees he apologised for his disobedience to the Archbishop's orders, and only obtained pardon through the influence of William of Wykeham. Short work was made of the Oxford Wycliffites; they were generally, and four of them by name, suspended from all academical functions. Rygge returned to Oxford, with a letter from Courtenay which repeated the condemnation of the four preachers, adding to their names the name of Wycliffe himself. The latter was likened by the Archbishop to a serpent which emits noxious poison. But the Chancellor protested he dared not execute this mandate, and a royal warrant had to be issued to compel him. Meanwhile he showed his real feeling in the matter by suspending a prominent opponent of the Wycliffites who had called them by the offensive name of Lollards ("idle babblers"). But the council in London went on to overpower the party by stronger measures.[20]Wycliffe had apparently retired before the storm burst upon Oxford. John of Gaunt was appealed to by the preachers named. But the great Duke of Lancaster had no desire to incur the charge of encouraging heresy. He pronounced the opinions of Hereford and Repyngdon on the nature of the eucharist utterly detestable. The last hope of Lollardism was gone. Wycliffe himself retired unmolested to Lutterworth, where he died and was buried. "Admirable," says Fuller "that a hare so often hunted with so many packs of dogs should die at last quietly sitting in his form." Just as he owed his influence as a Reformer to the skill and fame as a schoolman which he had acquired at Oxford, so now his immunity was due to his reputation as the greatest scholastic doctor in the "second school of the Church."

The statute "De haeretico Comburendo" did its work quickly in stamping out Lollardy in the country. The tares were weeded out. In Oxford alone the tradition of Wycliffe died hard. A remarkable testimonial was issued in October 1406 by the Chancellor and Masters, sealed with the University seal. Some have thought it a forgery, and at the best it probably only represented, as Maxwell Lyte suggests, the verdict of a minority of the Masters snatched in the Long Vacation. But it is in any case of considerable significance. It extols the character of John Wycliffe, and his exemplary performances as a son of the University; it extols his truly Catholic zeal against all who blasphemed Christ's religion by voluntary begging, and asserts that he was neither convicted of heretical pravity during his life, nor exhumed and burned after death. He had no equal, it maintains, in the University as a writer on logic, philosophy, theology or ethics.

Here then, Archbishop Arundel (1407) an Oriel man, who with his father had built for that College her first chapel, found it necessary to take strong steps. He held a provincial council at Oxford and ordered that all books written in Wycliffe's time should pass through the censorship, first of the University of Oxford or Cambridge, and secondly of the Archbishop himself, before they might be used in the schools. The establishment of such a censorship was equivalent to a fatal muzzling of genius. If it silenced the Wycliffite teaching, it silenced also the enunciation of any original opinion or truth. Two years later Arundel risked a serious quarrel with the University in order to secure the appointment of a committee to make a list of heresies and errors to be found in Wycliffe's writings. He announced his intention of holding a visitation of the University with that object. He met with violent opposition. The opponents of the Archbishop were not all enthusiastic supporters of Wycliffe's views. Not all masters and scholars were moved by pure zeal either for freedom of speculation or for evangelical truth. The local patriotism of the north countryman reinforced the religious zeal of the Lollard. The chronic antipathy of the secular scholars to the friars, of the realists to the nominalists, of the artists to the higher faculties, and the academic pride of the loyal Oxonians—these were all motives which fought for Wycliffe and his doctrines. Least tangible but not least powerful among them was the last, for when civil or ecclesiastical authority endeavoured to assert itself over corporate privileges in the Middle Ages, a very hornet's nest of local patriotism and personal resentment was quickly roused.

The Oxford masters were impatient of all interference ecclesiastical as well as civil. They had thrown off the yoke of the Bishop of Lincoln and the Archdeacon of Oxford. And, with a view to asserting their independence of the Primate, they had succeeded in obtaining a bull from Boniface IX. in which he specifically confirmed the sole jurisdiction of the Chancellor over all members of the University whatever, Priests and Monks and Friars included. The University, however, was compelled to renounce the bull, and to submit to the visitation of the Archbishop. But the submission was not made without much disturbance and bitterness of feeling. The Lollards, the younger scholars and the northerners, with their lawless allies the Irish, were in favour of active resistance.

The behaviour of three Fellows of Oriel will show how the University was divided against itself. These men, so runs the complaint against them, "are notorious fomenters of discord."

"They lead a band of ruffians by night, who beat, wound, and spoil men and cause murder. They haunt taverns day and night, and do not enter college before ten or eleven or twelve o'clock, and even scale the walls to the disturbance of quiet students, and bring in armed strangers to spend the night. Thomas Wilton came in over the wall at ten and knocked at the Provost's chamber, and woke up and abused him as a liar, and challenged him to get up and come out to fight him. Against the Provost's express orders, on the vigil of S. Peter, these three had gone out of college, broken the Chancellor's door and killed a student of law. The Chancellor could neither sleep in his house by night nor walk in the High Street by day for fear of these men."

The arrival of the Archbishop at Oxford then, to hold a visitation at S. Mary's was a signal for an outbreak. S. Mary's was barricaded and a band of scholars armed with bows, swords and bucklers awaited the Primate. Notwithstanding the interdict laid on the Church, John Birch of Oriel, one of the Proctors, took the keys, opened the doors, had the bell rung as usual, and even celebrated High Mass there. S. Mary's, it will be remembered, belonged to Oriel. Hence, perhaps, the active resistance of these Oriel Fellows and of the Dean of Oriel, John Rote, who asked "why should we be punished by an interdict on our church for other people's faults?" And he elegantly added, "The Devil go with the Archbishop and break his neck." The controversy was at last referred to the king. The Chancellors and Proctors resigned their office. The younger students who had opposed the Archbishop were soundly whipped, much to the delight of Henry IV. The bull of exemption was declared invalid; the University acknowledged itself subject to the See of Canterbury, thanks to the mediation of the Prince of Wales, mad-cap Harry, and the Archbishop Arundel made a handsome present of books to the public library of Oxford.

The committee desired by Arundel was eventually constituted. Two hundred and sixty-seven propositions were condemned and the obnoxious books solemnly burnt at Carfax. Not long after, a copy of the list of condemned articles was ordered to be preserved in the public libraries, and oaths against their maintenance were enjoined upon all members of the University on graduation.

The methods of the Archbishop met with the success which usually attends a well-conducted persecution. History notices the few martyrs who from time to time have laid down their lives for their principles, but it often fails to notice the millions of men who have discarded their principles rather than lay down their lives.

So the Wycliffite heresy was at length dead and buried. But the ecclesiastical repression which succeeded in bringing this about succeeded also in destroying all vigour and life in the thought of the University. Henceforth the Schoolmen refrained from touching on the practical questions of their day. They struck out no new paths of thought, but revolved on curves of subtle and profitless speculation, reproducing and exaggerating in their logical hair-splitting all the faults without any of the intellectual virtues of the great thinkers of the thirteenth and fourteenth centuries. It was against these degenerate dullards that the human mind at last rebelled, when intellect was born again in the New Birth of letters. What wonder then if, suddenly freed from the dead weight of their demoralising stupidities, men broke out in the exuberance of their spirits into childish excesses, confused the master with his foolish and depressing pupils, strewed the quadrangle of New College with the leaves of Dunce, and put them to the least noble of uses, as though they had been the Chronicles of Volusius.

The Archbishop's right of Visitation was confirmed in Parliament and with it the suppression of Lollardy, of free speech and thought, in the schools and pulpits of Oxford.

The issue of the struggle practically closes the history of Lollardism as a recognised force in English politics, and with it the intellectual history of mediæval Oxford.

Up to that time the University had shown itself decidedly eager for reform, and for a few years the same spirit survived. Oxford had consistently advocated the summoning of a General Council to settle the claims of the rival popes and to put an end to the schism which was the scandal of Christendom. But for fifteen years such pacific designs were eluded by the arts of the ambitious pontiffs, and the scruples or passions of their adherents. At length the Council of Pisa deposed, with equal justice, the Popes of Rome and Avignon. In their stead, as they intended, but in addition to them as events were to prove, the conclave, at which the representatives of Oxford and Cambridge were present, unanimously elected Peter Philargi. This Franciscan friar from Crete, who had taken his degree of Bachelor of Theology at Oxford, assumed the title of Alexander V., and remains the only wearer of the tiara who has graduated at Oxford or Cambridge. He was shortly afterwards succeeded by John XXIII., the most profligate of mankind. It remained for the Council of Constance to correct the rash proceedings of Pisa, and to substitute one head of the Church in place of the three rival popes (1414).

But before the opening of this Council the University of Oxford had drawn up and presented to the King a document of a very remarkable character. It consisted of forty-six articles for the reformation of the Church. The Oxford masters suggested that the three rival popes should all resign their claims; they complained of the simoniacal and extortionate proceedings of the Roman Court, and of the appointment of foreigners to benefices in England; they accused the Archbishops of encroaching on the rights of their suffragans, and charged the whole Order of prelates with nepotism and avarice. Abbots, they contended, should not be allowed to wear mitres and sandals as if they were bishops, and monks should hot be exempt from ordinary episcopal jurisdiction. Friars should be restrained from granting absolution on easy terms, from stealing children, and from begging for alms in the house of God. Secular canons should be made to abandon their luxurious style of living, and masters of hospitals to pay more regard to the wants of the poor. Parish priests, who neglected the flocks committed to their care, are described as ravening wolves. The Masters also complained of the non-observance of the Sabbath and of the iniquitous system of Indulgences.

Shades of the founder of Lincoln College, what a document is this! It is Wycliffism alive, rampant and unashamed. Not perhaps altogether unashamed or at least not indiscreet, for the Masters go out of their way to call for active measures against the Lollards. But the whole of this manifesto is a cry from Oxford, in 1414, for reformation; it is a direct echo of the teaching and declamation of Wycliffe, and an appeal for reformation as deliberate and less veiled than "the vision of William Langland concerning Piers Plowman," that sad, serious satirist of those times, who, in his contemplation of the corruption he saw around him in the nobility, the Government, the Church and the Friars, "all the wealth of the world and the woe too," saw no hope at all save in a new order of things.

Oxford's zeal for reformation at this time was made very clear also by her representatives at Constance, where a former Chancellor, Robert Halam, Bishop of Salisbury, and Henry Abingdon, a future Warden of Merton, very greatly distinguished themselves. Yet it was by a decree of this very Council of Constance (1415) that the remains of Wycliffe were ordered to be taken up and cast out far from those of any orthodox Christian. This order was not executed till twelve years later, when Bishop Fleming, having received direct instructions from the Pope, saw to it.

Wycliffe's remains were dug up, burnt and cast into the Swift, but, as it has been said, the Swift bore them to the Avon, the Avon to the Severn, and the Severn to the sea to be dispersed unto all lands: which things are an allegory. For though in England the repression of his teaching deferred the reformation, which theologically as well as politically Wycliffe had begun, for more than a hundred years, yet abroad, in Bohemia, the movement which he had commenced grew into a genuine national force, destined to react upon the world.

Bishop Fleming, who had been proctor in 1407, seems to have thought that the snake was scotched but not killed. For though he had been a sympathiser with the Lollards in his youth, in his old age he thought it worth while to found a "little college of theologians," who should defend the mysteries of the sacred page "against these ignorant laics, who profaned with swinish snout its most holy pearls." The students in this stronghold of orthodox divinity were to proceed to the degree of B.D. within a stated period; they must swear not to favour the pestilent sect of Wycliffites, and if they persisted in heresy were to be cast out of the College "as diseased sheep." It was in 1427 that Fleming obtained a charter permitting him to unite the three parish churches of All Saints', S. Michael's, and S. Mildred's into a collegiate church, and there to establish a "collegiolum," consisting of a rector and seven students of Theology, endowed with the revenue of those churches. No sooner had he appointed the first rector, purchased a site and begun to erect the buildings just south of the tower, than he died. The energy of the second rector, however, Dr John Beke, secured the firmer foundation of the College. He completed the purchase of the original site, which is represented by the front quadrangle and about half the grove; and thereon John Forest, Dean of Wells, completed (1437) the buildings as Fleming had planned them, including a chapel and library, hall and kitchen, and rooms. Modern Lincoln is bounded by Brasenose College and Brasenose Lane, the High Street and the Turl,[21] the additional property between All Saints' Church and the front quadrangle having been bestowed upon the College during the period 1435-1700. Of Forest's buildings the kitchen alone remains untouched, and a very charming fragment of the old structure it is.

The foundation of Lincoln was remodelled and developed by Thomas Rotherham, Chancellor of Cambridge, and afterwards Archbishop of York. His benefactions to the cause of learning were munificent and unceasing, and, so far as Lincoln is concerned, he may fairly be called the College's second founder. The origin of his interest in the College arose from a picturesque incident. When he visited the College as bishop of the diocese in 1474, the rector, John Tristrope, urged its claims in the course of a sermon. He took for his text the words from the psalm, "Behold and visit this vine, and the vineyard which thy right hand hath planted," and he earnestly exhorted the bishop to complete the work begun by his predecessor. For the College was poor, and what property it had was at this time threatened. So powerful and convincing was his appeal that, at the end of the sermon, the bishop stood up and announced that he would grant the request. He was as good as his word. He gave the College a new charter and new statutes (1480)—a code which served it till the Commission of 1854; he increased its revenues and completed the quadrangle on the south side. There is a vine which still grows in Lincoln, on the north side of the chapel quadrangle, and this is the successor of a vine which was either planted alongside the hall in allusion to the successful text, or, being already there, suggested it.

CHAPTER V

THE MEDIÆVAL STUDENT

"A clerk ther was of Oxenford also,
That unto logik hadde longe ygo....
For him was lever have at his beddes heed
Twenty bokes, clad in blak or reed,
Of Aristotle and his philosophye
Than robes riche, or fithele or gay sautrye.
But al be that he was a philosophre,
Yet hadde he but litel gold in cofre;

But al that he mighte of his freendes hente,
On bokes and on lerninge he it spente,
And bisily gan for the soules preye
Of hem that yaf him wherwith to scoleye.
Of studie took he most cure and most hede.
Noght o word spak he more than was nede,
And that was seyd in forme and reverence,
And short and quik, and ful of hy sentence.
Souninge in moral vertu was his speche,
And gladly wolde he lerne and gladly teche."

AS you drive into Oxford from the railway station, you pass, as we have seen, monuments which may recall to mind the leading features of her history and the part which she took in the life of the country. The Castle Mound takes us back to the time when Saxon was struggling against Dane; the Castle itself is the sign manual of the Norman conquerors; the Cathedral spire marks the site upon which S. Frideswide and her "she-monastics" built their Saxon church upon the virgin banks of the river. Carfax, with the Church of S. Martin, was the centre of the city's life and represents the spirit of municipal liberty which animated her citizens, and the progress of their municipal freedom.

The bell which swung in Carfax Tower summoned the common assembly to discuss and to decide their own public affairs and to elect their own mayor. And this town-mote of burghers, freemen within the walls, who held their rights as burghers by virtue of their tenure of ground on which their tenement stood, met in Carfax Churchyard. Justice was administered by mayor and bailiff sitting beneath the low shed, the "penniless bench"[22] of later times, without its eastern wall. And around the church lay the trade guilds, ranged as in some vast encampment.

Carfax Church, with all its significance of municipal life, stands at the top of High Street, the most beautiful street in the world. Still, by virtue of the splendid sweep of its curve comparable only to the Grand Canal of Venice or the bend of Windermere, and by virtue of the noble grouping of its varied buildings, the most beautiful street in the world; in spite of modern tramways and the ludicrous dome of the Shelley Memorial, "a thing resembling a goose pye," as Swift wrote of Sir John Vanburgh's house in Whitehall; in spite of the disquieting ornamentation of Brasenose new buildings and the new schools; in spite even of the unspeakably vulgar and pretentious façade of Lloyd's Bank, a gross, advertising abomination of unexampled ugliness and impertinence, which has done all that was possible to ruin the first view of this street of streets. Let us leave it behind us with a shudder and pass down the High till we find on our left, at what was once the end of "Schools Street," the lovely twisted columns of the porch which forms the modern entrance to S. Mary's Church.

What Carfax was to the municipal life of Oxford, S. Mary's was to the University. It was the centre of the academical and ecclesiastical life of the place. And the bell which swung in S. Mary's tower summoned the students of the University sometimes to take part in learned disputations among themselves, sometimes to fight the citizens of the town.

Here then, between the Churches of S. Martin and S. Mary, the life of this mediæval University town ebbed and flowed. In the narrow, ill-paved, dirty streets, streets that were mere winding passages, from which the light of day was almost excluded by the overhanging tops of the irregular houses, crowded a motley throng. The country folks filled the centre of the streets with their carts and strings of pack-horses; at the sides, standing beneath the signs of their calling, which projected from their houses, citizens in varied garb plied their trades, chaffering with the manciples, but always keeping their bow-strings taut, ready to promote a riot by pelting a scholar with offal from the butchers' stall, and prompt to draw their knives at a moment's notice. To and fro among the stalls moved Jews in their yellow gaberdines; black Benedictines and white Cistercians; Friars black, white and grey; men-at-arms from the Castle, and flocks of lads who had entered some grammar school or religious house to pass the first stage of the University course. Here passed a group of ragged, gaunt, yellow-visaged sophisters, returning peacefully from lectures to their inns, but with their "bastards" or daggers, as well as their leather pouches, at their waists. Here a knot of students, fantastically attired in many-coloured garments, whose tonsure was the only sign of their clerkly character, wearing beards, long hair, furred cloaks, and shoes chequered with red and green, paraded the thoroughfare, heated with wine from the feast of some determining bachelor. Here a line of servants, carrying the books of scholars or doctors to the schools, or there a procession of colleagues escorting to the grave the body of some master, and bearing before the corpse a silver cross, threaded the throng. Here hurried a bachelor in his cape, a new master in his "pynsons" or heelless shoes, a scholar of Exeter in his black boots, a full-fledged master with his tunic closely fastened about the middle by a belt and wearing round his shoulders a black, sleeveless, close gown. Here gleamed a mantle of crimson cloth, or the budge-edged hood of a doctor of law or of theology. And in the hubbub of voices which proceeded from this miscellaneous, parti-coloured mob, might be distinguished every accent, every language, and every dialect.[23] For French, German and Spanish students jostled in these streets against English, Irish, Scottish and Welsh; Kentish students mingled with students from Somersetshire or Yorkshire, and the speech of each was quite unintelligible to the other.

S. Mary's Church was the only formal meeting place of these students, thus drawn together in the pursuit of knowledge from various parts of Europe. It was here that all University business, secular and religious, was transacted, till the building of the Divinity school and the Sheldonian theatre allowed the church to be reserved for sacred purposes. Then at last it ceased to be the scene of violent altercations between Heads of Houses or the stage where the Terræ Filius of the year should utter his scurrilous banalities.[24]

But still every Sunday morning during term the great bell of S. Mary's rings out and summons the University to assemble in formal session there to hear a sermon. The bedels of the four faculties with their silver staves lead the way; and the Vice-chancellor is conducted to his throne, the preacher to his pulpit; the doctors of the several faculties in their rich robes follow and range themselves on either side of their official head; below them the proctors, representatives of the Masters of Arts, wearing the white hoods of their office, take their seats. The masters and bachelors fill the body of the church, the undergraduates are crowded into the galleries.

We must not think of S. Mary's as merely a meeting-house for University business or as merely a parish church. For centuries it has been the centre of Christian Oxford; where each successive movement in English theology has been expounded and discussed. From the old stone pulpit, of which a fragment is fixed over the southern archway of the tower, Peter Martyr delivered his testimony and Cole sent Cranmer to the stake; from its nineteenth century successor, John Keble began the Oxford movement; Dr Pusey preached a sermon for which he was suspended, and Newman (vicar 1831) entered on the path to Rome.

The church is mentioned in Domesday Book, and the north wall of the Lady Chapel, commonly known as Adam de Brome's Chapel because the tomb of the founder of Oriel is therein, may have been part of the church as it stood at the time of the Domesday survey. The tower and the spire date from the early fourteenth century.

S. Mary's as we have it now is very much a Tudor building. When William of Wykeham built New College Chapel he set a fashion which soon converted Oxford into a city of pinnacles. [25] In the perpendicular style pinnacles were erected on Merton tower and transept, on All Souls' Chapel, on Magdalen Chapel, hall and tower; nearly a hundred pinnacles decorated the Schools and Library; the nave, aisles and chancel of S. Mary's received the same ornaments, and pinnacles in the same style were added to the clusters of the fourteenth century tower and spire. These were not high but observed a true proportion.

It was the grave fault of the excessively lofty pinnacles (beautiful no doubt in themselves) which were added in 1848,[26] that they destroyed the true beauty of proportion and the effect of gradual transition which the fourteenth century builders had succeeded in giving to the tower and spire, and with which the ancient statues in their canopied niches were in perfect harmony. For the massive tower-buttresses are crowned with turrets, showing canopied niches containing twelve over-life-size statues and decorated with ball-flower ornament. Two of the statues on the buttresses facing south are modern; nine others are copies (1895) of the old statues, stored now in the ancient Congregation House, which still exhibit the carefully calculated gestures and the studied designs of the original fourteenth century workers. They form a series which recalls that on the west front of Wells Cathedral, a rare example of English sculpture in a *genre* which is so plentifully and superbly illustrated by the French cathedrals.

On the face of the south buttress of the west front stood the statue, beautifully posed, of the Virgin with the Infant Christ, the Lady of the Church thus occupying the most important angle of the tower; on the left, S. John the Evangelist with the cup. Between the Evangelist and S. John the Baptist, patron saint of the Chapel of Merton, Walter of Merton looks out towards the College he founded. These three are from new designs by Mr Frampton.

On the N.W. angle of the tower is S. Cuthbert of Durham, facing northwards. He holds in his hand the head of S. Oswald, the Christian King slain by Penda, and looks towards his own north country and Durham, the great diocese so intimately connected through its bishops and monastery with the early collegiate foundations of the Universities. Northwards, too, towards his cathedral church of Lincoln, faces S. Hugh, with the wild swan of Stowe nestling to him as was his wont, with its neck buried in the folds of his sleeve. This statue is on the eastern buttress at the N.E. angle, and on the eastern face of the same buttress is an equally noble statue of Edward the Confessor. On the S.E. angle stands, it may be, the murdered Becket, and among the other figures Edmund Rich may perhaps be counted.

The chancel and nave are, it will be seen, splendid examples of late perpendicular. The chancel, in fact, began to be rebuilt in 1462 and the nave 1487-1498. For the church "was so ruinated in Henry VII. reign that it could scarce stand," and though it was and is really a parish church, yet so closely was it bound up with the life and procedure of the University that the University at length took measures to collect money for its repair.

They begged, after the approved manner of the great church-builders of the Middle Ages, from the archbishop downwards, and their begging was so successful that they built the nave, as we now have it, and the chancel. In order to secure an appearance of uniformity, the architect unfortunately altered Adam de Brome's chapel, encasing the outer walls in the new style, and inserting larger windows. Not content with this, he likewise converted the old House of Congregation by substituting a row of large for two rows of small windows, giving thereby a false impression from the outside, as if the upper and lower stories were one.

The University had no right to the use of S. Mary's. The church was merely borrowed for sermons and meetings of Congregation, just as S. Peter's in the East was borrowed for English sermons and S. Mildred's for meetings of the Faculty of Arts. For the University in its infancy had little or no property of its own. It could not afford to erect buildings for its own use. The parish churches, therefore, were used by favour of the clergy, and lectures were delivered in hired schools.

The need for some University building was, however, severely felt. At last it was provided for in a small way. "That memorable fabric, the old Congregation House," and the room above it were begun in 1320 by the above-mentioned Adam de Brome, at the expense of Thomas Cobham, Bishop of Worcester. The latter had undertaken to enlarge the old fabric of S. Mary's Church by erecting a building two stories high immediately to the east of the tower, on the very site, that is, on which the University had previously endeavoured to found a chantry. He intended that the lower room should serve primarily as a meeting-place for the Congregations of regent-masters, and at other times for parochial purposes. The upper room was to be used partly as an oratory, and partly as a general library. But the good bishop's books, which were to form the nucleus of this library, met with the same fate as Richard de Bury's. His executors pawned them to defray the expenses of his funeral, and to pay his debts. Oriel College at their suggestion redeemed the books, and being also the impropriating rectors of the church, they claimed to treat both building and library as their own property. But the masters presently asserted their supposed rights by coming "with a great multitude" and forcibly carrying away the books from Oriel, "in autumn, when the fellows were mostly away." They lodged the books in the upper chamber, and Oriel presently acknowledged the University's proprietary rights.

The old University library, then, found its home in the upper room of the old Congregation House, and there remained until the books were moved to Duke Humphrey's library (1480). From that time till the erection of Laud's Convocation House, the upper room was used as a school of law, and also as another Congregation House, distinguished by the name of "Upper." Meantime a salary was provided for a librarian, who, besides taking care of the books in the upper chamber, was to pray for the soul of the donors. Other books were acquired by the University, either by purchase, bequest, or as unredeemed pledges. Some of these were kept in chests, and loaned out on security like cash from the other chests, whilst others were books given or bequeathed to the University, which were kept chained in the chancel of the church, where the students might read them. Others, in the upper room, were secured to shelves by chains that ran on iron bars. These shelves, with desks alongside, would run out from the walls, between the seven windows, in a manner clearly shown by such survivals of mediæval libraries as exist at the Bodleian, Merton and Corpus. The catalogue was in the form of a large board suspended in the room. At first these books were open for the use of all students at the specified times, but by later statutes (1412), made when the library had been increased by further donations and time had brought bitter experience, the use of them was stringently limited to graduates or religious of eight years' standing in Philosophia. These regulations were intended to provide against the overcrowding of the small library, the disturbance of readers and the destruction of books by careless, idle and not over-clean boy students. With the object of preserving the books, a solemn oath was also exacted from all graduates on admission to their degree, that they would use them well and carefully. The lower room fulfilled its founder's intention, and here the Congregation of regents met, whilst the Convocation, or Great Congregation of regents and non-regents, was held in the chancel of the church.

Here, then, we may imagine the Chancellor sitting, surrounded by doctors and masters of the Great Congregation as the scene was formerly depicted in the great west window of S. Mary's, and is still represented on the University seal.

I have referred to the "chests" which were kept in the upper chamber. This was in fact the treasure-house of the University, and here were stored in great chests doubly and trebly locked, like the "Bodley" chest in the Bodleian, the books and money with which the University had been endowed for the benefit of her scholars.

Mr Anstey (*Munimenta Academica*) has given a brilliant little sketch of the scene which the fancy may conjure up when the new guardians of the chests were appointed and the chests opened in their presence.

It is the eve of the Festival of S. John at the Latin Gate, in the year of Grace 1457. To-morrow is the commemoration day of W. de Seltone, founder of the chest known by his name. Master T. Parys, Principal of S. Mary Hall, and Master Lowson are the new guardians, the latter the north countryman of the two. High mass has just been sung with commemoration collects, and solemn prayers for the repose of the souls of W. de Seltone and all the faithful departed. It is not a reading (legible) day, so the church is full. But now all have left, except a few ragged-looking lads, who still kneel towards the altar, and seem to be saying their Pater Nosters and Ave Marias, according to their vow, for their benefactor. Master Parys and Master Lowson, however, have left earlier; they have passed out of the chancel and made their way into the old Congregation House for their first inspection of the Seltone Chest. Each of the guardians draws from beneath his cape a huge key, which he applies to the locks. At the top lies the register of the contents, in which is recorded particulars, dates, names and amounts of the loans granted. The money remaining in one corner of the chest is carefully counted and compared with the account in the register. Here and there among valuable MSS. lie other pledges of less peaceful sort but no less characteristic of a mediæval student's valuable possessions. Here perhaps are two or three daggers of more than ordinary workmanship, and there a silver cup or a hood lined with minever. That man in an ordinary civilian's dress, who stands beside Master Parys, is John More, the University stationer, and it is his office to fix the value of the pledges offered, and to take care that none are sold at less than their real value. It is a motley group that stands around; there are several masters and bachelors, but more boys and young men in every variety of coloured dress, blue, red, medley or green. Many of these lads are but scantily clothed, and all have their attention riveted on the chest, each with curious eye watching for his pledge, his book or his cup, brought from some country village, perhaps an old treasure of his family, and now pledged in his extremity. For last term he could not pay the principal of his hall seven and sixpence due for the rent of his miserable garret, or the maniple for his battels, but now he is in funds again. The remittance, long delayed on the road, has arrived, or perhaps he has succeeded in earning or begging a sufficient sum to redeem his pledge. He pulls out the coin from the leathern money-pouch at his girdle. But among the group you may see one master, whose bearing and dress plainly denote superior comfort and position. He is wearing the academical costume of a master, cincture and biretta, gown and hood of minever. Can it be that he too has been in difficulties? He might easily have been, for the post was irregular, and rents were not always punctual in those days. But in this case it is Master Henry Sever, Warden of Merton, who has lately been making some repairs in the College, and he has borrowed from the Seltone Chest the extreme sum permitted by the ordinance, sixty shillings, for that purpose. The scholars plainly disapprove of his action. They are jealous of his using the funds of the chest which, they think, were not intended for the convenience of such as he. Master Sever, however, is filled with anxiety at the present moment. He has pledged an illuminated missal which far exceeds in value the sum he has borrowed, and this he omitted to redeem at the proper time. It is not in the chest. He inquires, and is told that it has been borrowed for inspection by an intending purchaser, who has left a silver cup in its place, of more intrinsic value by the stationer's decision, but not in Mr Sever's opinion. Satisfied that he will be able to effect an exchange, he departs with the cup in search of the owner. Other cases are now considered. Some redeem their pledges, some borrow more monies, some are new customers, and they sorrowfully deposit their treasures and slink sadly away, not without a titter from the more hardened bystanders. But before the iron lid closes again, and the bolts slide back, "Ye shall pray," says Master Parys, addressing the borrowers, "for the soul of W. de Seltone and all the faithful departed."

We may pass from this scene in the old Convocation House to another not less typical of the mediæval University. The Chancellor's court is being held, and the Chancellor himself is sitting there, or, in his absence, his commissary. The two proctors are present as assessors, and these three constitute the court. It is before this tribunal that every member of the "Privilege" must be tried. For it was only in a University court that they could be sued in the first instance. Here then, if we attend this court and glance through the records of ages, we shall find the Chancellor administering justice, exercising the extensive powers which he holds as a Justice of the Peace and as almost the supreme authority over members of the University. True, he had not the power of life and death, but he could fine or banish, imprison and excommunicate. And as to the townsmen, he exercised over them a joint jurisdiction with the mayor and civic authorities. The accused was entitled to have an advocate to defend him, and he could appeal to the Congregation of Masters, and thereafter to the Pope. No spiritual cause terminable within the University could be carried out of it. But in all temporal cases the ultimate appeal was to the King.

The truculent student, however, was often inclined to appeal to force. Master John Hodilbeston, it is recorded in the Acts of the Chancellor's Court (1434), when accused of a certain offence, was observed to have brought a dagger into the very presence of the Chancellor, contrary to the statutes, "wherefore he lost his arms to the University and was put in Bocardo." The next case on the list of this mediæval police court is that of Thomas Skibbo. He is not a clerk, but he too finds his way to Bocardo, for he has committed many crimes of violence. Highway robbery and threats of murder were nothing to him, as a scholar of Bekis-Inn comes forward to depose, and, besides, he has stolen a serving boy. After the scholar and the ruffian, the Warden of Canterbury College steps forward. He has come to make his submission to the commissary, whom he had declared to be a partial judge, and whose summons he had refused to obey. Also, he has added injury to insult by encouraging his scholars to take beer by violence in the streets. The commissary graciously accepts his apology and his undertaking to keep the peace in future. The

Master of the Great Hall of the University now comes forward. Evil rumours have been rife, and he wishes to clear his character of vile slanders that have connected his name with those of certain women. He brings no charge of slander, but claims the right of clearing himself by making an affidavit. This was the system of compurgation, by which a man swore that he was innocent of a crime, and twelve good friends of his swore that he was speaking the truth. In this case the Master was permitted to clear himself by oath before the commissary in Merton College Chapel, and Mistress Agnes Bablake and divers women appeared and swore with him that rumour was a lying jade. On another occasion the Principal of White Hall wished to prove his descent from true English stock. He insisted on being allowed to swear that he was not a Scotsman. A discreditable rumour to that effect had doubtless got abroad, without taking tangible form. But he was, he maintained, a loyal Englishman. "It was greatly to his credit" doubtless. *Qui s'excuse, s'accuse*, we are inclined to think in such cases. The appalling penalties which awaited the perjurer probably gave the ceremony some force at one time. But Dr Gascoigne enters his protest in the Chancellor's book (1443) against the indiscriminate admission of parties to compurgation. National feeling and clan feeling ran high. Gascoigne says that he has known many cases in which people have privately admitted that they have perjured themselves in public. Moreover, he added, no townsman ventures to object to a person being admitted to compurgation, for fear of being murdered or at least maimed. No good end, therefore, can be answered by it.

But what is the cause of Robert Wright, Esquire-Bedel? He has some complaint against the master and fellows of Great University Hall (1456). The Chancellor listens for a moment, and then suggests, like a modern London police magistrate, that they should settle their quarrel out of court. They decide to appoint arbitrators, and bind themselves to abide by their award. The commissary is frequently appointed arbitrator himself, and his award is usually to the effect that one party shall humbly ask pardon of the other, pay a sum of money and swear to keep the peace. Other awards are more picturesque. Thus, when Broadgates and Pauline Halls decided to settle their quarrel in this way, the arbitrators ordered the principals mutually to beg reconciliation from each other for themselves and their parties, and to give either to the other the kiss of peace and swear upon the Bible to have brotherly love to each other, under a bond of a hundred shillings. David Phillipe, who struck John Olney, must kneel to him and ask and receive pardon.

As an earnest of their future good-will, it is often decreed that the two parties shall entertain their neighbours. Two gallons of ale are mentioned sometimes as suitable for this purpose; a feast is recommended at others, and the dishes are specified. As thus:—(1465) The arbiter decides that neither party in a quarrel which he has been appointed to settle, shall in future abuse, slander, threaten or make faces at the other. As a guarantee of their mutual forgiveness and reconciliation, they are commanded to provide at their joint charges an entertainment in S. Mary's College. The arbiter orders the dinner; one party is to supply a goose and a measure of wine, the other bread and beer.

Many and minute are the affairs of the Chancellor. At one time he is concerned with the taverners. He summons them all before him, and makes them swear that in future they will brew wholesome beer, and that they will supply the students with enough of it; at another he imprisons a butcher who has been selling "putrid and fetid" meat, or a baker who has been using false weights; at another banishes a carpenter for shooting at the proctors, or sends a woman to the pillory for being an incorrigible prostitute or to Bocardo for the mediæval fault of being a common and intolerable scold. Next he fines the vicar of S. Giles' for breaking the peace, and confiscates his club. Then he dispatches the organist of All Souls' to Bocardo, for Thomas Bentlee has committed adultery. But the poor man weeps so bitterly, that the Warden of that college is moved to have good hope of the said Thomas, and goes surety for him, and the "organ-player" is released after three hours of incarceration. The punishment of a friar who is charged with having uttered a gross libel in a sermon, and has refused to appear when cited before the Chancellor's court, is more severe. He is degraded in congregation and banished.

The jurisdiction which we have seen the Chancellor wielding in this court had not been always his, and it was acquired not without dust and heat. At the beginning of the thirteenth century he was both in fact and in theory the delegate of the bishop of the diocese; not the presiding head, but an external authority who might be invoked to enforce the decrees of the Masters' Guild.

Before that time the organisation of the University extended at least so far as to boast of a "Master of the Schools," who was probably elected by the masters themselves, and whose office was very likely merged into that of the Chancellor.

As an ecclesiastical judge, deriving his authority from the Bishop of Lincoln, the Chancellor exercised jurisdiction over students by virtue of their being "clerks," not members of the University. Over laymen he exercised jurisdiction only so far as they were subject to the authority of the ordinary ecclesiastical courts. At Oxford he had no prison or Cathedral dungeon to which he could commit delinquents. He was obliged to send them either to the King's prison in the Castle, or to the town prison over the Bocardo Gate.

But from this time forward by a series of steps, prepared as a rule by conflicts between town and gown, the office of Chancellor was gradually raised. First it encroached on the liberties of the town, and then shook itself free of its dependence on the See of Lincoln.

The protection of the great, learned and powerful Bishop of Lincoln and the fact that, in the last resort, the masters were always ready to stop lecturing and withdraw with all the students to another town, for the University, as such, had not yet acquired any property to tie them to Oxford, were weapons which proved of overwhelming advantage to the University at this early stage of its existence. Again and again we find that, when a dispute as to police jurisdiction or authority arose between the University and the town, pressure was brought to bear in this way. The masters ceased to lecture; the students threatened to shake the dust of Oxford off their feet;

the enthusiastic Grossetete, throwing aside the cares of State, the business of his bishopric, and the task of translating the Ethics of Aristotle, came forward to intervene on behalf of his darling University and to use his influence with the King. The Pope, Innocent IV. (1254), was also induced to take the University under his protection. He confirmed its "immunities and liberties and laudable, ancient and rational customs from whomsoever received," and called upon the Bishops of London and Salisbury to guard it from evil. Against the combined forces of the Church, the Crown, and the evident interests of their own pockets, it was a foregone conclusion that the citizens would not be able to maintain the full exercise of their municipal liberty.

It was in 1244 that the first important extension of the Chancellor's jurisdiction was made. Some students had made a raid upon Jewry and sacked the houses of their creditors. They were committed to prison by the civil authorities. Grossetete insisted on their being handed over to the ecclesiastical jurisdiction. As the outcome of this riot Henry III. presently issued a decree of great importance. By it all disputes concerning debts, rents and prices, and all other "contracts of moveables," in which one party was an Oxford clerk, were referred to the Chancellor for trial. This new power raised him at once to a position very different from that which he had hitherto enjoyed as the mere representative of the Bishop of Lincoln. "He was invested henceforth with a jurisdiction which no Legate or Bishop could confer and no civil judge could annul." A charter followed in 1248, which authorised the Chancellor and proctors to assist at the assaying of bread and beer by the mayor and bailiffs. On admission to office the latter were required to swear to respect the liberties and customs of the University, and the town, in its corporate capacity, was made responsible for injuries inflicted on scholars. The Chancellor's jurisdiction was still further extended in 1255. To his spiritual power, which he held according to the ordinary ecclesiastical law and to the civil jurisdiction conferred upon him in 1244, a new charter now added the criminal jurisdiction even over laymen, for breach of the peace. By this charter Henry III. provided that,

"for the peace, tranquillity and advantage of the University of scholars of Oxford, there be chosen four aldermen and eight discreet and legal burghers associated with them, to assist the Mayors and Bailiffs to keep the peace and hold the Assizes and to seek out malefactors and disturbers of the peace and night-vagabonds, and harbourers of robbers. Two officers shall also be elected in each parish to make diligent search for persons of suspicious character, and every one who takes a stranger in under his roof for more than three nights must be held responsible for him. No retail dealer may buy victuals on their way to market or buy anything with the view of selling again before nine in the morning, under penalty of forfeit and fine. If a layman assault a clerk, let him be immediately arrested, and if the assault prove serious, let him be imprisoned in the Castle and detained there untill he give satisfaction to the clerk in accordance with the judgment of the Chancellor and the University. If a clerk shall make a grave or outrageous assault upon a layman, let him be imprisoned in the aforesaid Castle untill the Chancellor demand his surrender; if the offence be a light one, let him be confined in the town prison untill he be set free by the Chancellor.

"Brewers and bakers are not to be punished for the first offence (of adulteration or other tradesman's tricks); but shall forfeit their stock on the second occasion, and for the third offence be put in the pillory." (One of these "hieroglyphic State machines" stood opposite the Cross Inn at Carfax; another, with stocks and gallows, at the corner of Longwall and Holywell Streets. In the former one Tubb was the last man to stand (1810), for perjury, though not the last to deserve it.) "Every baker," the charter continues, "must have his own stamp and stamp his own bread so that it may be known whose bread it is; every one who brews for sale must show his sign, or forfeit his beer. Wine must be sold to laymen and clerks on the same terms. The assay of bread and ale is to be made half yearly, and at the assay the Chancellor or his deputy appointed for that purpose must be present; otherwise the assay shall be invalid."

A few years later a Royal Writ of Edward I. (1275) conferred on the Chancellor the cognizance of all personal actions whatever wherein either party was a scholar, be he prosecutor or defendant. And in 1290, by judgment of King and Parliament, after a conflict between the town and University, when a bailiff had resisted the authority of the Chancellor in the students' playground, Beaumont Fields, which embraced the University Park and S. Giles', the Chancellor obtained jurisdiction in case of all crimes committed in Oxford, where one of the parties was a scholar, except pleas of homicide and mayhem. His jurisdiction over the King's bailiffs was affirmed, but leave was granted them to apply to the King's court if aggrieved by the Chancellor's proceedings.

From this time forward the authority of the Chancellor was gradually increased and extended. It was, indeed, not long before the office shook itself free from its historical subordination to the Bishop of Lincoln. After a considerable struggle over the point, the bishop was worsted by a Papal Bull (1368), which entirely abrogated his claim to confirm the Chancellor elect. Since that time the University has enjoyed the right of electing and admitting its highest officer without reference to any superior authority whatever (Maxwell Lyte).

The precinct of the University was defined in the reign of Henry IV. as extending to the Hospital of S. Bartholomew on the east, to Botley on the west, to Godstow on the north, and to Bagley Wood on the south.

These were the geographical limits of the University, and within them the following classes of people were held (1459) to be "of the privilege of the University":—The Chancellor, all doctors, masters and other graduates, and all students, scholars and clerks of every order and degree. These constituted a formidable number in themselves when arrayed against the town, for there were probably at least 3000 of them at the most flourishing periods. The Archbishop of

Armagh indeed stated confidently at Avignon (1357) that there had once been 30,000, but that must have been a rhetorical exaggeration. There can never have been more than 4000. But in addition to this army of scholars, all their "daily continual servants," all "barbers, manciples, spencers, cokes, lavenders," and all the numerous persons who were engaged in trades ancillary to study, such as the preparation, engrossing, illumination and binding of parchment, were "of the privilege" and directly controlled by the University. In what was afterwards known as Schools Street all these trades were represented as early as 1190. Over these classes, and within the limits defined, the jurisdiction of the Chancellor was by the end of the fifteenth century established supreme.

Citizens and scholars alike had now to be careful how they lived. The stocks, the pillory and the cucking stool awaited offenders among the townsmen, fines or banishment the students who transgressed. Local governments in the Middle Ages were excessively paternal. They inquired closely into the ways of their people and dealt firmly with their peccadilloes. Did a man brew or sell bad beer he was burnt alive at Nürnberg; at Oxford he was condemned to the pillory; if a manciple was too fond of cards he was also punished by the Chancellor's court. A regular tariff was framed of penalties for those breaches of the peace and street brawls, in which not freshmen only but heads of houses and vicars of parishes were so frequently involved.

Endeavours were made to promote a proper standard of life by holding "General Inquisitions" at regular intervals. The town was divided into sections, and a Doctor of Theology and two Masters of Arts were told off to inquire into the morals of the inhabitants of each division. Juries of citizens were summoned, and gave evidence on oath to these delegate judges who sat in the parish churches. The characters of their fellow-townsmen were critically discussed. Reports were made to the Chancellor, who corrected the offenders. Excommunication, penance or the cucking stool were meted out to "no common" scolds, notorious evil-livers and those who kept late hours.

It had formerly been enacted (1333) that since the absence of the Chancellor was the cause of many perils, his office should become vacant if he were to absent himself from the University for a month during full term. But in the course of the fifteenth century the Chancellor changed from a biennial and resident official to a permanent and non-resident one. He was chosen now for his power as a friend at court, and by the court, as it grew more despotic and ecclesiastically minded, he was used as an agent for coercing the University.

To-day the Chancellorship is a merely honorary office, usually bestowed on successful politicians. The Chancellor appoints a Vice-Chancellor, but usage compels him to appoint heads of houses in order of seniority. This right of appointment dates from the time when the Duke of Wellington, as Chancellor, dispensed with the formality of asking convocation for its assent to the appointment of his nominee.

Having sketched thus far the development of the office which represents the power and dignity of the University, we may now turn to consider the position of the young apprentices from their earliest initiation into this guild of learning.

The scholars of mediæval Universities were your true cosmopolitans. They passed freely from the University of one country to that of another by virtue of the freemasonry of knowledge. Despising the dangers of the sea, the knight-errants of learning went from country to country, like the bee, to use the metaphor applied by S. Athanasius to S. Anthony, in order to obtain the best instruction in every school. They went without let or hindrance, with no passport but the desire to learn, to Paris, like John of Salisbury, Stephen Langton or Thomas Becket, if they were attracted by the reputation of that University in Theology; to Bologna, if they wished to sit at the feet of some famous lecturer in Civil Law. Emperors issued edicts for their safe conduct and protection when travelling in their dominions—even when warring against the Scots, Edward III. issued general letters of protection for all Scottish scholars who desired to repair to Oxford or Cambridge—and when they arrived at their destination, of whatever nationality they might be, they found there as a rule little colonies of their own countrymen already established and ready to receive them. Dante was as much at home in the straw-strewn Schools Street in Paris as he would have found himself at Padua or at Oxford, had he chanced to study there.

It has indeed been suggested that he did study there in the year 1313. Like Chaucer, he may have done so, but probably did not. There is certainly a reference to Westminster in the "Inferno" (xii. 119); but it is not necessary to go to Oxford in order to learn that London and Westminster are on the banks of the Thames.

In attending lectures at a strange University the mediæval students had no difficulty in understanding the language of their teachers. For all the learned world spoke Latin. Latin was the Volapuk of the Middle Ages. Mediæval Latin, with all its faults and failing sense of style, is a language not dead, but living in a green old age, written by men who on literary matters talked and thought in a speech that is lively and free and fertile in vocabulary. The common use of it among all educated men gave authors like Erasmus a public which consisted of the whole civilised world, and it rendered scholars cosmopolitan in a sense almost inconceivable to the student of to-day. That was chiefly in the earlier days of Universities. Gradually, with the growth of national feeling and the more definite demarcation of nations and the ever-increasing sense of patriotism, that higher form of selfishness, cosmopolitanism went out of fashion. Nowadays only two classes of cosmopolitans survive—in theory, free traders, and in practice, thieves.

I have spoken of the dangers of the sea; they were very great in those days of open sailing boats, when the compass was unknown; but the dangers of land-travelling were hardly less. The roads through the forests that lay around Oxford were notoriously unsafe, not only in mediæval days but even a hundred years ago. Armed therefore, and if possible in companies, the students would ride on their Oxford pilgrimage. If they could not afford to ride, the mediæval pedagogue, the common carrier, would take them to their destination for a charge of fivepence a day. For there were carriers who took a regular route at the beginning of every University year for the purpose of bringing students up from the country. They would have a mixed company of all ages in their care. For though students went up to Oxford as a rule between the ages of thirteen and sixteen, many doubtless were younger and many older. It was indeed a common thing for ecclesiastics of all ages to obtain leave of absence from their benefices in order to go up to the University and study Canon Law or Theology there. You can fancy, then, this motley assembly of pack-horses and parish priests, of clever lads chosen from the monasteries or grammar schools, and ambitious lads from the plough, all very genuine philosophers, lovers of learning for its own sake or its advantages, working their way through the miry roads, passed occasionally by some nobleman's son with his imposing train of followers, and passing others yet more lowly, who were just trudging it on foot, begging their way, their bundles on their shoulders.

You can fancy them at last coming over Shotover Hill, down the "horse path" past S. Clement's, and so reaching safely their journey's end. Once in Oxford, they would take up their abode in a monastery to which they had an introduction; in a college, if, thanks to the fortune of birth or education, they had been elected to share in the benefits of a foundation; as menials attached to the household of some wealthier student, if they were hard put to it; in a hall or house licensed to take in lodgers, if they were foreigners or independent youths. On taking up his residence in one of these halls, the mediæval student would find that Alma Mater, in her struggles with the townsmen, had been fighting his battles. Lest he should fall among thieves, it had been provided that the rents charged should be fixed by a board of assessors; lest the sudden influx of this floating population should produce scarcity, and therefore starvation prices, the transactions of the retailers were carefully regulated. They were forbidden to buy up provisions from the farmers outside the city, and so establish a "corner"; they were forbidden even to buy in Oxford market till a certain hour in the morning. The prices of vendibles were fixed in the interests of the poor students. Thus in 1315 the King ordained that "a good living ox, stalled or corn-fed, should be sold for 16s., and no higher; if fatted with grass for 14s. A fat cow, 12s. A fat hog of two years old, 3s. 4d. A fat mutton, corn-fed or whose wool is not grown, 1s. 8d. A fat mutton shorn, 1s. 2d. A fat goose, 2d. A fat hen or two chickens, one penny. Four pigeons or twenty-four eggs, one penny."

The halls were, at any rate originally, merely private houses adapted to the use of students. A common room for meals, a kitchen and a few bedrooms were all they had to boast. Many of them had once belonged to Jews, for they were large and built of stone. And the Jews, being wealthy, had introduced a higher standard of comfort into Oxford, and at the same time, being a common sort of prey, they probably found that stone houses were safer as well as more luxurious. Moysey's Hall and Lombard's Hall bore in their names evident traces of their origin. Other halls derived their names from other causes. After the great fire in 1190 the citizens, in imitation of the Londoners, and the Jews, had rebuilt their houses of stone.

"Such tenements," says Wood, "were for the better distinction from others called Stone or Tiled halls. Some of those halls that were not slated were, if standing near those that were, stiled Thatched halls. Likewise when glass came into fashion, for before that time our windows were only latticed, that hall that had its windows first glazed was stiled, for difference sake, Glazen hall. In like manner 'tis probable that those that had leaden gutters, or any part of their roofs of lead were stiled Leaden hall, or in one instance Leaden porch. Those halls also that had staples to their doors, for our predecessors used only latch and catch, were written Staple halls."

Other halls were called after their owners (Peckwater's Inn, Alban Hall, etc.), or from their position in the street or town, or the patron Saint of a neighbouring church (S. Edward's Hall, S. Mary's Entry); many from other physical peculiarities besides those we have mentioned. Angle Hall, Broadgates Hall, White Hall and Black Hall explain themselves easily enough, whilst Chimney Hall is a name which recalls the days when a large chimney was a rarity, a louvre above a charcoal fire in the middle of the room being sufficient to carry off the smoke. Other halls, again, were named after signs that hung outside them, or over their gateways, like ordinary inns or shops. The towering and barbaric inn-signs always struck foreigners, when first visiting England, with astonishment not unmingled with dismay. They were thus probably thrown into a proper state of mind to receive their bills.

The Eagle, the Lion, the Elephant, the Saracen's Head, the Brazen Nose and the Swan were some of the signs in Oxford. There are a few survivals from this menagerie.

The Star Inn, now the Clarendon, was built on the site of one of these old Halls, and the richly-carved wooden gables were visible in the house next to it. The Roebuck was once Coventry Hall. The Mitre preserved traces of Burwaldscote Hall. The Angel had similar traces, but the Angel itself has now given place to the New Schools. Many students, however, lodged singly in private houses. Chaucer's *poor scholar* lodged with a carpenter who worked for the Abbot of Osney.

"A chamber had he in that hostelrie,
Alone, withouten any compagnie,
Ful fetisly ydight with herbes sote."...

Halls, it will have been observed, were known also by the name of entries and inns or (deriving from the French) hostels. And that in fact is what they were. The principal, who might originally have been the senior student of a party who had taken a house in which to study, or the owner of the house himself, derived a good income from keeping a boarding-house of this kind. He was responsible to the University for the good conduct of his men, and to his men, one must suppose, for their comfort. The position of principal was soon much sought after, and the ownership of a good hostel, with a good connection, would fetch a price like a public-house to-day.

It was found necessary, however, to decree that the principal of a hall should be a master, and should not cater for the other inmates. Payments for food were therefore made by the students to an upper servant, known as a maniciple, whose duty it was to go to market in the morning and there buy provisions for the day, before the admission of the retail-dealers at nine o'clock. The amount which each student contributed to the common purse for the purchase of provisions was known as "Commons." It varied from eight to eighteen pence a week. Extra food obtained from the maniciple to be eaten in private was called "Battels."

The principal could only maintain his position and fill his hall if he satisfied the students. The government of these halls was therefore highly democratic. A new principal could only succeed if he was accepted by the general opinion of the inmates and received their voluntary allegiance.

On coming up to Oxford the student, however little he might intend to devote his life to the Church, adopted, if he had not done so before, clerical tonsure and clerical garb. By so doing he became entitled to all the immunities and privileges of the clerical order. He was, now, so long as he did not marry, exempt from the secular courts, and his person was inviolable.

No examination or ceremony of any kind seems to have been required in order to become a member of the University. Attendance at lectures, after a declaration made to a resident master to the effect that the student purposed to attend them, was enough to entitle him to the privileges of that corporation.

The germ of the modern system of matriculation may perhaps be traced in the statute (1420), which required that all scholars and scholars' servants, who had attained years of discretion, should swear before the Chancellor that they would observe the statutes for the repression of riots and disorders.

Among the students themselves, however, some form of initiation probably took place, comparable to that of the Bejaunus, or Yellow-bill, in Germany, or of the young soldier, the young Freemason, or the newcomer at an *atelier* in Paris to-day. Horseplay at the expense of the raw youth, and much chaff and tomfoolery, would be followed in good time by a supper for which the freshman would obligingly pay. Initiation of this kind is a universal taste, and, if kept within bounds, is not a bad custom for testing the temper and grit of the new members of a community. At Oxford, then, freshmen were subject to certain customs at the hands of the senior scholars, or sophisters, on their first coming. So Wood tells us, but he cannot give details. He compares the ceremony, however, to the "salting" which obtained in his own day. Of this salting, as it was practised at Merton, he gives the following account:—

"On Feast days charcoal fires were lit in the Hall of Merton, and between five and six in the afternoon the senior undergraduates would bring in the Freshmen, and make them sit down on a form in the middle of the Hall. Which done, everyone in order was to speak some pretty apothegm or make a jest or bull or speak some eloquent nonsense, to make the company laugh. But if any of the Freshmen came off dull, or not cleverly, some of the forward or pragmatical seniors would *tuck* them, that is, set the nail of their thumb to their chin just under the lower lip, and by the help of their other fingers under the chin, would give him a mark which would sometimes produce blood." On Shrove Tuesday a brass pot was set before the fire filled with cawdle by the College Cook at the Freshmen's expense. Then each of them had to pluck off his gown and band and if possible make himself look like a scoundrel. 'Which done they were conducted each after the other to the High Table, made to stand upon a form and to deliver a speech.' Wood gives us the speech he himself made on this occasion, a dreary piece of facetiousness. As a 'kitten of the Muses and meer frog of Helicon he croaked cataracts of plumbeous cerebrosity.'

"The reward for a good speech was a cup of cawdle and no salted drink, for an indifferent one some cawdle and some salted drink, and for a bad one, besides the tucks, nothing but College beer and salt.

"When these ceremonies were over the senior cook administered an oath over an old shoe to those about to be admitted into the fraternity. The Freshman repeated the oath, kissed the shoe, put on his gown and band and took his place among the seniors."

When the freshmen of the past year were solemnly made seniors, and probationers were admitted fellows, similar ceremonies took place. At All Souls', for instance, on 14th January, those who were to be admitted fellows were brought from their chambers in the middle of the night, sometimes in a bucket slung on a pole, and so led about the college and into the hall, whilst some of the junior fellows, disguised perhaps, would sing a song in praise of the mallard, some verses of which I give:

"The griffin, bustard, turkey and capon,
Let other hungry mortals gape on,
And on their bones with stomachs fall hard,
But let All Souls' men have the mallard.

Hough the blood of King Edward, by the blood of
King Edward,
It was a swapping, swapping mallard.

"The Romans once admired a gander
More than they did their best commander,
Because he saved, if some don't fool us,
The place that's named from the scull of Tolus.

Hough the blood of King Edward, by the blood of
King Edward,
It was a swapping, swapping mallard.

"Then let us drink and dance a galliard
In the remembrance of the mallard,
And as the mallard doth in the pool,
Let's dabble, dive and duck in bowle.[27]

Hough, etc."

In any attempt to appreciate the kind and character of the mediæval students and the life which they led, it is necessary first of all to realise that the keynote of the early student life was poverty. It was partly for the benefit of poor scholars and partly for the benefit of their founders' souls, for which these scholars should pray, that the early colleges and chantries were founded. Morals, learning and poverty were the qualifications for a fellowship on Durham's foundation. Poverty, "the stepmother of learning," it is which the University in its letters and petitions always and truly represents as the great hindrance to the student "seeking in the vineyard of the Lord the pearl of knowledge." Books these poor seekers could not afford to buy, fees they could scarce afford to pay, food itself was none too plentiful.

But the pearl for which the young student as he sat, pinched and blue, at the feet of his teacher in the schools, and the Masters of Arts,

"When, in forlorn and naked chambers cooped
And crowded, o'er the ponderous books they hung,"

alike were searching, was a pearl of great price. For learning spelt success. There was through learning a career open to the talents. The lowliest and neediest might rise, by means of a University education, to the highest dignity which the Church, and that was also the world, could offer.

For all great civilians were ecclesiastics. The Church embraced all the professions; and the professors of all arts, of medicine, statesmanship or architecture, of diplomacy and even of law, embraced the Church. And the reward of success in any of them was ecclesiastical promotion and a fat benefice. The University opened the door to the Church, with all its dazzling possibilities of preferment, and the University itself was thrown open to the poorest by the system of the monastic houses and charitable foundations.

Promising lads, too, of humble origin were often maintained at the schools by wealthy patrons. From a villein one might rise to be a clerk, from a clerk become a master of the University—a fellow, a bursar, a bishop and a chancellor, first of Oxford, then of England.

At the University, of course, the students were not treated with the same absolute equality that they are now, regardless of birth or wealth. Sons of noblemen did not study there, unless they had a strong bent in that direction. The days were not yet come when a University training was valuable as a social and moral as well as an intellectual education: when noblemen, therefore, did attend the schools, more was made of them. They wore hoods lined with rich fur, and enjoyed certain privileges with regard to the taking of degrees.

Like those idyllic islanders who lived by taking in each other's washing, the masters supported themselves on the fees paid by the students who attended their lectures, whilst the poorest students earned a livelihood by waiting on the masters, or wealthier students. Servitors, who thus combined the careers of undergraduates with those of "scouts," continued in existence till the end of the eighteenth century. They were sent on the most menial errands or employed to transcribe manuscripts, and five shillings was deemed an ample allowance for their services. Whitfield was a servitor, and the father of the Wesleys also. Such students, lads of low extraction, drawn from the tap-room or the plough, but of promising parts, would be helped by the chests which we have described, and which were founded for their benefit. When Long Vacation came, they would turn again from intellectual to manual labour. For Long Vacation meant for them, not reading-parties, but the harvest, and in the harvest they could earn wages. But there was another method of obtaining the means to attend lectures at the University which was popularised in the Middle Ages by the Mendicants, by the theory of the poverty of Christ and by the insistence of the Church on the duty of charity. This was begging on the highway. "Pain por Dieu aus escoliers" was a well-known "street cry" in mediæval Paris, and in England during vacations the wandering scholar,

"Often, starting from some covert place,
Saluted the chance comer on the road,
Crying, 'An obolus, a penny give
To a poor scholar.'"

And as they made their way along the high-road a party of such begging scholars would come perhaps to a rich man's house, and ask for aid by prayer and song. Sometimes they would be put to the test as to their scholarship by being commanded to make a couplet of Latin verses on some topic. They would scratch their heads, look wistfully at one another and produce a passable verse or two. Then they would receive their reward and pass on. So popular, indeed, did this system become, that begging students had to be restricted. Only those licensed by the Chancellor and certified as deserving cases, like the scholars of Aristotle's Hall in 1461, were presently permitted to beg.

Where poverty was so prevalent, the standard of comfort was not likely to be high. The enormous advance in the general level of material comfort, and even luxury, which has taken place in this country during the last hundred years, makes it difficult to describe the comfortless lives of these early students without giving an exaggerated idea of the sacrifices they were making and the hardships they were enduring for the sake of setting their feet on the first rung of this great ladder of learning. But it should be remembered that, as far as the ordinary appliances of decency and comfort, as we understand them, are concerned, the labourer's cottage in these days is better supplied than was a palace in those when princes

"At matins froze and couched at curfew time,"

and when

"Lovers of truth, by penury constrained
Bucer, Erasmus or Melancthon, read
Before the doors or windows of their cells
By moonshine, through mere lack of taper light."

If we realise that this was the case, we shall not be surprised to find that the rooms in which these students and masters lived, so far from being spacious and luxurious, were small, dingy, overcrowded and excessively uncomfortable. It was rare for a student to have a room to himself —"alone, withouten any compagnie." The usual arrangement in halls and colleges would seem to have been that two or more scholars shared a room, and slept in that part of it which was not occupied by the "studies" of the inhabitants. For each scholar would have a "study" of his own adjoining the windows, where he might strain to catch the last ray of daylight. A "study" was a movable piece of furniture, a sort of combination of book-shelf and desk, which probably survives in the Winchester "toys." The students shared a room, and they frequently shared a bed too. The founder of Magdalen provided that in his college Demies under the age of fifteen should sleep two in a bed. And in addition to their beds and lodgings, the poorest students were obliged to share an academical gown also. Friends who had all things in common, might sleep at the same time, but could only attend lectures one by one, for lack of more than one gown amongst them. To these straits, it is said, S. Richard was reduced. But such deprivation accentuates rather than spoils the happiness of student life, as anyone who is acquainted with the Quartier Latin will agree. When the heart is young and generous, when the spirit is free and the blood is hot, what matters hardship when there are comrades bright and brave to share it; what matters poverty when the riches of art and love and learning are being outspread before your eyes; what matters the misery of circumstance, when daily the young traveller can wander forth, silent, amazed, into "the realms of gold?"

During the many centuries that the mansions of the wealthy and the palaces of princes were totally unprovided with the most indispensable appliances of domestic decency, it is not to be expected that the rooms of students should prove to be plentifully or luxuriously furnished. We know the stock-in-trade of Chaucer's poor student:

"His Almageste and bokes grete and smale
His astrelabie, longinge for his art,
His augrim-stones layen faire apart
On shelves couched at his beddes heed;
His presse y-covered with a falding reed.
And al above ther lay a gay sautrye
On which he made a nightes melodye
So swetely, that all the chambre rong;
And Angelus ad virginem he song."

We can supplement Chaucer's inventory of a poor student's furniture by an examination of old indentures. Therein we find specified among the goods of such an one just such a fithele or "gay sautrye" as Chaucer noted, an old cithara or a broken lute, a desk, a stool, a chair, a mattress, a coffer, a tripod table, a mortar and pestle, a sword and an old gown. Another student might boast the possession of a hatchet, a table "quinque pedum cum uno legge," some old wooden dishes, a pitcher and a bowl, an iron twister, a brass pot with a broken leg, a pair of knives, and, most prized of all, a bow and twenty arrows. Few could boast of so many "bokes at his beddes heed" as Chaucer's clerk of Oxenford. Manuscripts were of immense value in those days, and we need hardly be surprised if that worthy philosopher, seeing that he had invested his money in twenty volumes clad in black and red, had but little gold remaining in his coffer. The books that we find mentioned in such indentures, are those which formed the common stock of mediæval learning, volumes of homilies, the works of Boethius, Ovid's *De remedio amoris* and a book of geometry. These and other books, as articles of the highest intrinsic value, were always mentioned in detail in the last will and testament of a dying scholar. But, as the modern artist, on his death-bed in the Quartier Latin, summoned his dearest friend to his side and exclaimed, "My friend, I leave you my wife and my pipe. Take care of my pipe"; so the mediæval student would often feel that though his books might be his most valuable legacy in some eyes, his bow and arrows, his cap and gown or his mantle, "blodii coloris," these were the truest pledges of affection that he could bequeath to the comrade of his heart. Only the wealthier students, or the higher officials of the University, rejoiced in such luxuries as a change of clothes, or could reckon among their furniture several forms or chairs, a pair of snuffers and bellows. For of what use to the ordinary student were candlesticks and snuffers, when candles cost the prohibitive price of twopence a pound; or what should he do with bellows and tongs when a stove or fire was out of the question, save in the case of a Principal? To run about in order not to go to bed with cold feet was the plan of the mediæval student, unless he anticipated the advice of Mr Jorrocks and thought of ginger.

From his slumbers on a flock bed, in such quarters as I have described, the mediæval student roused him with the dawn. For lectures began with the hour of prime, soon after daybreak. He was soon dressed, for men seldom changed their clothes in those days, and in the centuries when the manuals of gallantry recommended the nobleman to wash his hands once a day and his face almost as often, when a charming queen like Margaret of Navarre, could remark without shame that she had not washed her hands for eight days, it is not to be expected that the ablutions of a mere student should be frequent or extensive. Washing is a modern habit, and not widespread. To attend a "chapel" or a "roll-call" is the first duty of the modern undergraduate, but a daily attendance at mass was not required till the college system had taken shape; the statutes of New College, in fact, are the first to enforce it. All therefore that the yawning student had to do, before making his way to the lecture-room in the hall of his inn or college, or in the long low buildings of Schools Street, was to break his fast, if he could afford to do so, with a piece of bread and a pot o' the smallest ale from the "Buttery." As a lecture lasted, not the one hour of a "Stunde," but for two or three hours, some such support would be highly desirable, but not necessary. Our forefathers were one-meal men, like the Germans of to-day. Civilisation is an advance from breakfast to dinner, from one meal a day to several. Late dinner is the goal towards which all humanity presses. For dinner-time, as De Quincey observed, has little connection with the idea of dinner. It has travelled through every hour, like the hand of a clock, from nine or ten in the morning till ten at night. But at Oxford it travelled slowly. Hearne growls at the colleges which, in 1723, altered their dinner hour from eleven to twelve, "from people's lying in bed longer than they used to do." Happily for him he did not live to see the beginning of the nineteenth century, when those colleges which had dined at three advanced to four, and those that had dined at four to five; or the close of it, when the hour of seven became the accepted time.

The mediæval student took his one meal at ten or eleven in the morning. Soup thickened with oatmeal, baked meat and bread was his diet, varied by unwholesome salt fish in Lent. These viands were served in hall on wooden trenches and washed down by a tankard of college beer. During the meal a chapter of the Bible or of some improving work in Latin was read aloud, and at its conclusion the founder's prayer and a Latin grace would be said. Conversation, it was usually ordained, might only be carried on in Latin; the modern student, on the contrary, is "sconced" (fined a tankard of beer) if he speaks three words of "shop" in hall. After dinner perhaps some disputations or exercises, some repetition and discussion of the morning's lecture would be held in hall, or the students would take the air, walking out two and two, as the founders directed, if they were good; going off singly, or in parties to poach or hawk or spoil for a row, if they were not. Lectures or disputations were resumed about noon.

Seated on benches, or more usually and properly, according to the command of Urban V., sitting on the rush-strewn floors of the school-room, the young seekers after knowledge listened to the words of wisdom that flowed from the regent master, who sat above them at a raised desk, dressed in full academical costume. Literally, they sat at the feet of their Gamaliels.

In the schools they were enjoined to "sit as quiet as a girl," but they were far from observing this injunction. Old and young were only too ready to quarrel or to play during lectures, to shout and interrupt whilst the master was reading the Sentences of Peter Lombard, and bang the benches with their books to express their approval or disapproval of his comments thereon.

Supper came at five, and after that perhaps a visit to the playing fields of Beaumont or a tavern, where wine would be mingled with song, and across the oaken tables would thunder those rousing choruses that students ever love:

"Mihi est propositum in taberna mori
Vinum sit appositum morientis ori,
Ut dicant, quum venerint, angelorum chori,
'Deus sit propitius huic potatori.'"

When curfew rang at length, all the students would assemble in hall and have a "drinking" or "collation." Then, before going to bed, they would sing the Antiphon of the Virgin (Salve Regina), and so the day was finished. A dull, monotonous day it seems to us, varied only by sermons—and there was no lack of them—at S. Mary's or S. Peter's in the East, with the chance excitement of hearing a friar recant the unorthodox views he had expressed the previous Sunday; but it was a day that was bright and social compared with the ordinary conditions of the time.

In this daily round, so far as one has been able to reconstruct it, the absence of any provision for physical recreation is a noticeable thing to us, who have exchanged the mediæval enthusiasm for learning for an enthusiasm for athletics. Both are excellent things in their way, but as the governor of an American State remarked when defending the practice of smoking over wine, both together are better than either separate. And nowadays in some cases the combination is happily attained. But in an age which inherited the monkish tradition of the vileness of the body and the need of mortifying it, games of all sorts were regarded as a weakness of the flesh. So far were founders from making any provision for recreation, that they usually went out of their way to prohibit it. Games with bat and ball, and tennis, that is, or fives, were strictly forbidden as indecent, though in some cases students were permitted to play with a soft ball in the college courts. But "deambulation in the College Grove" was the monastic ideal. Nor did the founders frown only on exercise; amusements of the most harmless sort were also under their ban. On the long, cold, dark winter evenings the students were naturally tempted to linger in the hall after supper, to gather round the fire, if there was one, in the middle of the room, beneath the louvre, to tell tales there and sing carols, to read poems, chronicles of the realm or wonders of the world. But it was only on the eve of a festival that William of Wykeham would allow this relaxation in his foundation. The members of Trinity College were allowed to play cards in hall on holidays only, "but on no account for money." Mummers, the chief source of amusement among the mediævals, were only permitted to enter New College once a year, on Twelfth Night. It was not till the dawn of the Renaissance that plays began to be acted in the colleges and halls, and to bring the academic intellect into touch with the views and literature of the people.

Not only was it forbidden to play marbles on the college steps, but even the hard exercise of chess was prohibited as a "noxious, inordinate and unhonest game." And the keeping of dogs and hawks was anathema.

By a survival of this mediæval view, the undergraduate is still solemnly warned by the statute book against playing any game which may cause injury to others; he is urged to refrain from hunting wild beasts with ferrets, nets or hounds, from hawking, "necnon ab omni apparatu et gestatione bombardarum et arcubalistarum." In the same way he is forbidden still to carry arms of any sort by day or night, unless it be bows and arrows for purposes of honest amusement. But to these injunctions, I fear, as to the accompanying threat of punishment at the discretion of the Vice-Chancellor, he does not pay over much attention. He does not consider them very seriously when he plays football or hunts with the "Bicester," takes a day's shooting or runs with the Christ Church beagles.

The restrictions which I have quoted above were mostly introduced by the founders of colleges. So far as the University was concerned, the private life of the student was hardly interfered with at all.

The offence of night-walking, indeed, was repressed by the proctor who patrolled the streets with a pole-axe and bulldogs (armed attendants), but the student might frequent the taverns and drink as he pleased. His liberty was almost completely unrestricted, except as to the wearing of academic dress, the attendance of lectures and the observance of the curfew bell. Offences against morality and order were treated as a rule, when they were dealt with at all, with amazing leniency. Murder was regarded as a very venial crime; drunkenness and loose-living as hardly matters for University police. A student who committed murder was usually banished, and banishment after all meant to him little more than changing his seat of learning. The punishment, though it might cause inconvenience, did not amount to more than being compelled to go to Cambridge. Fines, excommunication and imprisonment were the other punishments inflicted for offences; corporal punishment was but seldom imposed by the University. But with the growth of the college system the bonds of discipline were tightened. Not only did the statutes provide in the greatest detail for the punishment of undergraduate offences, stating the amount of the fine to be exacted for throwing a missile at a master and missing, and the larger amount for aiming true, but also the endowment of the scholar made it easy to collect the fine. The wardens and fellows, too, were in a stronger position than the principal of a hall, who owed his place to his popularity with the students, who, if he ceased to please them, might leave his hall and remove to another house where the principal was more lenient and could be relied upon to wink at their follies and their vices, even if he did not share them. Thus the founders of the early colleges were enabled to enforce upon the recipients of their bounty something of the rigour and decency of monastic discipline. As the system grew the authority entrusted to the heads of colleges was increased, and the position of the undergraduate was reduced to that of the earlier grammar-school boy. The statutes of B.N.C. (1509) rendered the undergraduate liable to be birched at the discretion of the college lecturer. He might now be flogged if he had not prepared his lessons; if he played, laughed or talked in lecture; if he made odious comparisons, or spoke English; if he were unpunctual, disobedient or did not attend chapel. Wolsey allowed the students of Cardinal College to be flogged up to the age of twenty.

Impositions by a dean were apparently a sixteenth-century invention. Then we find offending fellows who had played inordinately at hazard or cards, or earned a reputation for being notorious fighters or great frequenters of taverns, being ordered to read in their college libraries for a fortnight from 6 to 7 A.M. And the loss of a month's commons occasionally rewarded the insolence of undergraduates who did not duly cap and give way to their seniors, or who, yielding to that desire to adorn their persons which the mediæval student shared with his gaudy-waistcoated successors, wore "long undecent[28] hair," and cloth of no clerical hue, slashed doublets and boots and spurs beneath their gowns.

As to the academic career of the mediæval student; the course of his studies and "disputations" in the schools; the steps by which the "general sophister" became a "determining bachelor" and the bachelor, if he wished to teach, took a master's degree, first obtaining the Chancellor's licence to lecture, and then, on the occasion of his "inception," when he "commenced master" and first undertook his duty of teaching in the schools, being received into the fraternity of teaching masters by the presiding master of his faculty—of these ceremonies and their significance and the traces of them which survive in modern academic life, as of the high feastings and banquetings with which, as in the trade guilds, the new apprentices and masters entertained their faculties, I have no space here to treat.

The inceptor besides undertaking not to lecture at Stamford, recognise any University but Oxford and Cambridge, or maintain Lollard opinions, was also required to swear to wear a habit suitable to his degree. As an undergraduate he had had no academical dress, except that, as every member of the University was supposed to be a clerk, he was expected to wear the tonsure and clerical habit. The characteristic of this was that the outer garment must be of a certain length and closed in front. It was the cut and not the colour of the "cloth" which was at first considered important. But later regulations restricted the colour to black, and insisted that this garment must reach to the knees. In the colleges, however, it was only parti-coloured garments that were regarded as secular, and the "liveries" mentioned by the founders were usually clothes of the clerical cut but of uniform colour. The fellows of Queen's, for instance, were required to wear blood-red. The colour of the liveries was not usually prescribed by statute, but differences of colour and ornament still survive at Cambridge as badges of different colleges.

The masters at first wore the cappa, which was the ordinary out-door full-dress of the secular clergy. And this "cope," with a border and hood of minever, came to be the official academical costume. The shape of the masters' cappa soon became stereotyped and distinctive; then a cappa with sleeves was adopted as the uniform of bachelors. As to the hood, it was the material of which it was made—minever—which distinguished the master, not the hood itself; for a hood was part of the ordinary clerical attire. Bachelors of all faculties wore hoods of lamb's-wool or rabbit's-fur, but undergraduates were deprived of the right of wearing a hood in 1489—nisi liripipium consuetum ... et non contextum—the little black stuff hood, worn by sophisters in the schools till within living memory.

The cappa went out of use amongst the Oxford M.A.'s during the sixteenth century. The regents granted themselves wholesale dispensations from its use. Stripped of this formal, outer robe, the toga was revealed, the unofficial cassock or under-garment, which now gradually usurped the place of the cappa and became the distinctively academical dress of the Masters of Arts. But it was not at first the dull prosaic robe that we know. The mediæval master was clad in bright colours, red or green or blue, and rejoiced in them until the rising flood of prejudice in favour of all that is dull and sombre and austere washed away these together with almost all other touches of colour from the landscape of our grey island.

The distinctive badge of mastership handed to the inceptor by the father of his faculty, was the biretta, a square cap with a tuft on the top, from which is descended our cap with its tassel. Doctors of the superior faculties differentiated themselves by wearing a biretta (square cap) or pilea (round) as well as cappas, of bright hues, red, purple or violet. Gascoigne, indeed, in his theological dictionary, declares that this head-dress was bestowed by God himself on the Doctors of the Mosaic Law. Whatever its origin, the round velvet cap with coloured silk ribbon, came to be, and still is, the peculiar property of the Doctors of Law and Medicine.

The Oxford gowns of the present day have little resemblance to their mediæval prototypes. For the ordinary undergraduate or "commoner" to-day, academical dress, which must be worn at lectures, in chapel, in the streets at night, and on all official occasions, consists of his cap, a tattered "mortar-board," and a gown which seems a very poor relation of the original clerical garb. The sleeves have gone, and the length; only two bands survive, and a little gathering on the shoulders, and this apology for a gown is worn as often as not round the throat as a scarf, or carried under the arm.

Some years ago it was a point of honour with every undergraduate to wear a cap which was as battered and disreputable as possible. Every freshman seized the first opportunity to break the corners of his "mortar-board" and to cut and unravel the tassel. Yet once the tufted biretta, when it was the badge of mastership, was much coveted by undergraduates. First, they obtained the right of wearing a square cap without a tassel, like those still worn by the choristers of Oxford colleges, and then they were granted the use of a tassel. The tuft in the case of the gentlemen commoners took the form of a golden tassel. Snobs who cultivated the society of these gilded youths for the sake of their titles or their cash, or tutors,

"Rough to common men,
But honeying at the whisper of a Lord,"

gained from this fact the nick-name of tuft-hunters.

The commoner, it should be explained, is one who pays for his commons, a student not on the foundation. The colleges were, in most cases, intended originally only for the fellows and scholars on the foundation. The admission of other students as commoners or boarders was a subsequent development, and various ranks of students came to be recognised—noblemen, gentlemen commoners, commoners, fellow-commoners, batterlers, or servitors. These grades are now practically obsolete, the only distinction drawn among the undergraduates being between the scholars or students on the foundation and commoners, the ordinary undergraduates, who do not enjoy any scholarship or exhibition.

The scholar, who must wear a larger gown with wide sleeves, is known by various names at various colleges. At Merton he is a post-master, at Magdalen a demy, so-called because he was entitled to half the commons of a fellow.

The history of the commoner, the growth of an accretion that now forms the greater part of a college, may be illustrated by the records of the latter foundation.

The statutes of New College had not made any provision for the admission of *commensales*, but William of Waynflete, in drawing up the statutes of Magdalen, was the first definitely to recognise the system that had grown up by which men who were not on the foundation lived as members of the college. Waynflete limited the number of non-foundationers to twenty. They were to live at the charges of their own kindred; they were to be vouched for by "creancers"; and the privilege of admission was to be reserved for the sons of noble and powerful friends of the college.

But within a hundred years the number of the commoners or batterlers increased far beyond that allowed by the statutes. The position of these commoners was anomalous and led to "disorder and confusion," as certain fellows did most bitterly complain to the Visitor. No provision, it appears, was made either for the instruction or the discipline of these supernumeraries. They were, in fact, regarded as the private pupils of the President or of one of the fellows. In attendance upon the wealthier of them or upon other members of the college came numerous "poore scholars," acting as their servants and profiting in their turn from such free teaching as the Grammar School and the college lecturers might afford.

The system, however, was already justified to some extent by the fact that among the pupils of the President were numbered Bodley, Camden, Lyly and Florio. The Visitor, therefore, contented himself with enforcing the observation of the limits imposed by the statutes. The poor scholars were in future not to be more than thirteen in number, and were to be attached to the thirteen senior fellows. Before long, however, the matriculations of non-foundationers began to increase very rapidly. A new block of buildings even was erected near the Cherwell for their accommodation by 1636. This is that picturesque group of gables which nestles under the great tower and forms so distinct a feature of the view from Magdalen Bridge. The number of "poore scholars" had also increased—servitors whose office forestalled that of the college "scout." They bridged the days when the junior members of a foundation "did" for themselves and the modern days of an organised college service. It was decided, and this is where the scout has the advantage of his forerunners, that they should be required to attend the Grammar School, and afterwards to perform all disputations and exercises required of members of the foundation. All commoners, also, "the sonnes of Noblemen and such as are of great quality only excepted" were to be "tyed to the same rules."

Little more than a hundred years later Edward Gibbon matriculated at Magdalen (1752) as a "gentleman commoner," and as a youth of fifteen commenced those fourteen months which he has told us were the most idle and unprofitable of his whole life. There are prigs of all ages. Gibbon must have been intolerable in a common room. One can forgive the "Monks of Magdalen" for not discussing the Early Fathers with him after dinner, but one has no inclination on the other hand to revere the men who had already (1733), in their enthusiasm for the Italian style, begun the "New Buildings," and were still threatening to pull down the cloisters and to complete a large quadrangle in the same style, of which the New Buildings were to form one end. The damage done by the succeeding generation was directed chiefly against the chapel and the hall, where under the guidance of the outrageous James Wyatt, plaster ceilings were substituted for the old woodwork. The generosity of a late fellow has enabled Mr Bodley, with the aid of Professor Case, to repair this error by an extraordinarily interesting and successful restoration (1903). Magdalen Hall is now worthy of its pictures, its "linen-fold" panelling and splendid screen. Bitter as is the account which Gibbon has left us, it cannot be denied that there was much reason in his quarrel with the Oxford of his day. I say Oxford, for the state of Magdalen was better rather than worse than that of the University at large. It should, however, in fairness be pointed out that as a gentleman commoner in those days he was one of a class which was very small and far from anxious to avail itself of the intellectual advantages of a University training. The commoners at Magdalen were now very few in number. The founder's limitation was now so interpreted as to restrict them to the particular class of gentlemen commoners, sons of wealthy men, at liberty to study, but expected to prefer, and as a matter of fact usually preferring, to enjoy themselves.

But the efforts of the more liberal-minded fellows were at length crowned with success. By the first University Commission the college was allowed to admit as many non-foundationers as it could provide with rooms. The last gentleman commoner had ceased to figure in the *Calendar* by 1860. The system of licensed lodgings introduced by the University soon caused the numbers of the ordinary commoners to increase, so that in 1875 one-third of the resident undergraduates were living in lodgings outside the college. It was clearly time for the college to provide accommodation for as many of these as possible within its own walls. The change which took place in Magdalen during the last century, a change "from a small society, made up almost wholly of foundation-members and to a great extent of graduates, to a society of considerable numbers, made up of the same elements, in about the same proportion as most of the other Colleges," is recorded therefore in the architecture of Oxford. For it was to lodge the commoners that the buildings which are known as S. Swithun's (so-called from the statue in a niche on the west side of the tower which is placed at the entrance of these buildings, and which reminds one that S. Swithun was buried in Winchester Cathedral close to the beautiful shrine of William of Waynflete) were designed by Messrs Bodley & Garner and completed in 1884. They face the High Street, and you will pass them on your left as you come down to the new entrance gateway, which is in the line of the outer wall, parallel to the High. The old gateway, which was designed by Inigo Jones, stood almost at right angles to the site of the present gateway and lodge, looking west. It was removed in 1844, and a new one designed by A. W. Pugin erected in its stead. The present gateway (1885) follows the lines of the old design of Pugin, and the niches are filled with statues of S. John the Baptist, S. Mary Magdalen and of the founder, William of Waynflete. S. John the Baptist was the patron Saint of the old hospital, and after S. John the quadrangle into which you now enter is called. Opposite to you are the President's lodgings, built by Messrs Bodley & Garner in 1887 on the site of the old President's lodgings. With the exquisite architecture of the chapel and cloisters on the right to guide them, these famous architects have not failed to build here something that harmonises in style and treatment with the rest. One might wish that S. Swithun's were a little quieter. There is a slight yielding to the clamorous desire for fussy ornamentation which is so typical of this noisy age. But the President's lodgings are perfect in their kind. As you stand, then, in S. John's Quadrangle you have, in the chapel and founder's tower, and the cloisters on your right, and in the picturesque old fragment of the Grammar School, known as the Grammar Hall, facing you on your left, an epitome, as it were, of the old college foundations of Oxford; and in those buildings of S. Swithun and the gateway, which faces in a new direction, an epitome of the new Oxford that has been grafted on the old. On the extreme right you see a curious open-air pulpit of stone, from which the University sermon used to be preached on S. John the Baptist's Day. On that occasion the pulpit, as well as the surrounding buildings, was strewn with rushes and boughs in token of S. John's preaching in the wilderness.

In the Middle Ages the chief executive officers of the University were the Proctors, who are first mentioned in 1248. The origin of their office is obscure. They were responsible for the collection and expenditure of the common funds of the University, and as a record of this function they still retain in their robes a purse, a rudimentary organ, as it were, atrophied by disuse, but traceable in a triangular bunch of stuff at the back of the shoulder. Apart from this duty and that of regulating the system of lectures and disputations, their chief business was to keep order. One can imagine that a Proctor's life was not a happy one. He had to endeavour not only to keep the peace between the students and the townsmen, but also between the numerous factions among the scholars themselves. The Friars and the secular clergy, the Artists and the Jurists, the Nominalists and the Realists, and, above all, the Northerners and Southerners were always ready to quarrel, and quarrels quickly led to blows, and blows to a general riot. For the rivalry of the nations was a peculiar feature of mediæval Universities. At Bologna and Paris the Masters of Arts divided themselves into "Four Nations," with elective officers at their head. At Oxford the main division was between Northerners and Southerners, between students, that is, who came from the north or the south of the Trent. Welshmen and Irishmen were included among the Southerners. And over the northern and southern Masters of Arts presided northern and southern Proctors respectively, chosen by a process of indirect election, like the rectors of Bologna and Paris. Contests and continual riots arising out of the rivalry of these factions took the place of modern football matches or struggles on the river.

In 1273, for instance, we read of an encounter between the Northerners and the Irish, which resulted in the death of several Irishmen. So alarming, apparently, was this outbreak that many of the leading members of the University departed in fear, and only returned at the stern command of the King. The bishops, too, issued a notice, in which they earnestly exhorted the clerks in their dioceses to "repair to the schools, not armed for the fight, but rather prepared for study." But the episcopal exhortation had about as much effect as a meeting of the Peace League in Exeter Hall would have now. Quarrel after quarrel broke out between the rival nations. They plundered each others' goods and broke each others' heads with a zest worthy of an Irish wake.

In spite of their reputation for riotousness, however, the Irish students were specially exempted by royal writ from the operation of the statute passed by Parliament in 1413, which ordered that all Irishmen and Irish clerks, beggars called Chamberdekens, should quit the realm. Graduates in the schools had been exempted in the statute. This exemption does not appear to have conduced to the state of law and order painfully toiled after by the mere Saxon. For a few years later, in the first Parliament of Henry VI., the Commons sent up a petition complaining of the numerous outrages committed near Oxford by "Wylde Irishmen." These turbulent persons, it was alleged, living under the jurisdiction of the Chancellor, set the King's officers at defiance, and used such threatening language, that the bailiffs of the town did not dare to stir out of their houses for fear of death. The Commons therefore prayed that all Irishmen, except graduates in the schools, beneficed clergy, professed monks, landowners, merchants and members of civic corporations, should be compelled to quit the realm. It was also demanded that graduates of Irish extraction should be required to find security for their good behaviour, and that they should not be allowed to act as principals of halls. This petition received the royal assent. But it was stipulated that Irish clerks might freely resort to Oxford and Cambridge, if they could show that they were subjects of the English king.

It was in vain that students were compelled to swear that they would not carry arms; in vain were seditious gatherings and leagues for the espousal of private quarrels forbidden.

In vain, after one great outbreak in 1252, were formal articles of peace drawn up; in vain were the combatants bound over to keep the peace, and to give secret information to the Chancellor if they heard of others who were preparing to break it. In vain was the celebration of the national festivals forbidden, and the masters and scholars prohibited, under pain of the greater excommunication, from "going about dancing in the churches or open places, wearing masks or wreathed and garlanded with flowers" (1250). In vain was it decreed that the two nations should become one and cease, officially, to have a separate existence (1274). Though the Faculty of Arts might vote from this time forward as a single body, yet one Proctor was always a Borealis and the other an Australis; and when, in 1320, it was decreed that one of the three guardians of the Rothbury Chest should always be a Southerner and another a Northerner, the University admitted the existence of the two rival nations within its borders once more. Only a few years after this, in fact (1334), its very existence was threatened by the violence of the factions. The Northerners gave battle to the Southerners, and so many rioters were arrested that the Castle was filled to overflowing. Many of the more studious clerks resolved to quit this riotous University for ever, and betook themselves to Stamford, where there were already some flourishing schools.

They were compelled at last to disperse or to return by the King, who refused to listen to their plea, that their right to study in peace at Stamford was as good as that of any other person whatever who chose to live there. So serious was this secession, and so much was the rivalry of Stamford feared, that all candidates for a degree were henceforth (till 1827) required to swear that they would not give or attend lectures there "as in a University."

It was on the occasion of this migration that the members of Brasenose Hall, which adjoined S. Mary's Entry, Salesbury Hall, Little University Hall and Jussel's Tenement, carried with them, as a symbol of their continuity, the famous Brazen Nose Knocker to Stamford. There the little society settled; an archway of the hall they occupied there still exists, and now belongs to Brasenose College. The knocker itself was brought back in 1890 to a place of honour in the college hall. For in the meantime the old hall, after a career of over two hundred years, had been converted into a college, founded by William Smyth, Bishop of Lincoln, and Master Sotton, very much as a protest against the new learning which was then being encouraged at Corpus Christi. The continuity of the society is indicated by the fact that the first Principal of the college was the last Principal of the old "Aula Regia de Brasinnose." The foundation stone was laid in 1509, as the inscription in the old quadrangle, to which a story was added in the time of James I., records.

They were a turbulent crew, these Oxonian forbears of ours. Dearly they loved a fight, and they rose in rebellion against the masters when they were bringing in new statutes for the preservation of the peace. Several were slain on both sides. Nor was it easy to punish the unruly students.

Sometimes, after a brawl in which they were clearly in the wrong, the delinquents would flee to Shotover, and there maintain themselves in the forest. At other times, when they had gone too far, and the thunder of the Chancellor's sentence of excommunication had fallen on their heads as a punishment for attempting to sack the Abbey of Abingdon, or defiling the Church of S. Mary with bloodshed, for sleeping in a tavern, or fighting with the King's foresters, they would simply leave the University altogether and get away scathless. For the Chancellor's jurisdiction did not extend beyond Oxford.

A joust or tourney was a certain cause of riot. The passions are easily roused after any athletic contest, whether it be a football match or a bull-fight. Remembering this, we shall best be able to understand why the King found it necessary to forbid any joust or tournament to be held in the vicinity of Oxford or Cambridge (1305).

"Yea, such was the clashing of swords," says Fuller, "the rattling of arms, the sounding of trumpets, the neighing of horses, the shouting of men all day time with the roaring of riotous revellers all the night, that the scholars' studies were disturbed, safety endangered, lodging straitened, charges enlarged. In a word, so many war-horses were brought thither that Pegasus was himself likely to be shut out; for where Mars keeps his terms, there the Muses may even make their vacation."

Any excuse, indeed, was good enough to set the whole town in an uproar. A bailiff would hustle a student; a tradesman would "forestall" and retail provisions at a higher price than the regulations allowed; a rowdy student would compel a common bedesman to pray for the souls of certain unpopular living townsmen on the score that they would soon be dead. The bailiffs would arrest a clerk and refuse to give him up at the request of the Chancellor; the Chancellor, when appealed to by the townsmen to punish some offending students, would unsoothingly retort: "Chastise your laymen and we will chastise our clerks." The records of town and University are full of the riots which arose from such ebullitions of the ever-present ill-feeling; of the appeals made by either party; and of the awards given by the King, who might be some English Justinian, like Edward I., or might not.

The answer of the townsmen (1298) to the Chancellor's retort quoted above was distinctly vigorous. They seized and imprisoned all scholars on whom they could lay hands, invaded their inns, made havoc of their goods and trampled their books under foot. In the face of such provocation the Proctors sent their bedels about the town, forbidding the students to leave their inns. But all commands and exhortations were in vain. By nine o'clock next morning, bands of scholars were parading the streets in martial array. If the Proctors failed to restrain them, the mayor was equally powerless to restrain his townsmen. The great bell of S. Martin's rang out an alarm; ox-horns were sounded in the streets; messengers were sent into the country to collect rustic allies. The clerks, who numbered three thousand in all, began their attack simultaneously in various quarters. They broke open warehouses in the Spicery, the Cutlery and elsewhere. Armed with bows and arrows, swords and bucklers, slings and stones, they fell upon their opponents. Three they slew, and wounded fifty or more. One band, led by Fulk de Neyrmit, Rector of Piglesthorne, and his brother, took up a position in High Street between the Churches of S. Mary and All Saints, and attacked the house of a certain Edward Hales. This Hales was a long-standing enemy of the clerks. There were no half measures with him. He seized his crossbow, and from an upper chamber sent an unerring shaft into the eye of the pugnacious rector. The death of their valiant leader caused the clerks to lose heart. They fled, closely pursued by the townsmen and country-folk. Some were struck down in the streets, and others who had taken refuge in the churches were dragged out and driven mercilessly to prison, lashed with thongs and goaded with iron spikes.

Complaints of murder, violence and robbery were lodged straightway with the King by both parties. The townsmen claimed three thousand pounds' damage. The commissioners, however, appointed to decide the matter, condemned them to pay two hundred marks, removed the bailiffs, and banished twelve of the most turbulent citizens from Oxford. Then the terms of peace were formally ratified.

Following the example of their Chancellor, who was gradually asserting his authority more and more in secular matters, and thought little of excommunicating a mayor for removing a pillory without his leave (1325), the clerks became continually more aggressive. Quarrels with the townsmen were succeeded by quarrels with the Bishop of Lincoln, when the latter, in his turn, tried to encroach upon the jurisdiction of the Chancellor. Peace, perfect peace, it will be seen, had not yet descended upon the University. The triumph of Dulness had not arrived, when the enraptured monarch should behold:

"Isis' elders reel, their pupils sport,
And Alma Mater lie dissolved in port."

Certainly the elders gave their pupils sport enough after their kind, but the intellectual quarrels of the schoolmen, the furious controversies of the Dominicans and the Franciscans, the Scotists and the Thomists, the Nominalists and the Realists, were a part of it. When the excitement of local riots, theological disputes and political dissension failed, there were the exactions of a Papal representative to be resisted. And when such resistance led to the citation of the Chancellor and Proctors and certain masters to appear within sixty days before the Cardinal appointed by the Pope to hear the case at Avignon, there was the whole principle that no Englishman should be dragged across the seas to judgment to be fought for (*circa* 1330). For every man was a politician in those days, and the scholars of Oxford not least. Their quarrels and riotings were therefore not without political significance. Thus when the Mad Parliament met in the "new house of the Black Friars at Oxford," the behaviour of the barons was reflected by that of students. The "nations" pitched their field in "Beaumont," and after a fierce fight in battle array, divers on both sides were slain and pitifully wounded. The Northerners and Welshmen were at last acknowledged to be conquerors.

The position of the students with regard to the country, is indicated by the old rhyme:

"Mark the Chronicles aright
When Oxford scholars fall to fight
Before many months expired
England will with war be fired."

It was Oxford, the centre of English ecclesiasticism, which, by the riot that hounded the Papal Legate out of the city, gave the signal for a widespread outbreak of resistance to the wholesale pillage of excessive Papal taxation.

Regardless of the gathering storm, the Legate Cardinal Otho had arrived at Oxford with his retinue of Italians, and taken up his abode at Osney.

Some members of the University, having sent him some delicacies for his table, went to pay their respects in person, and to ask of him a favour in return. The doorkeeper, however, a suspicious Italian, absolutely refused to admit them to the guests' hall. Irritated by this unexpected rebuff, they collected a great number of their comrades, and made a determined attack on the foreigners, who defended themselves with sticks, swords and flaming brands plucked from the fire. The fury of the clerks reached its height when the Legate's chief cook took up a cauldron full of boiling broth, and threw its contents in the face of a poor Irish chaplain, who had been begging for food at the kitchen door. A student thereupon drew his bow, and shot the cook dead on the spot, whilst others tried to set fire to the massive gates which had been closed against them. The terrified Legate, hastily putting on a canonical cope, fled for refuge to the belfry of the abbey, and there lay hid for several hours, while the clerks assailed the building with bows and catapults.

News of the fray soon reached Henry III., who happened to be staying at Abingdon, and he lost no time in despatching some soldiers to the rescue. Under their powerful escort the Legate managed to ford the river by night, accompanied by the members of his suite. Still as he galloped away, he seemed to hear the shouts of his adversaries ringing in his ears, "Where is that usurer, that simoniac, that spoiler of revenues, and thirster after money, who perverts the King, overthrows the realm, and enriches strangers with plunder taken from us?"

It was not long before the Papal Legate was forbidden the English shores, and his bulls of excommunication were flung into the sea.

Simon de Montfort was the friend of Adam Marsh, and the confidant of Grossetete, and it was appropriately enough at Oxford that the great champion of English freedom secured the appointment of a council of twenty-four to draw up terms for the reform of the State. Parliament met at Oxford; the barons presented a long petition of grievances, the council was elected, and a body of preliminary articles known as the Provisions of Oxford was agreed upon. In the following year Henry repudiated the Provisions; civil war ensued, and ended by placing the country in the hands of Simon de Montfort.

The struggle between Henry and the barons then did not leave Oxford unaffected. For any disturbance without was sure to be reflected in a conflict between clerks and laymen, in a town and gown row, of some magnitude. In the present case the appearance of Prince Edward with an armed force—he took up his quarters at the King's Hall—in the northern suburb gave occasion for an outbreak. The municipal authorities closed the gates against him, and he resumed his march towards Wales.

The scholars now thought it was time that they should be allowed to go out of the city, and finding themselves prevented by the closed wooden doors of Smith Gate, they hewed these down and carried them away, like Samson, into the fields, chanting over them the office of the dead:

"A Subvenite Sancti fast began to sing
As man doth when a dead man men will to pit bring."

The mayor retorted by throwing some of them into prison, in spite of the Chancellor's protest. Further arrests were about to be made by the irate townsmen, but a clerk saw them advancing in a body down the High Street, and gave the alarm by ringing the bell of S. Mary's. The clerks were at dinner, but hearing the well-known summons they sprang to arms and rushed out into the street to give battle. Many of the foe were wounded; the rest were put to flight. Their banners were torn to pieces, and several shops were sacked by the victorious students, who, flushed with victory, marched to the houses of the bailiffs and set them on fire.

"In the South half of the town, and afterwards the Spicery
They brake from end to other, and did all to robberie."

The mayor, they then remembered, was a vintner. Accordingly a rush was made for the vintnery; all the taps were drawn, and the wine flowed out like water into the streets.

Their success for a moment was complete, but retribution awaited them. The King was appealed to, and refused to countenance so uproarious a vindication of their rights. When they saw how the wind blew, they determined to leave Oxford. It was a question whither they should go and where pitch their scholastic tents. Now it happened that at Cambridge, a town which had ceased to be famous only for eels and could boast a flourishing University of its own, similar disturbances had recently occurred with similar results. Many masters and scholars had removed to Northampton, and to Northampton accordingly, to aid them in their avowed intention of founding a third University, the disconsolate Oxford scholars departed. The situation was evidently serious. But the King induced the Oxonians to return by promising that they should not be molested if they would only keep the peace.

They returned, but almost immediately all scholars were commanded by a writ from the King to quit the town and stay at home until he should recall them after the session of Parliament then about to be held at Oxford. The King, it was officially explained, could not be responsible for the conduct of the fierce and untamed lords who would be assembled together there and would be sure to come into conflict with the students. Perhaps the more urgent motive was fear lest the students should openly and actively side with the barons, with whom, it was known, the majority of them were in sympathy.

The fact was that in the great struggle against the Crown in which England was now involved, the clergy and the Universities ranged themselves with the towns on the side of Simon de Montfort. Ejected from Oxford, many of the students openly joined his cause and repaired at once to Northampton.

For a time all went well with the King. As if to demonstrate his faith in the justice of his cause, he braved popular superstition and passing within the walls of Oxford paid his devotions at the shrine of S. Frideswide. The meeting of Parliament failed to bring about any reconciliation. Reinforced by a detachment of Scottish allies—"untamed and fierce" enough, no doubt—Henry left Oxford and marched on Northampton. Foremost in its defence was a band of Oxford students, who so enraged the King by the effective use they made of their bows and slings and catapults, that he swore to hang them all when he had taken the town. Take the town he did, and he would have kept his oath had he not been deterred by the reminder that he would by such an act lose the support of all those nobles and followers whose sons and kinsmen were students. But the victorious career of the King was almost at an end. The vengeance of S. Frideswide was wrought at the battle of Lewes. Simon de Montfort found himself head of the State, and one of his first acts was to order the scholars to return to their University.

Such keen, occasionally violent, interest in politics seems, in these days, characteristic of the German or Russian rather than the English University student. Nowadays the political enthusiasm of the undergraduate is mild, and his discussion of politics is academic. In the debating hall of the Union, or in the more retired meeting-places of the smaller political clubs, like the Canning, the Chatham, the Palmerston or the Russell, he discusses the questions of the day. But his discussions lack as a rule the sense of reality, and they suffer accordingly.

Occasionally, when a Cabinet Minister has been persuaded to dine and talk with one or other of these clubs, or when the speaker is one who is deliberately practising for the part he means to take in after-life, the debates are neither uninteresting nor entirely valueless. And at the worst they give those who take part in them a facility of speech and some knowledge of political questions. But it is not so that the University exercises any influence on current events. Nor, except in so far as they warn practical men to vote the other way, are those occasional manifestoes, which a few professors sign and publish, of any great importance. But it is through the press and through Parliament that the voice of young Oxford is heard. It is through the minds and the examples of those statesmen and administrators, who have imbibed their principles of life and action within her precincts, and have been trained in her schools and on her river or playing-fields, that the influence of the University is reflected on the outer world. Nor is it only the men like Lord Salisbury, Lord Rosebery and Mr Gladstone, who guide the country at home, or like Lord Milner and Lord Curzon, who give their best work to Greater Britain, that are the true sons of the University; it is the plain, hard-working clergymen and civilians, also, who, by their lives of honest and unselfish toil, hand on the torch of good conduct and high ideals which has been entrusted to them.

Oxford had some share in the events which led to the deposition of Edward II. The King wrote to the Chancellor, masters and scholars calling upon them to resist his enemies. On the approach of Roger de Mortimer, a supporter of the Queen, he wrote again enjoining them not to allow him to enter the city, but to keep Smith Gate shut, lest he should enter by that way. But when the King was a refugee in Wales, the Queen came to Islip. She would not come to Oxford till "she saw it secure." But when the burghers came to her with presents she was satisfied. She took up her residence at the White Friars, and the Mortimers theirs at Osney. And a sermon was preached by the Bishop of Hereford, who demonstrated from his text, "My head grieveth me," that an evil head, meaning the King, not otherwise to be cured, must be taken away. The majority of scholars apparently agreed with him.

The terrible scourge of the Black Death, which carried off half the population of England, fell hardly on Oxford. Those who had places in the country fled to them; those who remained behind were almost totally swept away. The schools were shut, the colleges and halls closed, and there were scarcely men enough to bury the dead. The effect upon learning was disastrous. There were not enough students forthcoming to fill the benefices, and the scarcity of students affected the citizens severely.

The disorder of the time, which was to issue in Wat Tyler's Rebellion, was shadowed forth at Oxford by the extraordinary riot of S. Scholastica's Day (1355). The story of this riot, which was to bear fruit in further privileges being vouchsafed to the University at the expense of the town, has been recorded with infinite spirit by Wood.

"On Tuesday, February 10, being the feast of S. Scholastica the Virgin, came Walter de Springheuse, Roger de Chesterfield, and other clerks to the Tavern called Swyndlestock (the Mermaid Tavern at Quatervoix), and there calling for wine, John de Croydon, the vintner, brought them some, but they disliking it, as it should seem, and he avouching it to be good, several snappish words passed between them. At length the vintner giving them stubborn and saucy language, they threw the wine and vessel at his head. The vintner therefore receding with great passion, and aggravating the abuse to those of his family and neighbourhood, several came in, who out of propensed malice seeking all occasions of conflict with the scholars, and taking this abuse for a ground to proceed upon, caused the town bell at S. Martin's to be rung, that the commonalty might be summoned together in a body. Which being begun, they in an instant were in arms, some with bows and arrows, others with divers sorts of weapons. And then they, without any more ado, did in a furious and hostile manner suddenly set upon divers scholars, who at that time had not any offensive arms, no, not so much as anything to defend themselves. They shot also at the Chancellor of the University, and would have killed him, though he endeavoured to pacify them and appease the tumult. Further, also, though the scholars at the command of the Chancellor did presently withdraw themselves from the fray, yet the townsmen thereupon did more fiercely pursue him and the scholars, and would by no means desist from the conflict. The Chancellor, perceiving what great danger they were in, caused the University bell at S. Mary's to be rung out, whereupon the scholars got bows and arrows, and maintained the fight with the townsmen till dark night, at which time the fray ceased, no one scholar or townsman being killed, or mortally wounded, or maimed.

"On the next day albeit the Chancellor of the University caused public proclamation to be made in the morning both at S. Mary's church in the presence of the scholars there assembled in a great multitude, and also at Quatervois among the townsmen, that no scholar or townsman should wear or bear any offensive weapons, or assault any man, or otherwise disturb the peace (upon which the scholars, in humble obedience to that proclamation, repaired to the Schools, and demeaned themselves peaceably till after dinner) yet the very same morning the townsmen came with their bows and arrows, and drove away a certain Master in Divinity and his auditors, who were then determining in the Augustine Schools. The Baillives of the town also had given particular warning to every townsman, at his respective house, in the morning, that they should make themselves ready to fight with the scholars against the time when the town bell should ring out, and also given notice before to the country round about, and had hired people to come in and assist the townsmen in their intended conflict with the scholars. In dinner time the townsmen subtily and secretly sent about fourscore men armed with bows and arrows, and other manner of weapons into the parish of S. Giles in the north suburb; who, after a little expectation, having discovered certain scholars walking after dinner in Beaumont, issued out of S. Giles's church, shooting at the same scholars for the space of three furlongs: some of them they drove into the Augustine Priory, and others into the town. One scholar they killed without the walls, some they wounded mortally, others grievously, and used the rest basely. All which being done without any mercy, caused an horrible outcry in the town: whereupon the town bell being rung out first, and after that the University bell, divers scholars issued out armed with bows and arrows in their own defence and of their companions, and having first shut and blocked up some of the gates of the town (lest the country people, who were then gathered in innumerable multitudes, might suddenly break in upon their rear in an hostile manner and assist the townsmen who were now ready prepared in battle array, and armed with their targets also) they fought with them and defended themselves till after Vesper tide; a little after which time, entered into the town by the west gate about two thousand countrymen, with a black dismal flag, erect and displayed. Of which the scholars having notice, and being unable to resist so great and fierce a company, they withdrew themselves to their lodgings: but the townsmen finding no scholars in the streets to make any opposition, pursued them, and that day they broke open five inns or hostels of scholars with fire and sword. Such scholars as they found in the said halls or inns they killed or maimed, or grievously wounded. Their books and all their goods which they could find, they spoiled, plundered and carried away. All their victuals, wine and other drink they poured out; their bread, fish, &c. they trod under foot. After this the night came on and the conflict ceased for that day, and the same even public proclamation was made in Oxen, in the King's name, 'that no man should injure the scholars or their goods under pain of forfeiture.'

"The next day being Thursday (after the Chancellor and some principal persons of the University were set out towards Woodstock to the King, who had sent for them thither) no one scholar or scholar's servant so much as appearing out of their houses with any intention to harm the townsmen, or offer any injury to them (as they themselves confessed) yet the said townsmen about sun rising, having rung out their bell, assembled themselves together in a numberless multitude, desiring to heap mischief upon mischief, and to perfect by a more terrible conclusion that wicked enterprize which they had begun. This being done, they with hideous noises and clamours came and invaded the scholars' houses in a wretchless sort, which they forced open with iron bars and other engines; and entering into them, those that resisted and stood upon their defence (particularly some chaplains) they killed or else in a grievous sort maimed. Some innocent wretches, after they had killed, they scornfully cast into houses of easement, others they buried in dunghills, and some they let lie above ground. The crowns of some chaplains, viz. all the skin so far as the tonsure went, these diabolical imps flayed off in scorn of their clergy. Divers others whom they had mortally wounded, they haled to prison, carrying their entrails in their hands in a most lamentable manner. They plundered and carried away all the goods out of fourteen inns or halls, which they spoiled that Thursday. They broke open and dashed to pieces the scholars' chests and left not any moveable thing which might stand them in any stead; and which was yet more horrid, some poor innocents that were flying with all speed to the body of CHRIST for succour (then honourably carried in procession by the brethren through the town for the appeasing of this slaughter) and striving to embrace and come as near as they could to the repository wherein the glorious Body was with great devotion put, these confounded sons of Satan knocked them down, beat and most cruelly wounded. The Crosses also of certain brethren (the friers) which were erected on the ground for the present time with a 'procul hinc ite profani,' they overthrew and laid flat with the cheynell. This wickedness and outrage continuing the said day from the rising of the sun till noon tide and a little after without any ceasing, and thereupon all the scholars (besides those of the Colleges) being fled divers ways, our mother the University of Oxon, which had but two days before many sons, is now almost forsaken and left forlorn."

The casualty list was heavy. Six members of the University were killed outright in the fray; twenty-one others, chiefly Irishmen, were dangerously wounded, and a large number was missing. The Bishop of Lincoln immediately placed the town under an interdict. The King sent a commission to inquire into the cause of the riot. The sheriff was summarily dismissed from his office, two hundred of the townsmen were arrested, and the mayor and bailiffs committed to the Tower. With a view to settling the deep-rooted differences, which, it was perceived, were the origin of this bloody combat, the University and the city were advised to surrender their privileges into the King's hands. Edward III. restored those of the University in a few days. The town was kept some time in suspense, whilst the King and the Archbishop were striving to induce the scholars to return to Oxford. In the end all their ancient rights were restored to the citizens, with the exception of those which had been transferred to the University. For by the new charter the King granted to the latter some of the old liberties of the town.

This charter (27th June 1355) granted a free pardon to all masters and scholars and their servants who had taken part in the great riot. The University, the King declared, was the main source and channel of learning in all England, more precious to him than gold or topaz. To the Chancellor, then, or his deputy, was granted the assay of bread and ale, the supervision of weights and measures, the sole cognisance of forestallers, retailers and sellers of putrid meat and fish; the power of excommunicating any person who polluted or obstructed the streets, and of assessing the tax to be paid by scholars' servants. It was also decreed that the sheriff and under-sheriff of the county should henceforth swear, on taking office, to uphold the privileges of the University. In compensation for the damage done in the recent riot, the city had to restore the goods and books of all scholars wherever found, and to pay down £250 in cash. Such was the price, in money and rights, that the commonalty had to pay before they could satisfy the civil authorities. From that time forth the University practically governed the town. The wrath of the Church was not so soon appeased. It was not till 1357 that the interdict was removed, nor were the offences of the citizens against the Holy Church forgiven even then, except at the price of further humiliation. The mayor and bailiffs, and sixty of the chiefest burghers, such were the conditions, were to appear personally, and defray the expenses of a mass to be celebrated every year in S. Mary's on S. Scholastica's Day, when prayers should be said for the souls of the clerks and others slain in that conflict. The mayor and these sixty substantial burghers were also to offer on that occasion one penny each at the great altar. Forty pence out of this offering were to be given by the proctors to forty poor scholars, and the remainder to the curate.

So humiliating did this condition appear, that it gave rise to the popular saying and, perhaps, belief that the mayor was obliged, on the anniversary of the riot, to wear round his neck a halter or, at best, a silken cord. It may well be imagined that the procession, as it took its way to S. Mary's, did not escape the taunts and jeers of the jubilant clerks. Under Elizabeth, when prayer for the dead had been forbidden, this function was changed for a sermon, with the old offering of a penny. The service was retained in a modified form down to the time of Charles II.

The political and religious divisions introduced by the Lollard doctrines found their expression, of course, in students' riots. For the Northerners sided with Wycliffe, himself a Yorkshireman, and the Southerners, supported by the Welsh, professed themselves loyal children of the Church. A general encounter took place in 1388; several persons were killed, and many Northerners left Oxford. The Chancellor was deposed by Parliament for failing to do his duty in the matter. The strife was renewed at the beginning of Lent next year. A pitched battle was arranged to be fought between the contending parties in the open country. This was only prevented by the active interference of the Duke of Gloucester. Some turbulent Welshmen were expelled. But this banishment only gave rise to a fresh outbreak. For as the Welshmen knelt down to kiss the gates of the town, they were subjected to gross indignities by their exultant adversaries. And a party of Northerners, headed by a chaplain named Speeke, paraded the streets in military array, threatening to kill anyone who looked out of the window, and shouting, "War, war. Slay the Welsh dogs and their whelps." Halls were broken open, and the goods of Welsh scholars who lodged there were plundered. The Welshmen retaliated, and the University only obtained peace, when, on the outbreak of Owen Glendower's rebellion, the Welsh scholars returned to Wales.

The effect of the lawlessness of these mediæval students upon the history of the University was considerable. It is reflected in the statute book. It came to be recognised that their riotous behaviour was not only scandalous but also a veritable danger, which threatened the very existence of Oxford as a seat of learning. Politically, too, their behaviour was intolerable. Each outbreak, therefore, and each revelation of the licence of unattached students, who were credited with the chief share in these brawls, were arguments in favour of the college system inaugurated by the founder of Merton College.

As early as 1250 it had been found necessary to provide that every scholar should have his own master, on whose roll his name should be entered, and from whom he should hear at least one lecture daily. And in 1420 Henry V. issued some ordinances for academical reform, with the object of tightening the bonds of discipline. They were reduced to a statute of the University immediately. Fines were imposed for threats of personal violence, carrying weapons, pushing with the shoulder or striking with the fist, striking with a stone or club, striking with a knife, dagger, sword-axe or other warlike weapon, carrying bows and arrows, gathering armed men, and resisting the execution of justice, especially by night.

All scholars and scholars' servants, it was enacted, were, on first coming to Oxford, to take the oath for keeping the peace, which had hitherto been taken by graduates only; they were no longer to lodge in the houses of laymen, but must place themselves under the government of some discreet principal, approved by the Chancellor and regents. Chamberdekens were to lodge at a hall where some common table was kept. Thus the "unattached student," who has been recently revived, was legislated out of existence.

It is not, then, surprising to find that, whilst the thirteenth century saw the beginning of the college system, the fourteenth was the era which saw its great development. Already, sixteen years after the foundation of Oriel, a North Country priest, Robert Eglesfield, chaplain of Queen Philippa, had anticipated in conception the achievement of William of Wykeham by proposing to establish a college which should be a Merton on a larger scale. But the ideas of the founder of Queen's were greater than his resources. In the hope of assistance, therefore, and not in vain, he commended his foundation to the Queen and all future Queens-consort of England. He himself devoted his closing years and all his fortune to the infant society, for whose guidance he drew up statutes of an original character. His aim seems to have been to endow a number of students of Theology or Canon Law; to provide for the elementary education of many poor boys, and for the distribution of alms to the poor of the city. The ecclesiastical character of the college was marked by the endowment of several chaplains, and by precise directions for the celebration of masses, at which the "poor boys" were to assist as choristers, besides being trained in Grammar and afterwards in Logic or Philosophy. The bent of Eglesfield's mind is further indicated by the symbolism which pervades his ordinances. The fellowships, which were tenable for life and intended to be well endowed, were practically restricted to natives of the North Country. And as there had been twelve apostles, so it was ordained that there should be twelve fellows, who should sit in hall on one side of the High Table, with the provost in their centre, even as Christ and His apostles, according to tradition, sat at the Last Supper. And, as a symbol of the Saviour's blood, they were required to wear mantles of crimson cloth. The "poor boys," who were to sit at a side-table clad in a distinctive dress, from which they derived their name of tabarders, and who were to be "opposed" or examined by one of the fellows at the beginning of every meal, symbolised the Seventy Disciples.

Some traces of the symbolism which pleased the founder still survive at Queen's. The students are still summoned to hall, as the founder directs, by the blasts of a trumpet; still on Christmas Day the college celebrates the "Boar's Head" dinner (see p. 23); still on 1st January the bursar presents to each guest at the Gaudy a needle and thread (aiguille et fil = Eglesfield), saying, "Take this and be thrifty." And the magnificent wassail cup given to the college by the founder is still in use. But of the original buildings scarcely anything remains. The old entrance in Queen's Lane has been supplanted by the front quadrangle opening on the High (1710-1730), in which Hawksmoor, Wren's pupil, achieved a fine example of the Italian style. Wren himself designed the chapel. The magnificent library in the back quadrangle (late seventeenth century) is housed in a room, which, with its rich plaster ceiling and carving by Grinling Gibbons, is a remarkable specimen of the ornate classical style.

Eglesfield had attempted a task beyond his means. Forty years later William of Wykeham adopted his ideas, developed them and carried them out. It is the scale on which he founded S. Mary College, or New College, as it has been called for five hundred years to distinguish it from Oriel, the other S. Mary College, and the completeness of its arrangements that mark an era in the history of college foundations. Son of a carpenter at Wickham, William had picked up the rudiments of education at a grammar school and in a notary's office. Presently he entered the King's service. He was promoted to be Supervisor of the Works at Windsor; and made the most of his opportunity. *Hoc fecit Wykeham* were the words he inscribed, according to the legend, on the walls of the castle at Windsor; and it is equally true that he made it and that it made him, for so, to stop the mouths of his calumniators, he chose to translate the phrase. The King marked the admirable man of affairs; and rewarded him, according to custom, with innumerable benefices. Wykeham became the greatest pluralist of his age. He grew in favour at court, until soon "everything was done by him and nothing was done without him." He was "so wise of building castles," as Wycliffe sarcastically hinted, that he was appointed Bishop of Winchester and Chancellor of England. Yet in the midst of the cares of these offices he found time (1370) to set about establishing his college. His great genius as an architect, and his astonishing powers of administration under two kings, point him out as one of the greatest Englishmen of the Middle Ages. He has left his mark on his country, not only in such architectural achievements as Windsor and Queenborough Castles, the reconstruction of the nave of Winchester Cathedral (where is his altar tomb) or the original plan of his Collegiate Buildings, but also as the founder of the public school system and the new type of college.

It was as a lawyer-ecclesiastic that he had succeeded. But it was against the administration of ecclesiastical statesmen that the discontent of the time was being directed by the Wycliffites and John of Gaunt. Himself a staunch supporter of the old régime in Church and State, Wykeham set himself to remedy its defects and to provide for its maintenance as well as for his own soul's health after death.

Oxford had reached the height of its prosperity in the fourteenth century. Then the Black Death, the decadence of the Friars, the French Wars, the withdrawal of foreign students and the severance of the ties between English and foreign Universities, commenced a decay which was accelerated by the decline of the ecclesiastical monopoly of learning, by the Wycliffite movement and, later, by the Wars of the Roses.

Wykeham marked some of these causes and their effect. He believed in himself, and therefore in the Canon Law and lawyer-ecclesiastics; he noted the falling off in the number of the students, and therefore of the clergy, caused by the Black Death; he knew the poverty of those who wished to study, and the weak points in the system of elementary education. He wished to encourage a secular clergy who should fight the Wycliffites and reform the Church. Therefore he determined to found a system by which they might be trained, and by which the road to success might be opened to the humblest youths—a system which should pay him in return the duty of perpetual prayers for his soul.[29]

As early as 1370, then, he began to buy land about the north-eastern corner of the city wall; and ten years later, having obtained licence from Richard II., he enclosed a filthy lane that ran alongside the north wall and began to build a home for the warden, seventy scholars, ten stipendiary priests or chaplains, three stipendiary clerks and sixteen chorister boys of whom his college was to be composed. Eglesfield had proposed to establish seventy-two young scholars on his foundation. Wykeham borrowed and improved upon the idea. He provided a separate college for them at Winchester, and in so doing he took a step which has proved to be of quite incalculable consequence in the history of the moral and intellectual development of this country. For he founded the first English public school.

From the scholars of Winchester, when they had reached at least the age of fifteen years, and from them only the seventy scholars of "S. Marie College" were to be chosen by examination. A preference was given to the founder's kin and the natives of certain dioceses. These young scholars, if they were not disqualified by an income of over five marks or by bodily deformity, entered at once upon the course in Arts, and, after two years of probation and if approved by examination, might be admitted true and perpetual fellows. Small wonder if golden scholars became sometimes silver bachelors and leaden masters!

A fellow's allowance was a shilling a week for commons and an annual "livery." But it was provided that each young scholar should study for his first three years under the supervision of one of the fellows, who was to receive for each pupil five shillings. This was a new step in the development of the college system. Though designed merely to supplement the lectures of the regents in the schools, the new provision of tutors was destined to supplant them. Another step of far-reaching consequence taken by Wykeham was the acquisition of benefices in the country, college livings to which a fellow could retire when he had resided long enough or failed to obtain other preferment.

The government of the college was not entrusted to the young fellows, but to the warden, sub-warden, five deans, three bursars and a few senior fellows. But even the youngest of the fellows was entitled to vote on the election of a warden.

The warden of this new foundation was to be a person of no small importance. Wykeham intended him to live in a separate house, with a separate establishment and an income (£40) far more splendid than the pittance assigned to the Master of Balliol or even the Warden of Merton. The buildings of Merton had been kept separate; only by degrees, and as if by accident, had they assumed the familiar and charming form of a quadrangle. The genius of Wykeham adopted and adapted the fortuitous plan of Merton. At New College we have for the first time a group of collegiate buildings, tower-gateway (the tower assuredly of one "wise of building castles!") chapel, hall, library, treasury, warden's lodgings, chambers, cloister-cemetery, kitchen and domestics offices, designed and comprised in one self-sufficing quadrangle (1380-1400). Just as the statutes of New College are the rule of Merton enormously elaborated, so the plan of the buildings is that of Merton modified and systematised. The type of New College served as a model for all subsequent foundations. The most noticeable features in this arrangement are that the hall and chapel are under one roof, and that the chapel consists of a choir, suitable to the needs of a small congregation, and of a nave of two bays, stopping short at the transepts, and forming an ante-chapel which might serve both as a vestibule and as a room for lectures and disputations. The chapel, which contains much very beautiful glass and the lovely if inappropriate window-pictures of Sir Joshua Reynolds, must have been in Wykeham's day, when it was adorned with a magnificent reredos and "works of many colours," a thing of even greater beauty than it now is. The chapels of Magdalen, All Souls' and Wadham were directly imitated from it. But, with the hall, it suffered much at the hands of Wyatt and Sir Gilbert Scott. The latter was also responsible for the atrocious New Buildings. The proportions of the front quadrangle were spoilt by the addition of a third story and the insertion of square windows in the seventeenth century.

The importance of the chapel architecturally, dominating the quadrangle as it does and absorbing the admiration of the visitor or the dweller in those courts, is indicative of the ecclesiastical aspect of the new foundation, which the great opponent of Wycliffe intended to revivify the Church by training secular priests of ability. This ecclesiastical aspect is still more prominent in the case of All Souls', which, like Magdalen, may fitly be described as a daughter of New College, so much do they both owe, as regards their rule and their architectural design, to the great foundation of Wykeham. The deterioration and ignorance of the parochial clergy were amongst the most serious symptoms of the decadence of the fifteenth century. Himself a Wykehamist and a successful ecclesiastical lawyer, the great Archbishop Chichele therefore followed Wykeham's example and founded a college which might help to educate and to increase the secular clergy. Out of the revenues of the suppressed alien priories he endowed a society consisting of a warden and forty fellows, of doctors and masters who were to study Philosophy, Theology and Law. His college was not, therefore, and happily is not (though now it takes its full share of educational work), a mere body of teachers, but of graduate students. The prominence given to the study of Law and Divinity resulted in a close connection with the public services which has always been maintained. But "All Souls'" was a chantry as well as a college. As head of the English Church and a responsible administrator of the Crown, Chichele had devoted all his powers to the prosecution of that war with France, for which Shakespeare, following Hall, has represented him as being responsible. The college is said to have been the Archbishop's expiation for the blood so shed. Whatever his motive, his object is stated clearly enough. It was to found a

"College of poor and indigent clerks bounden with all devotion to pray for the Souls of the glorious memory of Henry V., lately King of England and France, the Duke of Clarence and the other lords and lieges of the realm of England, whom the havoc of that warfare between the two realms hath drenched with the bowl of bitter death, and also for the souls of all the faithful departed."

Chichele had already undertaken the foundation of S. Bernard's College. He now (September 1437) purchased Bedford Hall, or Charleton's Inn, at the corner of Cat Street,[30]directly opposite the eastern end of S. Mary's Church. On this site, in the following February, was laid the foundation stone of the college afterwards incorporated under the title of "The Warden and All Soulen College," or "The Warden and College of All Faithful Souls deceased at Oxford." As Adam de Brome had persuaded Edward II. to be the foster-founder of Oriel, so Chichele asked Henry VI. to be the nominal founder of his college. The royal patronage proved advantageous in neither case.

The front quadrangle of All Souls' remains very much as the founder left it; the hall and the noble Codrington Library in the Italian style, the cloister of the great quadrangle and the odd twin towers belong to the first half of the eighteenth century. The latter are curious specimens of that mixture of the Gothic and Renaissance styles (Nicholas Hawksmoor), of which the best that can be said is that "the architect has blundered into a picturesque scenery not devoid of grandeur" (Walpole).

The political and social troubles of the fifteenth century brought about a period of darkness and stagnation in the University. The spirit of independence and reform had been crushed by the ecclesiastics. Oxford had learnt her lesson. She took little part in politics, but played the time-server, and was always loyal—to one party or the other. She neglected her duties; she neither taught nor thought, but devoted all her energies and resources to adorning herself with beautiful colleges and buildings. And for us the result of this meretricious policy is the possession of those glorious buildings which mark the interval between the Middle Ages and the Renaissance. For the University now built herself schools that were worthy of her dower of knowledge.

There was a vacant spot at the end of Schools Street belonging to Balliol College, lying between the town wall on the north and Exeter College on the west. On this site it was determined to erect a School of Divinity (1424). Donations flowed in from the bishops and monasteries.

But in spite of all economy funds ran short. The building had to be discontinued for a while (1444). The gift of 500 marks from the executors of Cardinal Beaufort, a former Chancellor, enabled the graduates to proceed with their work. They made strenuous efforts to raise money. They put a tax on all non-resident masters and bachelors; they offered "graces" for sale; they applied to the Pope and bishops for saleable indulgences. In return for a contribution of one hundred pounds from the old religious orders, they agreed to modify the ancient statutes concerning the admission of monks to academical degrees. Some of these methods of raising the necessary monies are doubtless open to criticism, but we cannot cavil when we look upon the noble building which the graduates were thus enabled to raise. The Divinity School, to which, Casaubon declared, nothing in Europe was comparable, was, with its "vaulting of peculiar skill," used, though not completed, in 1466.

It remained to construct an upper story where the books belonging to the University might be kept and used. For generous gifts of books (1439-1446) by Humphrey, Duke of Gloucester, uncle of Henry VI., had greatly increased the University Library. The fashion of large and gorgeous libraries was borrowed by the English from the French princes. The duke had taken his opportunity during his campaigns in France. He seized the valuable collection of books at the Louvre, and many of them had now found their way to Oxford. They were stored at first in the Cobham Library, but more room was needed. Accordingly, in 1444, the University addressed a letter to the duke in which they informed him of their intention to erect a new building suitable to contain his magnificent gift, and on a site far removed from the hum of men. Of this building, with that gratitude which is in part at least a lively sense of favours to come, they asked permission of the very learned and accomplished duke to inscribe his name as founder. The Duke Humphrey Library forms now the central portion of the great Reading Room of the Bodleian Library. It still answers, by virtue of its position and the arrangement of its cubicles, to the description and intention of the promotors—to build a room where scholars might study far removed *a strepitu sæculari*, from the noise of the world.

The three wheat-sheaves of the Kempe shield, repeated again and again on the elaborate groined roof of the Divinity School, commemorate the bounty of Thomas Kempe, Bishop of London, who (1478) promised to give 1000 marks for the completion of the school and the library. A grateful University rewarded him with anniversary services; his name is still mentioned in the "bidding prayer" on solemn occasions. Nor was Duke Humphrey forgotten. His name still heads the list of benefactors recited from time to time in S. Mary's. Religious services were instituted also for his benefit. He was more in need of them, perhaps, than the bishop. For the "Good Duke Humphrey" was good only so far as his love of learning and his generosity to scholars may entitle him to be considered so. The patron of Lydgate and Occleve, and the donor of hundreds of rare and polite books to the University was as unscrupulous in his political intrigues as immoral in his private life. But in his case the good he did lived after him.

The "Good Duke" was a reader as well as a collector. It was not merely the outsides of books or the title-pages which attracted him.

"His courage never doth appal
To study in books of antiquity."

So wrote Lydgate, who knew. Even when he presented his books to the University, he took care to reserve the right of borrowing them, for were they not, according to the inscription which he was wont to insert lovingly in them, all his worldly wealth (*mon bien mondain*)? It is perhaps not surprising to find from the list of books which he gave to the University, that the duke's taste in literature was for the Classics, for the works of Ovid, Cato, Aulus Gellius and Quintilian, for the speeches of Cicero, the plays of Terence and Seneca, the works of Aristotle and Plato, the histories of Suetonius and Josephus, of Beda and Eusebius, Higden and Vincent of Beauvais. A fancy for medical treatises and a pretty taste in Italian literature are betrayed by the titles of other books, for the duke gave seven volumes of Boccaccio, five of Petrarch and two of Dante to the University.

Duke Humphrey promised to give the whole of his collection to the University, together with a hundred pounds to go towards the building of the library. But he died suddenly, and the University never, as it appears, received full advantage of his generosity. It was not till 1488 that the books were removed from S. Mary's. For the completion of the library was delayed by an order from Edward IV. The workmen employed upon the building were summoned by him to Windsor, where he had need of them, to work at S. George's Chapel. Those who were not employed on the chapel were handed over to William of Waynflete, who restored them to the University along with some scaffolding which had been used in the building of Magdalen. William Patten or Barbour of Waynflete, an Oxford man, who had been master of the school at Winchester, had been appointed first master and then Provost of Eton by the founder, Henry VI., and was rewarded for his success there by the Bishopric of Winchester. In 1448 he had founded a hall for the study of Theology and Philosophy, situated between the present schools and Logic Lane, and called it, probably after the almshouse at Winchester, of which he had been master, the Hall of S. Mary Magdalen. When he became Lord Chancellor he immediately took steps to enlarge this foundation, transferred it to the site of the Hospital of S. John, and styled it the College of S. Mary Magdalen (September 1457).

Waynflete resigned the Chancellorship just before the battle of Northampton. After some years, during which he was "in great dedignation with Edward IV.," he received full pardon from his late master's conqueror. The Yorkist monarch (whose fine statue is over the west doorway of the chapel) also confirmed the grants made to Waynflete's College in the last reign. After an interval, then, the foundation stone of the most beautiful college in the world, "the most absolute building in Oxford," as James I. called it when his son matriculated there, was laid "in the midst of the High Altar" (5th May 1474).

Already enclosing walls had been built about the property, which was bounded on the east by the Cherwell, on the south by the High Street, on the west by what is now Long Wall Street, and on the north by the lands of Holywell. The "Long Wall" bounded the "Grove," famous, since the beginning of the eighteenth century, for its noble timber and herd of deer. Most of the trees in the present grove are elms planted in the seventeenth century, but there are two enormous wych elms, measured by Oliver Wendell Holmes in 1886, which would have dwarfed that venerable oak which stood near the entrance into the water-walk, and was blown down "into the meadow" in 1789. It was over seven hundred years old (girth 21 ft. 9 in., height 71 ft. 8 in.), and thought to be the same as that named by the founder for a northern boundary.

In the arrangement of his buildings Waynflete followed Wykeham. Chapel, hall and library were designed on the same plan. But the beautiful "Founder's Tower," rendered now still more lovely by the drapery of creepers which hangs about it, formed the principal entrance into cloisters, which were part of the buildings of the main quadrangle, carried an upper story of chambers, and were adorned with grotesques symbolical of the Vices and Virtues. The entrance now used was originally meant to serve only as the entrance from the cloister to the chapel. It was adorned (*circa* 1630) with a gateway similar to that designed by Inigo Jones for the main entrance to the college.

The statutes were based on those of New College, but, in addition to those of which we have already had occasion to speak, there were certain notable improvements. The society was to consist of a President and seventy scholars besides four chaplains, eight clerks and sixteen choristers. Forty of these scholars were fellows forming one class, and thirty were demies, forming another, whose tenure was limited and who were given half the allowance of the fellows. They had no special claim to promotion to fellowships. For their instruction a Grammar Master and an usher were provided; when they were well skilled in Grammar, they were to be taught Logic and Sophistry by the college lecturers, whilst three "Readers," in Natural and Moral Philosophy and Theology, chosen out of the University, were to provide the higher teaching in Arts and Theology. And all this teaching, in Theology and Philosophy and also in Grammar, was to be given free to all comers at the expense of the college.

In 1481 Waynflete, full of pride in his new foundation, "the most noble and rich structure in the learned world," persuaded Edward IV. to come over from Woodstock and see it. The King came at a few hours' notice. But as the royal cavalcade drew near the North Gate of the town, a little after sunset, it was met by the Chancellor and the masters of the University and a great number of persons carrying lighted torches. The King and his courtiers were hospitably received at Magdalen. On the morrow the President delivered a congratulatory address, and the King made a gracious reply; then he and his followers joined in a solemn procession round the precincts and the cloisters of the college.

Two years later Richard III. was very similarly welcomed by the University and entertained at Magdalen. On this occasion the King was regaled with two disputations in the hall. Richard declared himself very well pleased; and it is just possible that he was. For one of the disputants was William Grocyn, who was rewarded with a buck and three marks for his pains.

The University continued its policy of political time-serving, and, after the battle of Bosworth Field, congratulated Henry VII. as fulsomely as it had congratulated Richard III. a few months before. Henry retorted by demanding the surrender of Robert Stillington, Bishop of Bath and Wells, who was staying within the limits of the University. This prelate was accused of "damnable conjuracies and conspiracies," which may have included complicity in the rebellion of Lambert Simnel. For the future scullion was a native of Oxford. The University prevaricated for a while; and at last, when hard pressed, they explained that they would incur the sentence of excommunication if they used force against a prelate of the Catholic Church. The King then took the matter into his own hands, and committed the offender to prison at Windsor for the remainder of his life. He soon afterwards visited Oxford, offered a noble in the chapel of Magdalen College, and, by way of marking his approval of the University, undertook the maintenance of two students at Oxford. In 1493 he established at University College an obit for the widow of Warwick the king-maker.

Some years later, in 1504, he endowed the University with ten pounds a year in perpetuity for a religious service to be held in memory of him and his wife and of his parents. On the anniversary of his burial a hearse, covered with rich stuff, was to be set up in the middle of S. Mary's Church before the great crucifix, and there the Chancellor, the masters and the scholars were to recite certain specified prayers. Among the articles in the custody of the verger of the University is a very fine ancient pall of rich cloth of gold, embroidered with the arms and badges of Henry VII., the Tudor rose and the portcullis, that typify the union of the houses of York and Lancaster. Penurious in most matters, Henry VII. showed magnificence in building and in works of piety. In Westminster Abbey he erected one of the grandest chantries in Christendom; and it was for the exclusive benefit of the monks of Westminster that he established at Oxford three scholarships in Divinity, called after his name, and each endowed with a yearly income of ten pounds (Maxwell Lyte).

Of Henry's parents, his mother, the Lady Margaret, Countess of Richmond,[31] took a warm interest in Oxford as in Cambridge, where she founded two colleges. It was she who founded the two Readerships in Divinity at Oxford (1497) and Cambridge, the oldest professorial chairs that exist in either University.

His characteristically frugal offering was not the only sign of his favour which Henry vouchsafed to Magdalen. He sent his eldest son, Prince Arthur, frequently to Oxford. When there the boy stayed in the President's lodgings and the purchase of two marmosets for his amusement is recorded in the college accounts. One of the old pieces of tapestry preserved in the President's lodgings represents the marriage of the prince with Catherine of Aragon. It was probably presented to the President (Mayhew) by him.

It is possible that Henry VII. also contributed to the cost of building that bell tower, which is the pride of Magdalen and the chief ornament of Oxford.

The tower was built between the years 1492 and 1505. Wolsey was a junior fellow when the tower was begun, and though popular tradition ascribes to him the credit of the idea and even the design of that exquisite campanile, the fact that not he, but another senior fellow (Gosmore by name) was appointed to superintend the work, is evidence, so far as there is any evidence, that Wolsey had no particular share in the design. He was, however, senior bursar in 1499. But the story that he left the college because he had wrongly applied some of its funds to the building of the tower, is not borne out by any evidence in the college records. He ceased to be a fellow of Magdalen about 1501, having been instituted to the Rectory of Lymington. But he had filled the office of Dean of Divinity after his term as senior bursar was over.

We have referred to the close connection of the house of Lancaster with Waynflete's foundation. By a curious freak of popular imagination the name of Henry VII. as well as that of the future cardinal has been intimately connected with this tower. Besides other benefactions, he granted a licence for the conveyance to the college of the advowsons of Slymbridge and of Findon.

In return the college undertook to keep an obit for him every year. This celebration was originally fixed on the 2nd or 3rd of October, but it has been held on the 1st of May since the sixteenth century. The coincidence of this ceremony with the most interesting and picturesque custom of singing on Magdalen Tower has given rise to the fable that a payment made to the college by the Rectory of Slymbridge was intended to maintain the celebration of a requiem mass for the soul of Henry VII. And the hymn that is now sung is the survival, says the popular myth, of that requiem.

For in the early morning of May Day all the members of Waynflete's foundation, the President and fellows and demies with the organist and choir, clad in white surplices ascend the tall tower that stands sombre, grey and silent in the half-light of the coming day. There are a few moments of quiet watching, and the eye gazes at the distant hills, as the white mists far below are rolled away by the rising sun. The clock strikes five, and as the sound of the strokes floats about the tower, suddenly from the throats of the well-trained choir on the morning air rises the May Day hymn.

The hymn is finished, and a merry peal of bells rings out. The tower rocks and seems to swing to the sound of the bells as a well made bell tower should. And the members of the college having thus commemorated the completion of their campanile, descend once more to earth, to bathe in the Cherwell, or to return to bed.

For a repetition of an inaugural ceremony is what this function probably is, and it has nothing to do, so much can almost certainly be said, with any requiem mass. The hymn itself is no part of any use. It was written by a fellow of the college, Thomas Smith, and set to music as part of the college "grace" by Benjamin Rogers, the college organist, towards the end of the seventeenth century.

Whether or no the origin and meaning of the singing was to commemorate the completion of the tower, the singing itself would appear to have borne originally a secular character.

"The choral ministers of this house," says Wood, "do, according to an ancient custom, salute Flora every year on the First of May, at four in the morning, with vocal music of several parts. Which having been sometimes well performed, hath given great content to the neighbourhood, and auditors underneath."

The substitution of a hymn from the college grace for the "merry concert of both vocal and instrumental music, consisting of several merry ketches, and lasting almost two hours," which was the form the performance took in the middle of the eighteenth century, was made on one occasion when the weather was very inclement. Once made it was found easier and more suitable to continue it, and the observance came to be religious.[32]

Magdalen Tower is one of those rarely beautiful buildings, which strike you with a silent awe of admiration when first you behold them, and ever afterwards reveal to your admiring gaze new aspects and unsuspected charms. It is changeable as a woman, but its changes are all good and there is nothing else about it that is feminine. It conveys the impression that it is at once massive and slender, and its very slenderness is male.

The chaste simplicity of the lower stories carries the eye up unchecked to the ornamented belfry windows, the parapet and surmounting pinnacles, and thus enhances the impression of perfect and reposeful proportion.

The growth of the colleges had influenced the halls. Statutes imposed by the authority of the University, began to take the place of the private rule of custom and tradition approved and enforced by the authority of the self-governing scholars. The students quickly ceased to be autonomous scholars and became disciplined schoolboys. The division between don and undergraduate began to be formed and was rapidly accentuated. Thus, at the close of the mediæval period, a change had been wrought in the character of the University, which rendered it an institution very different from that which it had been in the beginning. The growth of Nationalism, the separation of languages and the establishment of the collegiate system—these and similar causes tended to give the Universities a local and aristocratic character. The order introduced by the colleges was accompanied by the introduction of rank, and of academical power and influence stored in the older, permanent members of the University. Learning, too, had ceased to be thought unworthy of a gentleman; it became a matter of custom for young men of rank to have a University education. Thus, in the charter of Edward III., we even read that "to the University a multitude of nobles, gentry, strangers and others continually flock"; and towards the end of the century we find Henry of Monmouth, afterwards Henry V., as a young man, a sojourner at Queen's College. But it was in the next century that colleges were provided, not for the poor, but for the noble. Many colleges, too, which had been originally intended for the poor, opened their gates to the rich, not as fellows or foundation students, but as simple lodgers, such as monasteries might have received in a former age. This change has continued to be remarkably impressed upon Oxford and Cambridge even down to this day.

The influence of other political classes was now also introduced. Never, as Newman said, has a learned institution been more directly political and national than the University of Oxford. Some of its colleges came to represent the talent of the nation, others its rank and fashion, others its wealth; others have been the organs of the Government of the day; while others, and the majority, represented one or other division, chiefly local, of opinion in the country. The local limitation of the members of many colleges, the West Country character of Exeter, the North Country character of Queen's or University, the South Country character of New College, the Welsh character of Jesus College, for instance, tended to accentuate this peculiarity. The whole nation was thus brought into the University by means of the colleges, which fortunately were sufficiently numerous, and no one of them overwhelmingly important. A vigour and a stability were thus imparted to the University such as the abundant influx of foreigners had not been able to secure. As in the twelfth and thirteenth centuries, French, German and Italian students had flocked to Oxford, and made its name famous in distant lands; so in the fifteenth all ranks and classes of the land furnished it with pupils, and what was wanting in their number or variety, compared with the former era, was made up by their splendour or political importance. The sons of the nobles came up to the University, each accompanied by an ample retinue; the towns were kept in touch with the University by means of the numerous members of it who belonged to the clerical order. Town and country, high and low, north and south, had a common stake in the academical institutions, and took a personal interest in the academical proceedings. The degree possessed a sort of indelible character which all classes understood; and the people at large were more or less partakers of a cultivation which the aristocracy were beginning to appreciate. Oxford, in fact, became the centre of national and political thought. Not only in vacations and term time was there a stated ebbing and flowing of the academical youth, but messengers posted to and fro between Oxford and all parts of the country in all seasons of the year. So intimate was this connection, that Oxford became, as it were, the selected arena for the conflicts of the various interests of the nation.

CHAPTER VI

OXFORD AND THE REFORMATION

IN 1453 Christendom was shocked by the news that the Turks had taken Constantinople. The home of learning and the citadel of philosophy was no more. The wisdom of Hellas, so it seemed to contemporary scholars like Æneas Sylvius, was destined likewise to perish. In fact, it was but beginning to be diffused. Scholars fled with what MSS. they could save to the hospitable shores of Italy. And at the very time that these fugitives were hastening across the Adriatic, it is probable that the sheets of the Mazarin Bible were issuing from the press at Maintz. Thus whilst Italy was rescuing from destruction the most valuable thought of the ancient world, Germany was devising the means for its diffusion in lands of which Strabo never heard, and to an extent of which the Sosii never dreamed. The Italians acquired the Greek language with rapidity and ardour. The student flung aside his scholastic culture; cast away the study of an Aristotle that had been conformed to Christian Theology, and the Sentences in which that theology was enshrined, and tried to identify himself in feeling with the spirit of cultivated paganism. The cowl and the gown were discarded for the tunic and the toga.

But the New Learning did not make its way at once to England. And when at length the Englishmen who had travelled and studied in Italy brought back with them something of the generous enthusiasm with which they had been fired, their ideas were but coldly welcomed by the followers of Thomas or the disciples of Duns. At Oxford the New Movement took but a momentary hold of only a small part of the University, and then was shaken off by the massive inertness of the intellectual stagnation characteristic of the country. "They prefer their horses and their dogs to poets," wrote Poggio; "and like their horses and their dogs they shall perish and be forgotten."

The majority of Englishmen are always slow to accept new ideas. They move ponderously and protestingly in the wake of the Continent. The New Learning was as unwelcome at Oxford as if it had been a motor car. The schoolmen were still busily chopping their logic, when the Medicis were ransacking the world for a new play, when Poggio was writing his "Facetiæ" or editing Tacitus, and Pope Nicholas was founding the Vatican Library at Rome. And the Renaissance, when it did begin to work in England, took the form of a religious reformation; the religious genius of the nation led it to the worship, not of Beauty, but of Truth.

The English were equally late in adopting the new German art of printing. When Caxton introduced it, it had almost reached its perfection abroad. Block books—books printed wholly from carved blocks of wood—had come in and gone out. Arising out of them, the idea of movable types had long been invented and developed on the Continent.

The Bamberg and Mazarin Bibles, the first two books to be printed from movable type, had been produced by Gutenberg, Fust and Schöffer as early as 1453. But it was not till 1477 that Caxton set up his press at Westminster. A year later the first book was issued from an Oxford press. This was the famous small quarto of forty-two leaves, "Exposicio sancti Jeronimi in simbolum apostolorum," written by Tyrannius Rufinus of Aquileia. The colophon of this book, however, distinctly states that it was printed in 1468: "Impressa Oxonie et ibi finita anno domini M.CCCC.LXVIIJ, XVIJ die decembris." But there is every reason to suppose that an X has been omitted from this date and that the true year was 1478. Such a misprint is not uncommon.

Exactly the same error occurs in books published at Venice, at Barcelona and at Augsburg. The workmanship is very much the same as, but slightly inferior to, that of the next two books which came from the Oxford Press in 1479. And in the library of All Souls' there is a copy of each of these, which were originally bound up together. A break of eleven years between the production of the first and subsequent books is both inconceivable and inexplicable.

The press from which these books and twelve others were issued at Oxford during the eight years, 1478-1486, was apparently set up by one Theodore Rood of Cologne. The first three books, however, namely the "Exposicio" mentioned, the "Ægidius de originali peccato," and "Textus Ethicorum Aristotelis per Leonardum Aretinum translatus," bear no printer's name, but the type was either brought from Cologne or directly copied from Cologne examples. It strongly resembles that used by Gerard ten Raem de Berka or Guldenschaff. Still, it cannot be proved that Rood printed these first three books, or that he ever used the type in which they alone are printed. The colophon of the fourth book, a Latin commentary on the "De Anima" of Aristotle by Alexander de Hales, a folio printed from new type, gives the name of the printer, Theodore Rood, and bears the date 1481. A copy of it was bought in the year of publication for the library of Magdalen, where it still remains. The price paid was thirty-three shillings and fourpence. A very beautiful copy of the next book, "Commentary on the Lamentation of Jeremiah," by John Lattebury, 1482, is in the library of All Souls'. Four leaves survive in the Bodleian and four in the Merton Library, of the "Cicero pro Milone," the first edition of a classic printed in England. Two leaves of a Latin grammar are to be found in the British Museum.

Rood went into partnership with an Oxford stationer named Thomas Hunt, and together they produced eight other books with a type more English in character than the preceding ones. One of these books, "Phalaris," 1485 (Wadham and Corpus Libraries), has a curious colophon in verse, which describes the printers and their ambition to surpass the Venetians in their work. The partners ceased to produce books after 1486. Rood probably returned to Cologne, and the German art found no exponents in Oxford for the remainder of the century. Subsequently we find Leicester advancing money to set up Joseph Barnes with a new press. Laud and Fell were other great patrons of the University Press.

Meantime the return of the Pope to Rome had attracted many foreign travellers and students to Italy, who could not fail to be impressed by the new birth of art and intellectual life that was taking place in that country.

Among the pupils of Guarino of Verona at Ferrara the names of at least five students from Oxford occur. Of these, Robert Fleming, a relative of the founder of Lincoln College, was an author of some distinction, and he compiled a Græco-Latin dictionary at a time when Greek was almost unknown in England. He brought back from his travels in Italy many precious books, which he gave to the library of Lincoln College. William Grey, another of Guarino's pupils, enriched the library of Balliol with many fine manuscripts redolent of the New Learning. John

Tiptoft, Earl of Worcester, was another scholar who, before paying for his share in politics with his head, presented to the University the valuable collection of manuscripts, which he had made in the course of his travels.

William Selling, a member of the recent foundation of All Souls', was perhaps the earliest Englishman of influence to catch from Italy the inspiration of the Greek muse. On his return from that country, he was appointed to the conventual school at Canterbury. His knowledge of Greek, and his enthusiasm for Greek literature, became the germ of the study in England. Thomas Linacre was one of his pupils, who, after studying at Oxford under Vitelli, journeyed to Italy with Selling. He was introduced to Politian at Florence. Thence he proceeded to Rome, and there perhaps formed his taste for the scientific writings of Aristotle and his devotion to the study of medicine, which afterwards found expression in the foundation of the College of Physicians and of the two lectureships at Merton, now merged into the chair which bears his name. Linacre returned to Oxford and lectured there awhile before being appointed Physician to Henry VIII. His translation of five medical treatises of Galen was, Erasmus declared, more valuable than the original Greek.

We have said that he studied under Vitelli. It was Cornelio Vitelli who, some time before 1475, first "introduced polite literature to the schools of Oxford," by a lecture as prelector of New College, upon which the warden, Thomas Chandler, complimented him in a set Latin speech. This was probably that Cornelius who, in company with two other Italians, Cyprian and Nicholas by name, dined with the President of Magdalen on Christmas Day, 1488. And from the lips of this pioneer William Grocyn himself learned Greek. Grocyn was a fellow of New College (1467-1481), but he afterwards removed to Magdalen as Reader in Theology. He completed his study of Greek and Latin by a sojourn of two years (1488) at Florence, under Demetrius Chalcondylas and Politian. On his return to Oxford he took rooms in Exeter College (1491), and gave a course of lectures on Greek.

A few years later (1496-7) the first step in the revolution against the system under which the study of the Bible had been ousted by the study of the Sentences was taken. A course of lectures by John Colet on the Epistles of S. Paul was the first overt act in a movement towards practical Christian reform.

It was from Grocyn and Linacre that Thomas More and Erasmus learnt Greek. For Gibbon's epigram that Erasmus learned Greek at Oxford and taught it at Cambridge is true, if we qualify it by the reminder that he knew a little before he came to England and learned more in the years which intervened between the time when, much to the chagrin of Colet, he left Oxford and went to Cambridge as an instructor in that language.

Erasmus had taught at Paris. He went to Oxford (1498) to learn and to observe. His return home from London had been delayed unexpectedly. He determined to use the opportunity of paying a visit to Oxford. The reputation of the learned men there attracted him more than the company of "the gold-chained courtiers" of the capital. He was received as an inmate of S. Mary's College, which had been built as a house for students of his own Augustinian order (1435). This house, when it was dissolved (1541), was converted into a hall for students, and then into a charitable institution (Bridewell). The site, on the east side of New Inn Hall Street, is occupied by a house and garden, now called Frewen Hall, which was chosen in 1859 as the residence of the Prince of Wales during his studies at Oxford. The west gateway, a few remains of groining and the wall facing the street north of the gate are practically all that remains of the building as Erasmus saw it, unless we reckon the roof of the chapel of B.N.C., which is said to have been taken from the chapel of S. Mary's College. Erasmus had nothing to complain of in his welcome to Oxford. He found the prior of his college, Richard Charnock, an intelligent companion and useful friend. Colet, having heard from Charnock of his arrival, addressed to him a letter of welcome, which in the midst of its formal civility has a characteristic touch of Puritan sincerity. To this Erasmus replied in his own rhetorical fashion with a letter of elaborate compliment.

His wit, his learning and the charm of his brilliant conversation soon won him friends. Delightful himself, he found everybody delightful. The English girls were divinely pretty, and he admired their custom of kissing visitors. Erasmus made a fair show in the hunting-field, and was charmed with everything, even with our English climate.

"The air," he wrote from Oxford, "is soft and delicious. The men are sensible and intelligent. Many of them are even learned, and not superficially either. They know their classics and so accurately that I seem to have lost little in not going to Italy. When Colet speaks I might be listening to Plato. Linacre is as deep and acute a thinker as I have ever met. Grocyn is a mine of knowledge, and Nature never formed a sweeter and happier disposition than that of Thomas More. The number of young men who are studying ancient literature here is astonishing."

In one of his letters he gives a very lively picture of a gathering of witty divines at the house of his "sweet and amiable friend" Colet, when the latter "spoke with a sacred fury" and Erasmus himself, finding the conversation growing too serious for a social gathering, entertained the company with a happily invented tale.

At Oxford, then, the great centre of theological study, he was learning something of the methods of the theologians. They were not strange to him, for he knew Paris. But the Oxford school was in his mind when he poured forth his shafts of ridicule upon scholastic divines in his brilliant satire, "The Praise of Folly." Yet it was at Oxford that Colet had taught him to detest the authority of Thomas Aquinas, and to apply to the study of the New Testament the knowledge and methods indicated by the study of Greek literature. His "Moria" and his "Novum Instrumentum," therefore, the books which prepared the way for the Reformation, were his protest, and the protest of the Christian laity along with him, against the authority of the clergy and against the popular theology which was based on the errors of the Vulgate. Erasmus laid the egg and Luther hatched it—a very different bird, as the former declared. The fact was that throughout Europe the growing intelligence of the educated class was slowly but surely developing in antagonism, not merely to specific doctrines, but to the whole spirit of mediæval theology.

The Old Learning was threatened with destruction. It rose in arms against Greek and heresy. Bishops fulminated. The clergy cried Antichrist, and clamoured for sword and faggot. The Universities forbade the sale of Erasmus's writings, and, seeing what came of the study of Greek, declared that they would have no more of it. Oxford divided itself into two bodies, who called themselves Greeks and Trojans, the Trojans enormously preponderating. The "Greeks," the adherents of the New Learning, were assailed with every kind of ridicule. They were openly derided in the streets and abused from the pulpit. In after years Tyndale, who had been a student at Magdalen Hall, could recall how

"The old barking curs, Duns' disciples and like draff called Scotists, the children of darkness, raged in every pulpit against Greek, Latin and Hebrew, and what sorrow the schoolmasters that taught the true Latin tongue had with them, some beating the pulpit with their fists for madness, and roaring out with open and foaming mouth, that if there were but one Terence or Vergil in the world, and that same in their sleeve, and a fire before them, they would burn them therin, though it should cost them their lives."

News of what was going on reached the court at Abingdon. At the King's command, More wrote to the governing body of the University to rebuke the intemperance of the Trojan clique. But the Heads of Houses were sleeping over a volcano, and More's letter could not rouse them from their slumber. For the present the result was that the little band of pioneers in the New Learning one by one departed out of their coasts.

"The Cardinal of York," More writes, "will not permit these studies to be meddled with." Wolsey, of course, as well as the King, More and Archbishop Warham, the Chancellor, was on the side of the New Learning. He defrayed the expenses of many lectures, for which the University repeatedly thanked him. He engaged a famous Spanish scholar, Juan Luis Vives, to occupy his new Chair of Rhetoric; and he sent a rising English scholar, Thomas Lupset, from Paris to lecture on the Classics at Oxford.

Vives was the first Professor of Humanity (or Latin) at Corpus Christi, the first of the Renaissance colleges. His special function it was to banish all "barbarism" from the "bee-hive," as the founder fondly called his college, by lecturing daily on the Classics. Tradition says that the professor was welcomed to his new home by a swarm of bees, which, to signify the incomparable sweetness of his eloquence, settled under the leads of his chambers.

The founder of C.C.C., Richard Foxe, Bishop of Winchester, was a prelate, statesman, architect, soldier, herald and diplomatist, who, in the very encyclopædic nature of his talents, was a typical product of the Renaissance. He had been Bishop of Exeter, of Bath and Wells and of Durham before he was translated to Winchester; he had been Keeper of the Privy Seal and Secretary of State, and had played an important part in the history of his country; he had been Chancellor of Cambridge and Master of Pembroke College there; but it was chiefly upon Oxford that he lavished the wealth he had acquired.

Having bought some land between Merton and S. Frideswide's, he proposed at first to establish a college, after the manner of Durham College, directly in connection with the Monastery of S. Swithun at Winchester. But before the building was completed, he determined to make it a college for secular students. Holinshed gives us the words in which Hugh Oldham, Bishop of Exeter, who was intimately associated with him in the work—his arms are to be seen in various places in the existing buildings—persuaded him to this course.

"What, my Lord, shall we build houses and provide livelihood for a company of bussing monks, whose end and fall we ourselves may live to see? No, no. It is more meet a great deal that we should have care to provide for the increase of learning, and for such as by their learning shall do good in the Church and Commonwealth."

The broad-minded founder accepted this view. He drew up statutes, by means of which he hoped to train men who should help the Church to recognise, to lead and to control the New Movement. The verdict of his contemporaries with regard to his work and intentions is expressed by Erasmus, who wrote that "Just as Rhodes was once famous for the Colossus, and Caria for the tomb of Mausolus, so the new College at Oxford dedicated to the most profitable literature would be recognised throughout the civilised world as one of the chief ornaments of Britain."

The influence of the Renaissance is writ large over Foxe's statutes. What is remarkable in them is the provision he made for the teaching of the New Learning. As he furnished his students with a library, rich in classical MSS. and books in Greek, Latin and Hebrew, a "Bibliotheca trilinguis" which Erasmus declared would attract more students than Rome had done hitherto; so also, in addition to the twenty fellows and twenty scholars of his college, he endowed three Readers, in Greek, in Latin, and in Theology. Natives of Greece and Italy were to be specially eligible for these offices; Greek as well as Latin might be spoken in hall, and some acquaintance with the works of Roman poets, orators and historians, no less than with Logic and Philosophy, was to be required of candidates for scholarships, who must also prove their fitness by ability to compose verses and write letters in Latin.

Cicero, Sallust, Valerius Maximus, Suetonius, Pliny, Livy and Quintilian are enumerated in the statutes as the prose writers, and Vergil, Ovid, Lucan, Juvenal, Terence and Plautus as the poets to be expounded by the Professor of Humanity. The works of Lorenzo Valla, Aulus Gellius and Politian are recommended as suitable subjects of study during the three vacations. The Professor of Greek, an officer unknown in any earlier college, was required to lecture, and to lecture to the whole University, not only on Grammar, but also on the works of Isocrates, Lucian, Philostratus, Aristophanes, Theocritus, Euripides, Sophocles, Pindar, Hesiod, Demosthenes, Thucydides, Aristotle and Plutarch.

The third "Reader" appointed by Foxe was to expound the Old Testament and the New in alternate years. He was not, however, to be content with the comments of the schoolmen, but was "to follow so far as possible the ancient and holy doctors both Latin and Greek."

It will be seen that these statutes form, as it were, at once a charter and a corpus of the New Learning. Patristic theology was to be restored to the place of honour whence the quibbles of the schoolmen had banished it; the masterpieces of the ancient world were, in future, to be studied instead of the second-rate philosophers and slovenly writers of the Dark Ages.

Apart from the fascinating hall and library, the buildings of Corpus are less distinguished than her history. The curious sundial, surmounted by a pelican vulning herself in piety, which stands in the centre of the front quadrangle, was erected by a fellow in 1581. As at All Souls' and elsewhere, the name of the college is indicated by sculpture over the gateway—a group of angels bearing a pyx, the receptacle of the sacramental host, the body of Christ (Corpus Christi). The pastoral staff, a chalice and paten, which belonged to the founder, are still preserved. They rank among the finest examples of the work of English mediæval silversmiths.

The connection between Magdalen and C.C.C. was always close. Foxe, indeed, is said to have been at Magdalen, and to have

left Oxford on account of a pestilence. It is at any rate noteworthy that he makes special provision against plagues in his statutes. The severity and frequency of plagues of one sort or another were a serious obstacle to the prosperity of the University, and therefore of the city, throughout this century. The causes are not far to seek. For centuries filth and garbage had been allowed to accumulate in the ill-made, unswept streets. And though the King might write to the burghers and command them to remove the nuisances of this sort from before their doors, the efforts to deal with them were only spasmodic. Brewers and bakers, again, were forbidden by the King's edict (1293) to make use of the foul waters of Trill Mill Stream for the making of their bread and ale. But police was inefficient, and the health of the scholars frequently suffered from a renewal of this insanitary practice. Regrators, who burned before their doors stinking fat and suet, were also forbidden by Edward III. to pursue their habits, and the citizens were enjoined to repair the pavements in front of their houses.

But in spite of regulations and restrictions butchers persisted in slaughtering their beasts in their homes and fouling the Trill Mill Stream with offal. Inundations from the Cherwell and the Thames, not yet regulated and confined by the Conservancy Board, occasionally swamped even the cloisters of Magdalen and left behind a legacy of mud, damp and malaria.

Sweating sickness—a kind of rheumatic fever—struck Oxford hard in 1517. In the following years other loathsome diseases, attributed to the noisome smells which arose from the marshy grounds around the city and the obstructed state of the Thames, manifested themselves and caused the students to fly. Frequent instances are recorded of fellows obtaining permission to leave Oxford on account of the pestilence. In 1513 most of the members of Oriel removed to a farm at Dean; in 1522 the inmates of New College fled on the outbreak of some illness, and the fellows of University College dispersed on the same account in 1525. From Magdalen, in unhealthy seasons, there were frequent migrations of a large portion of the society to Witney or to Brackley, where the hospital had been indicated by the founder as a place to which such migrations might be made. But it was in 1528 that the sweating sickness broke out in its severest form. Many persons died within a few hours of being attacked by the disease; public business was postponed, and the lecture rooms were closed. The Festival of S. John was stopped. It was decreed that all clerks who thought themselves in danger might be absent until October. It might almost have been the influenza (1894).

The plague broke out in 1571, so that the University term had to be deferred. It broke out again in the following years, and culminated, in 1577, in the "Black Assizes." Rowland Jencks, a bookbinder, had been seized and sent to London for railing against the Commonwealth and the established religion. His house was searched for "bulls, libels, and suchlike things against the Queen and religion." He was returned to Oxford to be committed to prison. At the Assizes, held in the Court House at the Castle-yard, he was condemned to lose his ears. No sooner was the prisoner removed from the crowded court than, as Wood tells us,

"there arose such an infectious damp or breath among the people, that many there present, to the apprehensions of most men, were then smothered and others so deeply infected that they lived not many hours after. Above 600 sickened in one night; and the day after, the infectious air being carried into the next villages, sickened there an hundred more. The number of persons that died in five weeks' space were 300 in Oxford, and 200 and odd in other places; so that the whole number that died in that time were 510 persons, of whom many bled till they expired."

The description of the disease given by Wood reminds one of Thucydides' account of the plague at Athens. The outbreak was attributed by some to the Roman Catholics, who were said to have used magic to revenge themselves for the cropping of Jencks' ears, but the explanation suggested by a remark of Bacon is more probable. "The most pernicious infection next to the plague," he says, "is the smell of the Jail, when prisoners have been long and close nastily kept."

In 1582 the plague again threatened. This time measures were taken to improve the sanitary conditions of the place. Regulations were introduced, which do not greatly differ from the precautions of modern legislation. It was, for instance, ordained that—

"No person shall cast or lay any donge, dust, ordure, rubbish, carreyne or any other thing noyant into any the waters ryvers or streams or any the streets, wayes or lanes. But every person shall swepe together & take up the said things noyant out of the channel of the street so far as their ground reacheth and cause the same to be carried away twice every week. All privies & hogsties set or made over upon or adjoining to any the waters or streames leading to any brew-house shall be removed & taken away. No person shall keep any hogs or swine within the said City but only within their own several backsides; no butcher shall keep any slaughter house or kill any oxen kyne shepe or calves within the walls. All pavements shall be made and amended in places defective and all chimneys occupied with fire shall from henceforth be swept four times every year."

These ordinances, it will be seen, provided against the customary crying evils of a mediæval town. Similar provisions against similar evils are to be found in the archives of most cities in England or France in the sixteenth century. But ordinances are one thing and effective street-police is another. A hundred years later S. James's Square was still the receptacle for all offal and cinders, for all the dead cats and dead dogs of Westminster, whilst Voltaire's scathing description of the streets of Paris was no exaggeration. It was a state of affairs on which the Plague of London was the grimmest of all possible commentaries.

Another outbreak of plague in 1593 produced an order against plays, which were said to bring too many people, and the plague with them, from London. Regulations were also passed against overcrowding in the houses. At the beginning of the reign of James I., however, the infection spread once more from London to Oxford. Term was prorogued; the colleges broke up; and the citizens were so hard hit that they petitioned the University for aid. A weekly contribution from the colleges alleviated the distress that arose from this doleful sickness. The town was almost deserted; the shops were closed; and only the keepers of the sick or the collectors of relief appeared in the streets—"no not so much as dog or cat." The churches were seldom opened, and grass grew in the common market-place. Next year and the next plague broke out again, by which time some arrangements had been made for a system of isolation. Yet the mediæval attitude of mind towards medicine and sanitation would seem to have lasted on through the Age of Reason. For in 1774, when small-pox had many times scourged the town, all attempts at inoculation were formally forbidden by the Vice-Chancellor and Mayor.

Foxe had aided the rise and rejoiced in the success of Wolsey. But that success was not universally popular. In spite of his benefactions to learning, and the University, it was an Oxford

Laureate, one of our earliest satirists, who, when the Cardinal was at the height of his power, more monarch than the King himself, attacked him with the most outspoken virulence.

A crown of laurel would seem to have been the outward sign and symbol of a degree in Rhetoric, and rhetoricians were occasionally styled Poets Laureate. John Skelton, who was perhaps Court Poet to Henry VIII., was certainly tutor to Prince Henry and Laureate of both Universities. He was very proud of this distinction, and, not being troubled by any excess of modesty, he wrote a poem of 1600 lines in praise of himself:

"A Kynge to me myn habite gave;
At Oxforth the Universyte,
Auvaunsed to that degre
By hole consent of theyr Senate,
I was made Poete Laureate."

So he says; and Cambridge apparently followed suit and admitted him (1493) to a corresponding degree, and likewise encircled his brows with a wreath of laurel.

Skelton jeered at the Cardinal's pride and pomp; at his low birth (his "greasy original") and his lack of scholarship. There was more truth in Shakespeare's description of him as a "scholar and a right good one," for the "Boy Bachelor" had taken his degree of B.A. at fifteen years of age, "a rare thing and seldom seen." He held a fellowship at Magdalen, and was bursar for a short while, as we have seen; for six months he acted as master of Magdalen School, and in 1500 he was instituted to the Rectory of Lymington, thanks to the favour of the Marquis of Dorset, whose three sons had been his pupils at the school. It is not every man who is given even one chance in life, but at last to Wolsey, as to Wykeham, the opportunity came. He pleased the King by the speed with which he performed the first errand on which he was dispatched; and from that time he never ceased to advance in power and the confidence of his sovereign. The account of that episode, which he gave after his fall to George Cavendish, is one of the most profitable lessons in history. It is the secret of success as recorded by a bankrupt millionaire.

Wolsey never allowed his ecclesiastical and political work and honours to make him forget the University which had given him his start in life. In 1510 he took his degree of Bachelor of Divinity.

By the University the need for the codification of its statutes, and the unification of the mass of obscure customs and contradictory ordinances of which they were by this time composed, had long been felt. Some efforts had indeed already (1518) been made in this direction, but they had come to nothing. Graduates who swore to obey the statutes now found themselves in the awkward position of being really unable to find their way through the labyrinth of confused and contradictory enactments.

Now it happened that an outbreak of the sweating sickness in 1517 drove the King and his court from London to Abingdon. Queen Catherine availed herself of the opportunity to pay a visit to Oxford, to dine at Merton and to worship at the shrine of S. Frideswide, whilst Wolsey, who escorted her from Abingdon, attended a solemn meeting of the graduates at S. Mary's and informed them of his design to establish certain daily lectures for the benefit of the University at large. For this purpose it was necessary to alter existing regulations. The graduates seized the opportunity of inviting the Cardinal, their "Mæcenas," whom they even came to address as "His Majesty," to undertake a complete revision of their statutes. In so doing they disregarded the wishes of their Chancellor, the Archbishop Warham. But their action was fruitless, for the Cardinal had no time to examine and codify the chaotic enactments of the mediæval academicians.

It was at Wolsey's request that a charter was granted to the University (1523) which placed the greater part of the city at its mercy. It was now empowered to incorporate any trade, whilst all "members of the privilege" were exempted from having to apply to the city for permission to carry on business. Many minor rights and immunities were granted to the Chancellor, and no appeal was allowed from his court. "Any sentence, just or unjust, by the Chancellor against any person, shall be holden good, and for the same sentence, so just or unjust, the Chancellor or his deputy shall not be drawn out of the University for false judgment, or for the same vexed or troubled by any written commandment of the King."

Prior to the issue of this charter there had been grievances arising from the favour shown by the Crown to the University, as, for instance, when, a few years back, the colleges and other places of the University had been exempted from the subsidies charged upon the town. The jealousy which had been slumbering now burst into flames. The bailiffs flatly refused to summon a jury under the new terms. They were imprisoned. A writ was issued to enforce the University charter and for the appearance of the mayor and corporation to answer a suit in chancery.

The same year (1529) the University, not being able to obtain the assistance of the bailiffs, ordered the bedels to summon a jury for their leet. The city bailiffs closed the door of the Guildhall, so that the court thus summoned could not be held. This device they adopted repeatedly. On one occasion Wolsey proposed to submit the question to the arbitration of More. But the city perceived their danger and unanimously refused,

"for," they remarked, "by such arbitrements in time past, the Commissary & procters & their officers of the University hath usurped & daily usurpeth upon the town of divers matters contrary to their compositions."

The struggle passed through several stages. The mayor, one Michael Hethe by name, refused to take the customary oath at S. Mary's to maintain the privileges of the University. Proceedings were instituted against him. His answer, when he was summoned to appear at S. Mary's Church and show cause why he should not be declared perjured and excommunicate, was couched in very spirited terms:

"Recommend me unto your master and shew him, I am here in this town the King's Grace's lieutenant for lack of a better, and I know no cause why I should appear before him. I know him not for my ordinary."

The court pronounced him contumacious, and sentenced him to be excommunicated. He was obliged to demand absolution, but he did not abate the firmness of his attitude when he obtained it, for he flatly refused to promise "to stand to the law and to obey the commands of the Church," though that promise was proposed as a necessary condition of absolution being granted.

Before the end of this year (1530) the town made a direct petition to the King against the University, in which the chief incidents in the hard-fought battle are recounted in detail. Complaint is made, for instance, that the commissary

"Doth take fourpence for the sale of every horse-lode of fresh salmon, & one penny of every seme of fresshe herrings, which is extorcyon": and again "Another time he sent for one William Falofelde & demanded of him a duty that he should give him a pint of wine of every hogshead that he did set a-broach, for his taste. And the said William answered and said that he knew no such duty to be had, if he knew it he would gladly give it. And thereupon the said Commissary said he would make him know that it was his duty & so sent him to prison: and so ever since, for fear of imprisonment, the said William Falofelde hath sent him wine when he sent for it, which is to the great losse and hindrance of the said William Falofelde."

In order to compel submission on the part of the city, the mayor and twenty of the citizens were discommoned in 1533, so that

"no schollar nor none of their servants, should buy nor sell with none of them, neither eat nor drink in their houses, under pain of for every time of so doing to forfeit to the Commissary of 6s. and 8d."

For twenty years the quarrel dragged on, till at last both parties grew weary. In 1542 arbitrators were called in, and Wolsey's charter was repealed. But under Elizabeth, when in Leicester they had elected a Chancellor of sufficient power to represent their interests, the University began to endeavour to regain the privileges and franchises which, as they maintained, had only been in abeyance. An Act of Parliament was procured which confirmed the old obnoxious charter of 1523, but with a clause of all the liberties of the mayor and town. This clause led the way to fresh acts of aggression on either side, and renewed recriminations and disputes until, on the report of two judges, a series of orders was promulgated by the Privy Council (1575), intended to set at rest the differences between the two bodies for ever. But the result fell short of the intention. The opposition at this time had been led by one William Noble, who lived in the old house known as Le Swynstock. Smarting under the sting of false imprisonment, Noble commenced suits in the Star Chamber against the University, and presented petitions both against that body and the mayor and citizens. His popularity was such that he was elected Member of Parliament for the city.

Wolsey, as we have seen, had taken some steps towards establishing public lectureships in the University. But he provided no permanent endowment for these chairs. His designs developed into a grander scheme. He determined to found a college which, in splendour and resources, should eclipse even the noble foundations of Wykeham and Waynflete, a college where the secular clergy should study the New Learning and use it as a handmaid of Theology and in the service of the old Church. And as Wykeham had established in connection with his college a school at Winchester, so Wolsey proposed to found at his birth-place, Ipswich, and at Oxford, two sister-seats of learning and religion.

Through the darkness and stagnation of the fifteenth century a few great men had handed on the torch of learning and of educational ideals. The pedigree of Christ Church is clearly traceable through Magdalen and New College back to Merton. Wolsey at Magdalen had learnt to appreciate, in the most beautiful of all the homes of learning, something of the aims of the great school-master bishop, Waynflete. And Waynflete himself, can we doubt? had caught from Wykeham the enthusiasm for producing "rightly and nobly ordered minds and characters." At Oxford, at Winchester and at Windsor he had lived under the shadow of the great monuments of Wykeham's genius, and learned to discern "the true nature of the beautiful and graceful, the simplicity of beauty in style, harmony and grace." So that in the architecture of his college—and Architecture, as Plato tells us, as all the other Arts, is full of grace and harmony, which are the two sisters of goodness and virtue—he was enabled to fulfil the Platonic ideal and to provide the youth whom he desired to benefit with a home where they might dwell "in a land of health and fair sights and sounds, and receive the good in everything, and where beauty, the effluence of fair works, might flow into the eye and ear like a health-giving breeze from a purer region, and insensibly draw the soul from earliest years into likeness and sympathy with the beauty of reason." Inspired by such examples, Wolsey set himself to build a college which should eclipse them,

"Though unfinished, yet so famous,
So excellent in art and yet so rising,
That Christendom shall ever speak his virtue."

Indeed, says Fuller, nothing mean could enter into this man's mind.

Immense as were his private resources, they could not bear the strain of his magnificent plans. He therefore seized upon the idea of appropriating the property of the regular clergy and applying it to the foundation and endowment of Cardinal's College. The time was ripe for some such conversion. Monasticism was outworn. Whatever the merits of some few monasteries might be, whatever the piety of an occasional Abbot Samson, or the popularity of a monkish institution which did its duty of charity and instruction in this or that part of the country, the monks as a rule had ceased to live up to their original standard. They had accumulated wealth and lost their hold on the people. And where they were popular, it was in many cases with the people they had pauperised. To a statesman with so keen an insight and so broad a mind as Wolsey, it must have seemed both wise and safe to take this opportunity of suppressing some of the English priories. Had not Chicheley, when the alien priories had been suppressed on political grounds, secured some of their lands for the endowment of his foundation, All Souls' College?

His first step was to obtain a bull from the Pope and the assent of the King, authorising him (1524) to suppress the Priory of S. Frideswide and transfer the canons to other houses of the Augustinian order. Their house and revenues, amounting to nearly £300, were assigned to the proposed college of secular clerks. The scale of that college is indicated by the fact that it was to consist of a dean and sixty canons, forty canons of inferior rank, besides thirteen chaplains, twelve lay clerks, sixteen choristers and a teacher of music, for the service of the Church. Six public professors were to be appointed in connection with the college.

A few months later another bull, which premised that divine service could not be properly maintained in monasteries which contained less than seven professed members, empowered Wolsey to suppress any number of such small religious houses all over the country. This he proceeded to do, and to transfer the inmates to other monasteries. Their revenues, to an amount not exceeding 3000 golden ducats, were to be devoted to the new college.

The plan of thus concentrating the resources of the small and scattered religious houses was both economical and statesmanlike. But, in its execution, it gave rise to fear and irritation, of which Wolsey's political enemies were quick to avail themselves. The perturbation of the monks is well expressed in Fuller's happy metaphor:

"His proceedings made all the forest of religious foundations in England to shake, justly fearing the King would finish to fell the oaks, seeing the Cardinal began to cut the underwood."

Wolsey found it necessary to write to his royal master more than once to contradict the mis-representations of his opponents. The King had been informed that monks and abbots had been turned out to starve. Wolsey declared that what he had done was "to the full satisfaction, recompense and joyous contentation" of all concerned. The King complained that some of the monasteries would not contribute to his necessities as much as they had contributed to the Cardinal's scheme. Wolsey replied that he had indeed received "from divers mine old lovers and friends right loving and favourable aids towards the edifying of my said College," but added that these had been justly obtained and exaggerated in amount. But he promised in future to take nothing from any religious person.

Meantime he had set about building Cardinal's College with extraordinary energy and on an enormous scale. The foundation stone was laid on 15th July 1525. Whilst the Chapter-house and refectory of the old monastery were kept, the western bays of the church were removed to make way for the great quadrangle. The Chapel of S. Michael at South Gate was demolished, and part of the old town wall was thrown down. Room was thus made for the buildings on the south side of the quadrangle. These, the first portion of the college to be finished, were the kitchen and that hall which, in its practical and stately magnificence, can scarcely be equalled in England or surpassed in Europe. But the fact that it was the kitchen and dining-room which first reached completion gave an opportunity to the wits.

"Egregium opus. Cardinalis iste instituit Collegium, et absolvit popinam."

So runs one epigram, which being freely translated is:

"The Mountains were in labour once, and forth there came a mouse;— Your Cardinal a College planned, and built an eating-house!"

It was part of Wolsey's design to gather into his college all the rising intellect of Europe. In pursuance of this plan, he induced certain scholars from Cambridge to migrate thither. But they it was, so men afterwards complained, who first introduced the taint of heresy into Oxford. For at first the University was as strictly orthodox as her powerful patron, who hated "the Hellish Lutherans," could wish. When Martin Luther (1517) nailed his ninety-five theses on the church door of Wittenberg, in protest against what Erasmus had called "the crime of false pardons," the sale of indulgences, his protest found no echo here. On the contrary, the masters in convocation gladly elected three representative theologians who attended Wolsey's conference in London, and condemned the noxious doctrines of the German reformer. A committee of theologians was also held at Oxford, and their condemnation of Luther's teaching won the warm approval of the University. But the leaven of Lutheranism had already been introduced. The Cambridge students whom Wolsey had brought to be canons of Cardinal College, began to hold secret meetings and to disseminate Lutheran treatises. They made proselytes; they grew bolder, and nailed upon the church doors at nights some famous "libels and bills."

Archbishop Warham presently found himself obliged to take notice of the growing sect. He wrote to Wolsey invoking his aid,

"that the captains of the said erroneous doctrines be punished to the fearful example of all other. One or two cankered members," he explains, "have induced no small number of young and incircumspect fools to give ear unto them," and he proposes that the Cardinal should give "in commission to some sad father which was brought up in the University to sit and examine them."

Active measures were now taken to stamp out the heresy in Oxford. Wolsey ordered the arrest of a certain Thomas Garret of Magdalen, a pernicious heretic who had been busy selling Tyndale's Bible and the German reformer's treatises, not only to Oxford students, but even to the Abbot of Reading. His friends managed to get him safely out of Oxford, but for some reason or other he returned after three days. The same night he was arrested in bed in the house of one Radley, a singing-man, where it was well known that the little Lutheran community was wont to meet. Garret was not detained in Bocardo, but in a cellar underneath the lodgings of the commissary, Dr Cottisford, Rector of Lincoln. Whilst the commissary was at evensong he managed to escape, and made his way to the rooms of Anthony Dalaber, one of the "brotherhood," at Gloucester College. Dalaber has left an account—it is a most tearful tale—of the events which ensued. He had previously had some share in getting Garret away from Oxford, and was greatly surprised to see him back. He provided him with a coat in place of his tell-tale gown and hood, and sent him off with tears and prayers to Wales, whence he hoped to escape to Germany. After reading the tenth chapter of S. Matthew's Gospel with many a deep sigh and salt tear, Dalaber went to Cardinal College to give Master Clarke, a leading brother, notice of what had occurred. On his way he met William Eden, a fellow of Magdalen, who with a pitiful countenance explained to him that they were all undone. Dalaber was able to give him the joyful news of Garret's escape, and proceeded to S. Frideswide's.

"Evensong," he says, "was begun, and the Dean and the other Canons were there in their grey amices; they were almost at Magnificat before I came thither. I stood at the Choir door and heard Master Taverner play, and others of the Chapel there sing, with and among whom I myself was wont to sing also. But now my singing and music were turned into sighing and musing. As I thus and there stood, in cometh Dr Cottysford, as fast as ever he could go, bareheaded, as pale as ashes—I knew his grief well enough, and to the Dean he goeth into the Choir, where he was sitting in his stall, and talked with him very sorrowfully." Dalaber describes the interview which followed, outside the choir, between these two and Dr London, the Warden of New College, "puffing, blustering and blowing, like a hungry and greedy lion seeking his prey." The commissary was so much blamed, that he wept for sorrow. Spies were sent out in every direction; and when Dalaber returned to his rooms next morning, he found that they had been thoroughly searched. He had spent the night with the "brethren," supping at Corpus ("at which supper we were not very merry"), sleeping at S. Alban Hall, consulting together and praying for the wisdom of the serpent, and the harmlessness of the dove. This request would appear to have been in some measure vouchsafed to him, for, when he was interrogated by the prior as to his own movements and those of Garret, he was enabled to furnish forth a tale full of circumstantial detail but wholly untrue. "This tale," he observes, "I thought meetest, but it was nothing so." Although it were nothing so, he repeated his convincing narrative on oath, when he was examined at Lincoln College by Cottisford, Higdon (Dean of Cardinal's College) and London. He had sworn on a great Mass book laid before him to answer truly, but, as he complacently observes, "in my heart nothing so meant to do." Nor, perhaps, did he mean to betray twenty-two of his associates, and the storehouse of Garret's books, when examined by Dr London, whom he calls the "rankest, papistical Pharisee of them all"—at any rate he omits to mention the fact in his narrative.

Of Garret himself, however, no trace could be found; and the commissary, being "in extreme pensyfness," consulted an astrologer, who made a figure for him, and told him, with all the cheerful certainty of an eastern astrologer in these days, that Garret, having fled south-eastward in a tawny coat, was at that time in London, on his way to the sea-side. Consulting the stars was strictly forbidden by the Catholic Church, but the Warden of New College, though a Doctor of Divinity, was not ashamed to inform the bishop of the astrologer's saying, or afraid to ask him to inform the Cardinal, Archbishop of York, concerning it. Luckily for him the commissary did not rely wholly on the information either of Dalaber or the astrologer. The more practical method of watching the seaport towns resulted a few days later in Garret's recapture near Bristol. Many of the Oxford brotherhood were also imprisoned and excommunicated. Garret, who had written a piteous letter to Wolsey, praying for release, not from the iron bonds which he said he justly deserved, but from the more terrible bonds of excommunication, and who had also made a formal recantation of all his heresies, was allowed to escape. But first he took part in a procession, in which most of the other prisoners also appeared, carrying faggots from S. Mary's Church to S. Frideswide's, and on the way casting into a bonfire made at Carfax for the purpose certain books which had most likely formed part of Garret's stock.

At least three of the prisoners, however, died in prison without having been readmitted to Communion, either from the sweating sickness then raging, or, as Foxe asserts, from the hardships they endured. For they were kept, he says, for nearly six months in a deep cave under the ground, on a diet of salt fish. By Higdon's orders they did at least receive a Christian burial.

The heretics were crushed in Oxford, but elsewhere the movement grew apace. The printing press scattered wide-cast books and pamphlets which openly attacked the corruption of the Church and the monastic orders. Henry determined to proscribe all books that savoured of heresy. A joint committee of Oxford and Cambridge theologians was summoned to meet in London. They examined and condemned the suspected books which were submitted to them. The publication of English treatises upon Holy Scripture without ecclesiastical sanction was forbidden by royal proclamation. Versions of the Bible in the vulgar tongue were at the same time proscribed.

Yet this orthodox king, to whom as "Defender of the Faith," Leo X. had sent a sword still preserved in the Ashmolean, was on the brink of a breach with Rome. For Henry, with his curious mania for matrimony, had determined to marry Anne Boleyn, but he failed to obtain from the Papal Legates in England a decree for the dissolution of his marriage. It was a failure fraught with enormous consequences. The fortunes of Oxford were involved in it. The King gladly availed himself of the suggestion of a Cambridge scholar, Thomas Cranmer, that the Universities should be called on for their judgment. They were thus placed in a position analogous to that of an œcumenical council with power to control a pontifical decree. For the Pope's predecessor had granted a dispensation for Henry's marriage with Catherine, his brother's wife. Every learned man in Europe, but for bribery or threats, would have condemned Henry's cause on its merits. But it was evident that the question would not be decided on its merits.

From a packed commission at Cambridge a decision favourable to a divorce was with difficulty extorted; but even so it was qualified by an important reservation. The marriage was declared illegal, if it could be proved that Catherine's marriage with Prince Arthur had been consummated. Cambridge was praised by the King for her "wisdom and good conveyance." Yet that reservation, if the testimony of the Queen herself was to go for anything, amounted to a conclusion against the divorce.

It was not expected that a favourable verdict would be obtained so easily from Oxford. At the end of his first letter, in which the King called upon the University to declare their minds "sincerely and truly without any abuse," a very plain threat is added, which left no doubt as to the royal view of what could be considered "sincere and true":

"And in case ye do not uprightly according to divine learning handle yourselves herein, ye may be assured that we, not without great cause, shall so quickly and sharply look to your unnatural misdemeanour therein that it shall not be to your quietness and ease hereafter."

It was proposed that the question should be referred to a packed committee. But the Masters of Arts refused to entrust the matter wholly to the Faculty of Theology. They claimed to nominate a certain number of delegates. Their attitude provoked sharp reproval and further threats from the imperious monarch.

The youths of the University were warned not to play masters, or they would soon learn that "it is not good to stir up a hornets' nest."

Persuasion was used by the Archbishop and the Bishop of Lincoln. The example of Paris and Cambridge was quoted. The aid of Dr Foxe, who had proved his skill by obtaining the decree at Cambridge, was called in. Learned arguments were provided by Nicholas de Burgo, an Italian friar. But there was no doubt about the popular feeling on the question. Pieces of hemp and rough drawings of gallows were affixed to the gate of the bishop's lodging; both he and Father Nicholas were pelted with stones in the open street; the women of Oxford supported Catherine with such vehemence, that thirty of them had to be shut up in Bocardo. The King had dispatched two of his courtiers to Oxford: the Duke of Suffolk and Sir William Fitzwilliam. The former imprisoned the women; the latter distributed money to the more venal of the graduates. "No indifferency was used in the whole matter."

Threats and bribes at last prevailed. A committee carefully packed was appointed with power to decide in the name of the University. A verdict was obtained which corresponded to the Cambridge decree. The important reservation, "if the marriage had been consummated," was added to the decision that marriage with the widow of a deceased brother was contrary to the divine and human law.

Cranmer, who had succeeded Warham as Archbishop of Canterbury, pronounced the King's marriage with Catherine null and void. In the following year the University was asked to concur in the foregone decision in favour of separation from Rome. The authority of the Pope in England was abolished, and the monasteries were rendered liable to visitation by commission under the Great Seal. The Act of Supremacy followed. Bishop Fisher and Sir Thomas More were executed for denying the royal supremacy, and Thomas Cromwell was appointed Vicar-General of England.

His failure to procure a decree invalidating Henry's marriage meant the downfall of Wolsey. His downfall involved the fortunes of his college. It was rumoured at once that the buildings were to be demolished, because they bore at every prominent point escutcheons carved with the arms of the proud Cardinal. Wolsey had "gathered into his College whatsoever excellent thing there was in the whole realm." The rich vestments and ornaments with which he had furnished S. Frideswide's Church were quickly "disposed" by the King. The disposal of this and other property, lands, offices, plate and tapestries forfeited under the statute of Praemunire, and carefully catalogued for his royal master by the fallen minister, had obvious pecuniary advantages. And as in London, York Place, the palace which the Cardinal had occupied and rebuilt as Archbishop of York, was confiscated and its name changed to Whitehall; so, when "bluff Harry broke into the spence," he converted Cardinal's College into "King Henry VIII.'s College at Oxford" consisting of a dean and twelve canons only (1532).

Henry had been besought to be gracious to the college; but he replied that it deserved no favour at his hands, for most of its members had opposed his wishes in the matter of the divorce. The prospect of the dissolution of his college at Oxford, foreshadowed by that of his great foundation at Ipswich, caused Wolsey infinite sorrow. To Thomas Cromwell he wrote that he could not sleep for the thought of it, and could not write unto him for weeping and sorrow. He appealed with all the passion of despair to the King and those in power, that the "sharpness and rigour of the law should not be visited upon these poor innocents." In response to a petition from the whole college, Henry replied that he would not dissolve it entirely. He intended, he said, to have an honourable college there,

"but not so great or of such magnificence as my Lord Cardinal intended to have, for it is not thought meet for the common weal of our realm. Yet we will have a College honourably to maintain the service of God and literature."

The purely ecclesiastical foundation of 1532 was not calculated to maintain the service of literature. It was surrendered twelve years afterwards to the King, whose commissioners received on the same day the surrender of the Cathedral Church of Christ and the Blessed Virgin Mary at Osney, the new cathedral body formed at the ancient abbey upon the creation of the see and diocese of Oxford (1542). The way was thus cleared for the final arrangement by which (4th November 1546) the episcopal see was transferred from Osney and united with the collegiate corporation under the title it bears to-day, Ecclesia Christi Cathedralis Oxon; ex fundatione Regis Henrici Octavi. Thus S. Frideswide's Church became the Cathedral Church of Christ in Oxford, and also the chapel of the college now at last called Christ Church. The foundation now consisted of a dean, eight canons, eight chaplains, sixty scholars and forty children, besides an organist, singing men, servants and almsmen. It was still, then, a foundation of extraordinary magnificence.

Yet there were not wanting "greedy wretches to gape after the lands belonging to the Colleges." They urged Henry to treat them as he had treated the monasteries. But the King refused.

"Ah, sirrah," he replied to one, "I perceive the Abbey lands have fleshed you, and set your teeth on edge, to ask also those Colleges. And wheras we had a regard only to pull down sin by defacing the monasteries, you have a desire also to overthrow all goodness by subversion of Colleges. I tell you, sirs, that I judge no land in England better bestowed than that which is given to our Universities; for by their maintenance our realm shall be well governed when we be dead and rotten.... I love not learning so ill that I will impair the revenues of any one house by a penny, wherby it may be upholden."

Henry, in fact, may be credited with a genuine desire for the promotion of learning. He had, besides, no reason to quarrel with the University. It had proved subservient to his will; the colleges were nurseries of the secular clergy, who adopted the new order of things. They could not be regarded like the monks, as mercenaries of a foreign and hostile power.

But academic enthusiasm was not to be promoted by the despotic methods of Henry. The arbitrary restrictions of the Six Articles, "that sure touchstone of a man's conscience," struck at the root of intellectual liberty. The revival of academic life which had resulted from the stimulus of the Catholic Renaissance, was suddenly and severely checked by the early developments of the Reformation. The monasteries had been dissolved, and the poor students whom they had supported trudged a-begging. Another outbreak of plague helped to increase the depopulation of the University. The town suffered severely from both causes. The halls and hostels stood empty; very few degrees were taken. Religious controversy usurped the place of education. The University became a centre of politics and ecclesiasticism. The schools were deserted or occupied by laundresses; and, whilst commissioners were busy applying tests, expelling honest fellows, destroying MSS. and smashing organs, men began to discover that, through the invention of printing, it had become possible for them to educate themselves. They no longer needed to go to a monastery or college library to obtain a book; teaching needed no longer to be merely oral. The multiplication of books decentralised learning. With the monopoly of manuscripts and the universality of Latin were taken almost at a moment's notice two of the chief assets of mediæval Universities. A man might now read what he liked, and where he liked, instead of being obliged to listen to a master in the schools teaching set subjects that did not interest him. And no "test" was required of the independent reader. No wonder that, as one preacher dismally exclaimed, the Wells of Learning, Oxford and Cambridge, were dried up.

The King had taken the charters of both University and town into his own hands in 1530. He did not restore them till 1543. Two years later Parliament made over all colleges and chantries to the King, "who gave them very good counsel." Meanwhile, in 1535, a Visitation of the University had been held. Dr London and Richard Layton were the chief Visitors. Their object was to establish ecclesiastical conformity, to supplant the old scholastic teaching and to promote classical learning. They confirmed the public lectures in Greek and Latin which they found, and established others, at Magdalen, New College, and C.C.C., and they settled other lectures of the kind at Merton and Queen's. The other colleges, they found, could not afford to have such lectures, and accordingly they directed the students of these to attend the courses at the others daily. The study of Aristotle and the Holy Scriptures was enjoined, and the King founded Regius Professorships in Divinity, Hebrew, Greek, Medicine and Civil Law. The University meantime was rewarded for its compliance by being exempted from the payment of tithes. At the same time the professors of the Old Learning were ousted from the academic chairs. Duns Scotus was dragged from his pedestal with an ignominy which recalled the fate of Sejanus.

"We have set Duns in Bocardo," wrote Layton, "and have utterly banished him Oxford for ever with all his blind glosses.... The second time we came to New College, after we had declared your injunctions we found all the great Quadrant Court full of the leaves of Dunse, the wind blowing them into every corner. And there we found one Mr. Greenfield, a gentleman of Buckinghamshire gathering up part of the same book leaves, as he said, to make him sewells or blawnshers to keep the deer within his wood, therby to have the better cry with his hounds."

That day the downfall of scholasticism in England was at last complete.

During the minority of Edward VI. "there was great expectation in the University what religion would be professed." It was soon evident which way the wind was to blow. Young men began to "protest" in Magdalen Chapel. In 1548 the Protector Somerset and Cranmer determined to reform the University in the interests of the new Anglican Church. Theologians were invited from the Continent, and in default of Melancthon, Peter Martyr arrived and lectured in the Divinity Schools on the Epistles of S. Paul and the Eucharist. His teaching roused protest from the Roman Catholics, and polemical divinity, if no other study, flourished for a while in Oxford. But a commission was now appointed with large powers, which proceeded to draw up a code of statutes calculated to eliminate all popery from the constitution of the University. These "Edwardine statutes," as they were called, remained nominally in force till the "Laudian" statutes replaced them.

The commissioners dealt severely with the colleges. Many of the fellows who had opposed the Reformation fled forthwith; others they ejected and replaced by rigid Calvinists. "All things," the Roman Catholics thought, "were turned topsy turvy." The disciplinary injunctions and acts of the commissioners were wholly admirable. Unfortunately their fanaticism in other directions was of the deplorably iconoclastic sort.

The ancient libraries were rifled; many MSS., guilty of no other superstition than red letters in their titles, were condemned to the fire. "Treatises on scholastical divinity were let loose from their chains and given away or sold to mechanics for servile uses, whilst those wherein angles or mathematical diagrams appeared were destroyed because accounted Popish or diabolical or both." The works of the schoolmen were carried about the city "by certain rude young men" on biers and finally burnt in the market-place, a proceeding which they styled the funeral of Scotus and Scotists. Some of the books from monasteries were sold at this time to grocers and soapsellers, and some by shiploads to bookbinders abroad, "to the wondering of foreign nations," says Bale.

From wall and window, the order had gone forth giving sanction to the popular movement, every picture, every image commemorating saint or prophet or apostle was to be extirpated. Painted glass, as at New College, survives to show that the order was imperfectly obeyed. But everywhere the statues crashed from their niches, rood and rood-loft were laid low and the sun-light stared in white and stainless on the whitened aisles. At Magdalen the high altar and various images and paintings were destroyed, the organ burnt and the vestments sold. At Christ Church the dean and chapter decided that all altars, statues, images, tabernacles, missals and other matters of superstition and idolatry should be removed out of the Cathedral; and the other colleges and churches followed this example.

The magnificent reredos in the chapel of All Souls', of which the present work is a conjectural restoration, was smashed; most of the stained glass there was broken, and the altars were removed together with "the thing they call an organ."

The Edwardine commissioners proposed to abolish the grammar schools founded in connection with the colleges. The city, however, immediately petitioned the King on behalf of the schools:

"Where your poor orators have always had received and enjoyed by the means of your Colleges founded by your grace's most noble progenitor's singular treasure, help & commodity for the education of their sons, and especially the more part of us being not otherwise able to bring up our children in good learning and to find them at grammar.... There be in danger to be cast out of some college thirty, some other forty or fifty, some other more or fewer, & the most part of them children of your poor orators, having of the said college meat, drink, cloth & lodging & were verie well brought up in learning in the common grammar scoole at the College of S. Marie Magdalen, & so went forward & attained to logicke & other faculties at the charges of the said College & likewise of other houses and little or nothing at the charge of their parents, after their admission into any of the said colleges, wh. thing hath always heretofore been a great succour unto your said poor orators."

The petition was successful, though some schools were suppressed.

Magdalen College School, thus preserved, was intended by the founder to be to Magdalen what Winchester was to New College. It had been housed in his life-time in a building (1480), a picturesque fragment of which yet remains, in what is known as the Grammar Hall. The Grammar School buildings stood outside the west gate of the college, on the ground between the modern S. Swithun's buildings and the present "Grammar Hall," which belonged in part to this school building and in part (including the south portion and the little bell-tower) to other buildings that were added to it (1614). All these buildings, save the fragment that remains to be used as undergraduates' rooms, were removed in 1845 together with the houses that faced the gravel walk between them and Long Wall. The present school-room, facing the High, was erected shortly afterwards (Buckler), in the Perpendicular style, and recently (1894), across the bridge, on the site once occupied by Turrel's Hall, a handsome house for the master and fifty boarders has been built (Sir Arthur Blomfield). At the same time the ground by the river below the bridge was converted into gardens and a cricket ground for the choristers and schoolboys, a conversion which has greatly improved the aspect of the bridge.

CHAPTER VII

THE OXFORD MARTYRS

THE sufferings of the Protestants had failed to teach them the value of religious liberty. The use of the new liturgy was enforced by imprisonment, and the subscription to the Articles of Faith was demanded by royal authority from all the clergy and schoolmasters. The excesses of the Protestants led to a temporary but violent reaction.

The married priests were driven from their churches; the images were replaced, the new prayer book was set aside, the mass restored. Ridley and the others who had displaced the deposed bishops were expelled; Latimer and Cranmer were sent to the Tower. After the failure of Wyatt's rebellion and the defeat of the Protestants, Mary set herself to enforce the submission of England to the Pope.

With the restoration of the system of Henry VIII. the country was satisfied. But Mary was not content to stop there.

The statutes against heretics were revived. The bigotry of Mary knew no restraint. She ferreted out Protestants all over the country, and for three and a half years England experienced a persecution which was insignificant if judged by continental standards, but which has left an indelible impression on the minds of men. Nearly three hundred Protestants were burnt at the stake, and among them Latimer, Ridley and Cranmer—all Cambridge men—at Oxford.

The accession of Mary had caused much dismay in the hearts of the Protestants in that city. The Queen's proclamation as to religion on 18th August 1553, was followed two days after by letters to the Chancellors of Oxford and Cambridge enjoining the full observance of the ancient statutes. A special letter from the Queen was sent to Magdalen annulling the ordinances made contrary to the statutes since the death of Henry VIII. Prudent Protestants who had made themselves prominent in their colleges now wisely took leave of absence from Oxford. Peter Martyr left the country; and his place was soon afterwards taken by a Spanish friar from the court of Philip and Mary. Commissioners arrived, and were shocked to find that at Magdalen, for example, there was no priest to say mass, and no fellow who would hear it; there was no boy to respond, no altar and no vestments. Visitors were sent by Stephen Gardiner to New College, Magdalen and C.C.C. Many fellows were ejected, and mass was restored.

The work of death had now begun. Thomas Cranmer, Archbishop of Canterbury, Nicholas Ridley, Bishop of London, and Hugh Latimer, Bishop of Worcester, were removed from the Tower in March and placed in the custody of the mayor and bailiffs of Oxford. For preparations had been made to examine them before a commission appointed from both the Universities. They were lodged at first in Bocardo, the town prison, now become, as Ridley observed, "a very

College of Quondams." Shortly afterwards Ridley was removed to the house of an alderman, and Latimer elsewhere, in order that they might not confer together. Presently

"a solemn Convocation was held in S. Mary's Chancel concerning the business forthwith to be taken in hand; which being concluded all the Doctors and Masters went in a solemn procession to Carfax and thence to Christ Church, where they heard Divine service, and so they went to dinner;[33] afterwards they with some others, in number thirty-three, that were to dispute with the Bishops, met in Our Lady's Chapel on the North side of S. Mary's Church, and thence going into the Chancel, placed themselves in a semi-circle by the High Altar."

To support the platform where they sat the finials of the stalls are said to have been then levelled. "Soon after was brought in Cranmer (with a great number of rusty billmen), then Ridley, and last of all Latimer, to subscribe to certain articles then proposed. They all denied them."

On Monday, the 16th April, the Vice-Chancellor and proctors met at Exeter College and thence went to the Divinity School, there to dispute with the bishops on the nature of the Eucharist. The Oxford and Cambridge doctors took their places, and the Moderator of the schools presided in his lofty chair. Cranmer was brought in and set opposite to the latter in the respondent's place. By his side was the mayor of the city, in whose charge he was. Next day it was Ridley's turn, and on the third Latimer's. So the solemn farce of the disputations, punctuated by "opprobrious checks and reviling taunts," was gone through; the bishops were pronounced no members of the Church, Cranmer was returned to Bocardo, Ridley taken to the sheriff's house and Latimer to the bailiff's. The judicial sentence followed the academical judgment.

In September 1555 a commission was sent down from London, and sat in the Divinity School. The two bishops had looked death steadily in the face for two years, expecting it every day or hour. It was now come. Ridley was urged to recant, but this he firmly refused to do or to acknowledge by word or gesture "the usurped supremacy of Rome." His cap, which he refused to remove at the mention of the Cardinals and the Pope, was forcibly taken off by a beadle. Latimer when examined was equally firm. He appeared

"with a kerchief on his head and upon it a night cap or two and a great cap such as townsmen use, with two broad flaps to button under the chin, wearing an old threadbare Bristol frieze gown, girded to his body with a penny leather girdle, at the which hanged by a long string of leather his Testament and his spectacles without a case, depending about his neck upon his breast."

Bread was bread, the aged bishop boldly declared when asked for his views on transubstantiation, and wine was wine; there was a change in the Sacrament it was true, but the change was not in the nature but the dignity.

The two Protestants were reprieved for the day and summoned to appear next morning at eight o'clock in S. Mary's Church. There, after further examination, the sentence of condemnation was pronounced upon them as heretics obstinate and incurable. And on 16th October the sentence was fulfilled.

Ridley and Latimer were led out to be burnt, whilst Cranmer, whose execution had been delayed, since it required the sanction of Rome, remained in Bocardo, and ascending to the top of the prison house, or, as an old print represents it, to the top of S. Michael's Tower, kneeled down and prayed to God to strengthen them.

On the evening of the 15th there had been a supper at the house of Irish, the mayor, whose wife was a bigoted and fanatical Catholic. Ridley, as we have seen, was in their charge, and the members of his family were permitted to be present. He talked cheerfully of his approaching "marriage"; his brother-in-law promised to be in attendance and, if possible, to bring with him his wife, Ridley's sister. Even the hard eyes of Mrs Irish softened to tears as she listened and thought of what was coming. The brother-in-law offered to sit up through the night, but Ridley said there was no occasion; he "minded to go to bed and sleep as quietly as ever he did in his life." In the morning he wrote a letter to the Queen. As Bishop of London he had granted renewals of certain leases on which he had received fines. Bonnor had refused to recognise them; and he entreated the Queen, for Christ's sake, either that the leases should be allowed, or that some portion of his own confiscated property might be applied to the repayment of the tenants. The letter was long; by the time it was finished the sheriff's officers were probably in readiness.

Bocardo, the prison over the North Gate, spanned the road from the ancient tower of S. Michael's, and commanded the approach to Broad Street. Thither, to a place over against Balliol College, "those special and singular captains and principal pillars of Christ's church" were now led. The frontage of Balliol was then much further back than it is now; beyond it lay open country, before it, under the town wall, ran the water of the tower-ditch. Some years ago a stake with ashes round it was found on the site which is marked by a metal cross in the roadway, at the foot of the first electric lamp, as the site of the martyrs' death.[34] To this spot then came the two bishops.

Lord Williams of Thame was on the spot by the Queen's order; and the city guard was under arms to prevent disturbance. Ridley appeared first. He wore "a fair black gown furred and faced with foins, such as he was wont to wear being Bishop, and a tippet of velvet furs likewise about his neck, a velvet nightcap upon his head and a corner cap upon the same, going in a pair of slippers to the stake."

He walked between the mayor and aldermen, and Master Latimer followed him in the same shabby attire as that which he had worn on the occasion of his examination. As they passed towards Bocardo they looked up in the hope of seeing Cranmer at the little glass window. It was from this window[35] that the Bocardo

prisoners used to let down an old hat and cry, "Pity the Bocardo Birds." For prisoners in those days depended for their daily sustenance on the charity of strangers, even as the prisoners in Portugal or Morocco do to-day, and "Bread and meat for the prisoners" was a well-known cry in the London streets. The Parisian version was, "Aux prisonniers du Palais." Cranmer's attention at this moment was engrossed by a Spanish friar, who was busy improving the occasion, and the martyr could not see him. But Ridley spied Latimer hobbling after him. "Oh, be ye there?" he exclaimed. "Yea," answered the old man. "Have after as fast as I can follow!" When he reached the stake Ridley ran to Latimer, "and with a wondrous cheerful look embraced and kissed him" and comforted him, saying, "Be of good heart, brother, for God will either assuage the fury of the flame, or else strengthen us to abide it." With that he went to the stake, kneeled down by it, kissed it and effectually prayed, and behind him Master Latimer kneeled, as earnestly calling upon God as he.

The martyrs had now to listen to a sermon from Dr Smith, who denounced them as heretics, and exhorted them to recant. The Lord Williams of Thame, the Vice-Chancellor and other commissioners sat upon a form close at hand. The martyrs asked leave of them to reply, but the bailiffs and the Vice-Chancellor ran up to Ridley and stopped his mouth with their hands. The martyrs now commended their souls and their cause to God, and stripped themselves for the stake, Ridley giving away to the eager crowd his garments, dials, napkins and nutmegs, whilst some plucked the points off his hose; "happy was he that might get any rag of him." They were chained to the stakes, and gunpowder was hung about their necks, thanks to the humane care of Ridley's brother-in-law. Then men brought a faggot kindled with fire, and laid the same down at Dr Ridley's feet, to whom Master Latimer spake in this manner:

'Be of good comfort, Master Ridley, and play the man. We shall this day light such a candle, by God's grace, in England, as I trust shall never be put out.'

Then Latimer crying aloud, "O Father of Heaven, receive my soul," bathed his hands in the flame that blazed up about him, and stroked his face. The powder exploded, and he "soon died with very little pain or none." Ridley was less fortunate, for the fire being lit beneath and the faggots heaped above, the flames burnt his legs slowly away, and did not ignite the gunpowder round his neck. Amid cries to heaven of "Lord, Lord, receive my soul," and "Lord have mercy upon me," he screamed in his agony to the bystanders to let the fire come unto him. His brother-in-law with awkward kindness threw on more wood, which only kept down the flame. It was not till the lower part of his body had been burned away that he fell over, "and when the flame touched the gunpowder he was seen to stir no more."

The lot of Cranmer was still more pathetic, and made a yet deeper impression upon the popular mind. He, like the others, had been examined in S. Mary's (7th September 1555). He had appeared, clad in a fair black gown with his hood on his shoulders, such as Doctors of Divinity used to wear, and in his hand was a white staff. The aged Archbishop confronted there the Pope's Legate, who sat on a raised dais ten feet high, with cloth of state, very richly and sumptuously adorned, at the east end of the church. Summoned to answer to a charge of blasphemy, incontinency and heresy, he refused as firmly as the others to recognise the authority of the Bishop of Rome within this kingdom.

"I protest," he said, "I am no traitor. I have made an oath to the King and I must obey the King by God's law. By the Scripture the King is chief and no foreign person in his own realm above him. The Pope is contrary to the Crown. I cannot obey both, for no man can serve two masters at once. You attribute the keys to the Pope and the sword to the King. I say the King hath both."

Before further proceedings were taken against the Archbishop, it was necessary to obtain sanction of the Pope. It was not till the middle of the following February that the Papal breve arrived and a new commission came down to Oxford. Sitting before the high altar in the choir of Christ Church, Thirlby and Bonnor announced that Cranmer had been tried at Rome, where, according to the preamble of the Papal sentence, he had been allowed every opportunity to answer for himself. "O Lord!" commented Cranmer, "what lies be these!" They were directed, the commissioners continued, to degrade him, excommunicate him and deliver him up to the secular power. The form of degradation was begun when Cranmer appealed to the next Free General Council. The appeal was refused; the degradation was continued. Cranmer was stripped of his vestments, his hair was shorn, the sacred unction scraped from his finger-tips, and he was then dressed in a poor yeoman-beadle's gown, full bare and nearly worn, and handed over to the secular power.

"Now are you lord no longer!" cried Bonnor when the ceremony was finished. "All this needed not," the Archbishop replied; "I myself had done with this gear long ago."

Cranmer had been three years in prison; he was an old man, and his nerve may well have been upset by the prolonged delay and fear of death and the recent degradation which he had undergone. There is no authentic account of what happened to him during the next few hours. But Protestant tradition relates that he was taken from the Cathedral to the Deanery of Christ Church, where he was entertained at his ease and exposed to the arguments and exhortations of Soto, the Spanish friar. He was warned at the same time that the Queen's mind was so set, that she would either have Cranmer a Catholic or else no Cranmer at all. He was taken back to his cell that night, and there his constancy at last gave way. He signed a series of recantations. But the Queen refused to relent; she had humiliated her enemy, and now he must die. She fixed the 25th of March for the day of his execution. But first he was called upon to make a public confession of his recantation. It was a foul and rainy day when he was brought out of Bocardo to S. Mary's Church. Peers, knights, doctors, students, priests, men-at-arms and citizens thronged the narrow aisles, and through their midst passed the mayor and next the aldermen in their place and degree; after them came Cranmer between two Spanish friars, who, on entering the church, chanted the *Nunc Dimittis*. A stage was set over against the pulpit—the ledge cut for it may still be seen in the pillar to the left of the Vice-Chancellor's chair—and here Cranmer was made to stand in his bare and ragged gown, and old square cap, whilst Dr Cole, the Warden of New College, preached his funeral sermon, and justified the sentence that had been passed, by which, even though he had recanted, he was condemned to die.

Cole gave this reason and that, and added that there were others which had moved the Queen and Council "which were not meet and convenient for every one to understand." He congratulated the Archbishop on his conversion, and promised him that a dirge should be sung for him in every church in Oxford. Finally, he called upon the whole congregation to kneel where they were and to pray for him. When the prayer was finished the preacher called upon the Archbishop to make the public confession of his faith. "Brethren," cried he, "lest any man should doubt of this man's earnest conversion and repentance, you shall hear him speak before you." But the spirit of revenge had overreached itself. Cranmer's enemies had hoped to humiliate him to the uttermost; instead, they gave him the opportunity of redeeming his fame and adding his name to the roll of martyrs.

"The tongues of dying men
Enforce attention, like deep harmony....
More are men's ends marked than their lives before."

To the astonishment of friends and foes alike, Cranmer stood up before the congregation, and chanted the palinode of his forsworn opinions; he recanted his recantation. Face to face with that cruel death, which in his weakness he had so desperately striven to avoid, he made the declaration of his true belief. "And now I come," he concluded, "to the great thing which so much troubleth my conscience, more than anything that ever I did or said in my whole life, and that is the setting abroad of a writing contrary to the truth; which now here I renounce and refuse as things written with my hand, contrary to the truth which I thought in my heart, and written for fear of death, and to save my life if it might be;... And forasmuch as my hand offended, writing contrary to my heart, my hand shall first be punished therefore; for, may I come to the fire, it shall be first burned. As for the Pope I utterly refuse him, as Christ's enemy and Anti-Christ, with all his false doctrine; and as for the Sacrament, I believe as I have taught in my book against the Bishop of Winchester."

So far he was allowed to proceed before, amidst the infuriated cries of his enemies, he was pulled down from the stage and borne away to the stake. "Priests who did rue to see him go so wickedly to his death, ran after him exhorting him, while time was, to remember himself." But Cranmer had remembered himself at last. He had done with recantations at the bidding of Spanish priests and "bloody" Bonnor. He approached the stake with a cheerful countenance, we are told, undressed in haste and stood upright in his shirt. The Spanish friars finding they could do nothing with him, exclaimed the one to the other, "Let us go from him, for the devil is in him." "Make short," cried Lord Williams, and "Recant, recant," cried others. The wood was kindled. "This was the hand that wrote it," Cranmer said, extending his right arm, "therefore it shall suffer first punishment." He held his hand so steadfast and immovable in the flame that all men might see it burned before his body was touched. And so holding it he never stirred nor cried till the fire reached him and he was dead.

A portrait of Cranmer hangs in the Bodleian. But the chief monument to the Protestant martyrs was raised in 1841. The Martyrs' Memorial in S. Giles', opposite the west front of Balliol College, was happily designed by Sir Gilbert Scott in imitation of the beautiful crosses which Edward I. raised in memory of Queen Eleanor. The statues of the martyrs are by Weekes. The north aisle of the neighbouring Church of S. Mary Magdalene was restored at the same time in memory of the same event.

Cranmer had atoned for his inconstancy, and crowned the martyrdoms of the English Reformation. From that moment the cause of Catholic reaction was hopeless. Cranmer's career had not been that of a saint or a martyr. He was a weak man with a legal rather than a religious cast of mind. Nothing in his life became him like the leaving of it. Others more constant to their belief, and more noble in character, had died at the stake. But the very weakness of the man and the pathos of the humiliation of one so highly placed, appealed to the crowd who could not rise to heights of unshaken constancy. More easily understood by the people than the triumphant cry of heroic sufferers like Latimer, the dramatic end of the Archbishop filled every independent mind with sympathetic dread. In vain did Mary heap rewards on the University. In vain did Cardinal Pole institute a fresh visitation, hunt all heretics from the University, burn in the common market-place all English Bibles and Protestant books that could be found. In vain did he revise the University and college statutes. His work was undone as soon as finished. The lesson of Cranmer's death had gone home to a thousand hearts. England refused to be a province of Spain and of Rome. The news of Mary's death was received in Oxford with the ringing of bells and other signs of discreet delight.

The Catholic Reaction is marked in Oxford history by the institution of two colleges, Trinity and S. John's, both founded on the sites of old monastic houses by wealthy citizens of London who were lovers of the old order and adherents of the old religion. In 1555 Sir Thomas Pope, a faithful servant of the Tudors, who had acquired large tracts of abbey lands in Oxfordshire, bought the site and vacant buildings of Durham College, which were then "mere dog-kennels," and the half of the grove which had not been included in the grant of S. Bernard's College to Christ Church. Here he founded the College of the Holy and Undivided Trinity, consisting of a president, twelve fellows and eight scholars. And in drawing up his statutes he availed himself of the advice both of Elizabeth and Cardinal Pole. The hall was completed in 1620. In 1665 the decay of the old Durham buildings made reconstruction imperative. Wren was the architect. He wished to build a long range in the upper part of the grove, but the quadrangular form was preferred; and he designed the garden quadrangle, a block in the Renaissance style which was spoilt by additions and alterations in 1802. The chapel (1691), which boasts some magnificent carving by Grinling Gibbons, is, in style, closely akin to the advanced palladian of Dean Aldrich's Church of All Saints. He certainly made some suggestions for it, and so did Wren. The President's house and New Buildings, by T. G. Jackson (1883), form, with the iron railings and old halls, including the old Perilous or Kettle Hall (1615), that face "the Broad," a new and handsome quadrangle.

It was in 1555, also, that Sir Thomas White, a rich merchant tailor who had twice been Lord Mayor of London, chose the site of the suppressed College of S. Bernard for his foundation, being guided thereto, as tradition asserts, by a dream which warned him to build near a place where there was a triple elm having three trunks issuing from one root. Between his college and the Merchant Taylors' School in London White established a connection similar to that between Winchester and New College. The treasure of ecclesiastical vestments preserved in the library, and the fact that Edmund Campion, the Jesuit poet and conspirator, after whom the new Jesuit Hall in Oxford is called, was the fellow chosen to preach the founder's funeral sermon, indicate the Roman Catholic sympathies of the institution. Yet it was an alumnus of this college, William Laud, whose body was laid in the chapel (1530), and whose ghost, it is said, still haunts the library he built and the quadrangle which owes its completion (1635) to his munificence, who fixed the University in its sympathy with the High Church party of the Anglican Church. The classical colonnades and the charming garden front, wherein Inigo Jones combined the Oxford Gothic with the style which he had recently learned to love in Italy, form a fitting background to the most perfect of Oxford gardens (1750).

CHAPTER VIII

ELIZABETH, BODLEY AND LAUD

THE University had declined sadly under Mary. Affairs were not at first greatly improved when Elizabeth ascended the throne. "Two religions," says Wood, "being now as it were on foot, divers of the chiefest of the University retired and absented themselves till they saw how affairs would proceed." It was not long, however, before Queen Elizabeth appointed a body of Visitors to "make a mild and gentle, not rigorous reformation." The Edwardine system was for the most part restored; the ejected fellows were brought back, whilst those who refused to comply with the new Act of Supremacy were expelled in their turn. Of these the largest number were New College men. The loss of these scholars did not improve the state of learning at Oxford. But in 1564 the Earl of Leicester became Chancellor, and it is in some part due to him that order was restored and a regular course of studies once more established.

Queen Elizabeth had been imprisoned at Woodstock during her sister's reign, and some of the needlework which she did when she was there is preserved at the Bodleian. The University had dispatched a deputation to her, with a present of gloves and a congratulatory address upon her accession; she now (31st August 1566) paid to Oxford a long-promised visit.

She was welcomed by a deputation from the University at Godstow Bridge and at Bocardo by the civic authorities, who there yielded up to her the city mace, and presented her with a gilt cup and forty pounds of gold. A Latin oration at the North Gate and a Greek oration at Carfax were delivered. The Queen thanked the orator in Greek, and was then escorted to Christ Church. For three days Disputations were held in the royal presence in S. Mary's Church. Elizabeth was a good scholar, one remembers, taught by Roger Ascham, and she really seems to have enjoyed this learned function. On the last day, at any rate, so keen was the argument and the Queen's interest in it, that the disputants "tired the sun with talking and sent him down the sky," so that the lights had to be lit in the church. At the end of the Disputations a Latin oration was delivered in praise of the Queen and her victories over the hosts of Spain and the Pope. "Tuis auspiciis," the peroration ran, "Hispania Anglum non vidit nisi victorem, Anglia Hispanum nisi captivum."

Loud cries of "Vivat Regina" resounded through the church. Elizabeth was pressed to reply. She pretended to hesitate, suggesting that the Spanish Ambassador, or Leicester, or Cecil should speak for her. The courtiers were wise enough to bow dissent. At length she rose, and her opening words contained a happy allusion to the growing darkness: "Qui male agit odit lucem"; "Dominus illuminatio mea," she might have added.

Some relaxation was provided for Her Majesty in the shape of Latin and English plays which were acted in Christ Church Hall "upon a large scaffold erected, set about with stately lights of wax variously wrought." The Latin play was entitled "Marcus Geminus and Progne"; the

English play "Palamon and Arcite," written by Mr Richard Edwards, and acted, we are told, with very great applause. "In the said play was acted a cry of hounds in the Quadrant upon the train of a fox in the hunting of Theseus, with which the young scholars who stood in the windows were so much taken, supposing it was real, that they cried out 'Now, now. There, there. He's caught! He's caught!' All which the Queen merrily beholding said 'O excellent! Those boys in very troth are ready to leap out of the window, to follow the hounds.'" The play, indeed, was considered to surpass "Damon and Pythias," than which they thought nothing could be better.

The acting of plays of this kind and in this manner at the Universities as at the Inns of Law on occasions of high festivity throws considerable light on the development of the Elizabethan drama. The University Wits, as they were called, began at this period to lay the foundations of English fiction in their "Tales"; the early English drama received its classical tone and form from them also. For John Lyly, George Peele, Thomas Lodge and others were Oxford men.

The Bohemian extravagance of the life of the "University Wits" in London will help us to understand why it was that Henry Savile, Warden of Merton (1586), the austere and accomplished scholar, could not abide wits. He preferred the plodding scholar, and used to say that if he wanted wits he would look for them in Newgate. Neither Wits nor their plays, which were often scurrilous enough, were acceptable to the Puritans, and within a few years both city and University began to restrict the performances of plays.

Queen Elizabeth bade farewell to Oxford on 6th September, and on that day the walls of S. Mary's, All Souls' and University were hung with innumerable copies of verses bemoaning her departure. By Magdalen College she took leave of the civic authorities; the University officials attended her to Shotover, and there, at the conclusion of a speech from the Provost of Oriel, "she gave him her hand to kiss, with many thanks to the whole University, speaking then these words, as 'tis reported, with her face towards Oxford. 'Farewell the worthy University of Oxford; Farewell my good subjects there; Farewell my dear scholars and pray God prosper your studies. Farewell. Farewell.'" No wonder she won universal homage by "her sweet, affable and noble carriage."

The name of Robert Dudley, Earl of Leicester, lover of Elizabeth, is inseparably connected with Oxford, not only by his chancellorship, but also by the fact that it is here that his ill-fated wife, Amy Robsart, is buried. She was found dead at the foot of the stairs in Cumnor Place. After the inquest her body was brought to Gloucester Hall, and lay there till it was buried with full heraldic ceremonial on 22nd September 1560 in the choir of S. Mary's Church. The funeral sermon was preached by one of Dudley's chaplains, who had just been transferred from the mastership of Balliol to the rectorship of Lincoln. He, fumbling for a phrase to express her violent death, "tripped once or twice by recommending to his auditors the virtues of that Lady, so pitifully *murdered*." But there is no evidence that Amy Robsart was murdered, with or without the connivance of Leicester. The story which Sir Walter Scott has used in "Kenilworth" is the baseless invention of political enemies. What happened to the unfortunate lady was either accident or suicide.

The influence of Leicester and the interest which as Chancellor he took in the University, is marked by various Acts which had an important effect upon the course of its development. In 1571 the Chancellor, masters and scholars received the right of perpetual succession, and were thus relieved of the necessity of obtaining a new charter from each succeeding king. In this year too an Act was passed, supplemented by further enactments in 1575, by which one-third part at least of the rents to be reserved in college leases is required to be payable in corn or in malt. The continual rise in prices which has resulted ever since from the increase, and therefore depreciation, of the precious metals, has thus only impoverished the colleges so far as rents were fixed in money, but corn having more or less kept its value, the one-third of the rents so wisely reserved came to exceed the remainder by far.

Leicester revived the practice of nominating the Vice-Chancellor, and by an Act of the University passed at his instigation (1569) a great step was taken in the direction of establishing the monopoly of the colleges in the government of the University. The preliminary deliberations of the Black Congregation, consisting of resident masters, were henceforth to be conducted by the Vice-Chancellor, Doctors, Heads of Houses and Proctors.

Leicester earned the reputation of being meddlesome, and he certainly used his position as Chancellor in the dispensing of patronage. But many of his reforms were statesmanlike, and his endeavours to raise the standard of discipline and learning were evidently genuine. One of his chief aims was to prevent the possibility of Romanising priests obtaining a foothold once more in the University. With this object he introduced among other provisions a test which was destined to have the most potent influence on the history of the place. Every student above sixteen years of age was now required to subscribe on his matriculation to the Thirty-nine Articles and the royal supremacy. Intended to exclude the Romanising party only, this rule affected in the future mainly the descendants of the Puritans who enacted it. Thenceforth, Mr Brodrick remarks, the University, once open to all Christendom, was narrowed into an exclusively Church of England institution and became the favourite arena of Anglican controversy, developing more and more that special character, at once worldly and clerical, which it shares with Cambridge alone among the Universities of Europe.

The country, meanwhile, was filled with the Jesuits' propaganda. There was Robert Parsons, for instance, who had been compelled to resign his fellowship at Balliol and had since joined the Society of Jesus. Disguised as a soldier and armed with a secret printing press, he wandered about the country disseminating Romanist literature. He finally brought off an extraordinary *coup* at Oxford. In a wood near Henley he printed copies of a tract by Campian, a fellow Jesuit, and on Commemoration Day (1580) every member of the University found a copy of it in his seat at S. Mary's when he came there to listen to the University sermon.

Proceedings against the Roman Catholics became more severe as the struggle continued. Fellows were ejected from colleges; priests were hung, drawn and quartered. In the reign of James I. George Napier of Corpus, a seminary priest convicted of high treason, was so treated, parts of his quartered body being set over the gates of the city and over the great gate of Christ Church. Puritan Oxford, however, was not distinguished for learning or discipline, in spite of Leicester's fatherly exhortations. For the Chancellor rated the University for its deficiency in sermonising and lecturing, its lack of religious instruction and education of youth. And as to discipline, he finds fault with the prevailing excess in apparel "as silk and velvet, and cut doublets, hose, deep ruffs and such like, like unto or rather exceeding both Inns of Court men and Courtiers." The streets, he complains, are more full of scholars than of townsmen, and the ordinary tables and ale-houses, grown to great number, are overcrowded day and night with scholars tippling, dicing, carding, tabling and perhaps worse. Ministers and deacons were presently solemnly forbidden to go into the field to play at football or to wear weapons to maintain any quarrel under penalty of expulsion. Plays acted by common stage players were forbidden, and scholars were not allowed, under pain of imprisonment, to sit on bulks or penniless bench or other open places, or to gad up and down the streets. Leicester, however, made a reservation in favour of the "Tragedies and Comedies used to be set forth by University men," and he himself was entertained (1585) at Christ Church and at Magdalen with pleasant comedies.

The students, indeed, had shown themselves so unruly that the affrays and riots of the Middle Ages seemed to have been revived. The times were unsettled. Not only were the Roman Catholics and the Calvinists at feud alike with each other and the moderate party of the Reformed Church, whom the Queen favoured, but the old quarrels between North and South and the Welsh broke out again. And the old disputes between the town and the University had been reopened by a series of orders put forth by the Privy Council in 1575 which were intended to settle them for ever.

The lack of discipline resulting from these causes is vividly brought before us by the attack made on the retinue of Lord Norreys by some scholars of Magdalen who wished to revenge themselves for the punishment inflicted on one of their number for stealing deer in Shotover forest. They were repulsed and "beaten down as far as S. Mary's"; but when Lord Norreys was leaving the town, the scholars

"went up privately to the top of their tower and sent down a shower of stones that they had picked up, upon him and his retinew, wounding some and endangering others of their lives. It is said that upon the foresight of this storm, divers had got boards, others tables on their heads, to keep them from it, and that if the Lord had not been in his coach or chariot he would certainly have been killed."

Some progress, one hopes, had been made in the restoration of order when Elizabeth paid her final visit "to behold the change and amendment of learning and manners that had been in her long absence made." She was received with the same ceremonies as before, but this time, at the Divinity Disputations in S. Mary's, she did not hesitate to send twice to a prosy bishop and bid him "cut it short." The fact was that she was anxious to make a Latin speech herself. But the bishop either could not or would not sacrifice his beloved periods, and the Queen was obliged to keep her speech for the Heads of Houses next morning. In the middle of her oration she noticed the old Lord Treasurer, Burleigh (Cecil), standing on his lame feet for want of a stool. "Whereupon she called in all haste for a stool for him, nor would she proceed in her speech till she saw him provided with one. Then fell she to it, as if there had been no interruption. Upon which one that knew he might be bold with her, told her, that she did it on purpose to show that she could interrupt her speech, unlike the Bishop, and not be put out." In her speech she, "the only great man in her kingdom," gave some very good advice to the University, and took the opportunity of rebuking the Romanising and the Puritan factions of the Church, counselling moderation on all sides.

On her departure she again expressed her love for the place. "Farewell, farewell, dear Oxford," she exclaimed as she viewed its towers and spires from the heights of Shotover. "God bless thee and increase thy sons in number, holiness and virtue!"

Some outward and visible signs there certainly were that the Queen's encouragement of learning and her policy of selecting for her service "eminent and hopeful students" had borne fruit. In 1571 Jesus College, the first of the Protestant colleges, had been founded by Hugh ap Rees, a Welsh Oxonian, at a time when the increase of grammar schools in Wales was likely to produce an influx of Welsh students into the University. The statutes were free from any local or national restriction, but Welshmen always predominated, and Jesus soon came to be regarded, in Wales, as the National College. Elizabeth figured as a nominal foundress; and the college, the front of which in Turl Street dates from her time, the rest being mainly seventeenth-century Gothic, possesses a famous portrait of her by Zucchero.

A still more noble memorial of Elizabethan times exists in Bodley, as the great library is called after its founder, "whose single work clouds the proud fame of the Egyptian Library and shames the tedious growth o' the wealthy Vatican."

Scarcely had the Duke of Gloucester's library been completed than it began to be depleted of its treasures. Three volumes only out of that splendid collection now remain in the Bodleian; one volume has found its way to Oriel College, another to Corpus Christi; six others may be seen at the British Museum. The rest had by this time been lost through the negligence of one generation or the ignorant fanaticism of another. For scholars borrowed books on insufficient pledges, and preferred to keep the former and sacrifice the latter. The Edwardine commissioners, as we have seen, appointed to reform the University, visited the libraries in the spirit of John Knox. All the books were destroyed or sold. In Convocation (1556) "venerable men" were chosen to sell the empty shelves and stalls, and to make a timber-yard of Duke Humphrey's treasure-house!

But the room remained; and it was destined, in its very emptiness and desolation, to work upon the imagination of one Thomas Bodley, an accomplished scholar, linguist and diplomatist, who believed with Bury that a "library of wisdom is more precious than all wealth."

Born at Exeter, he accompanied his father when he fled to Germany from the Papist persecutions. Whilst other Oxonian Protestants were "eating mice at Zurich," he studied at Geneva, learning Hebrew under Chevalerius, Greek under Constantinus, and Divinity under Calvin. Queen Mary being dead and religion changed, young Bodley was sent to Magdalen. There, he tells us, he took the degree of Bachelor of Arts (1563). In the following year he was admitted fellow of Merton College, where he gave public Greek lectures, without requiring any stipend. He was elected proctor in 1569, and was subsequently University orator and studied sundry Faculties. He next determined to travel, to learn modern languages and to increase his experience in the managing of affairs. He performed several important diplomatic missions with great ability and success. On his return from the Hague Burleigh marked him out for the Secretaryship, but grew jealous of the support he received from Essex. Bodley found himself unsuited for party intrigue and, weary of statecraft and diplomacy, decided to withdraw into private life.

But whilst refusing all subsequent offers of high office, he felt that he was called upon "to do the true part of a profitable member in the State." All his life, whether immersed in affairs of State at home or lying abroad for the good of his country, he had never forgotten that ruined library at Oxford. That there once had been one, he has to remind the University, was apparent by the room itself remaining.

"Whereupon, examining exactly for the rest of my life what course I might take, and having sought, as I thought, all the ways to the wood, to select the most proper, I concluded at the last to set up my staff at the Library door in Oxford."

He wrote accordingly, offering (1597-8) to restore the place at his own charge. The offer was gratefully accepted. Bodley had married a rich widow, and his "purse-ability" was such that he was able to bear the expense of repairing the room, collecting books and endowing the library: a work, says Casaubon, rather for a king than a private man. Two years were spent in fitting up the room and erecting its superb heraldic roof. The ceiling is divided into square compartments, on each of which are painted the arms of the University, the open Bible with seven seals (I Rev. v. I) between three ducal crowns, on the open pages of which are the words, so truly fitting for a Christian school: "Dominus Illuminatio mea."

On bosses which intervene between each compartment are painted the arms of Bodley himself.

Bodley now began to solicit his great store of honourable friends to present books to the library. His proposal was warmly supported by his countrymen in Devonshire, where, as a contemporary records, "every man bethought himself now how by some good book or other he might be written in the scroll of benefactors."

This scroll was the register which Bodley had provided for the enrolment of the names of all benefactors, with particulars of their gifts. It consists of two large folios, ornamented with silver-gilt bosses on their massy covers, which lie on a table of the great room.

Bodley's own donations were large, and he employed a London bookseller to travel on the Continent and collect books for the library. Besides numerous private benefactors like Lord Buckhurst and the Earl of Essex in the early years, the Stationers Company agreed to give Bodley a copy of every book which they published on condition that they might borrow the books thus given if needed for reprinting. This arrangement, in making which Bodley said he met with many rubs and delays, was the precursor of the obligation of the Copyright Acts, by which a copy of every book published has to be presented to the Bodleian and the British Museum. In 1603 Sir Walter Raleigh made a donation of fifty pounds, and he no doubt had some share in influencing the bestowal of many of the books which had once belonged to the library of Bishop Hieron. Ossorius, and were carried off from Faro in Portugal, when that town was captured by the English fleet under Essex. Raleigh, an Oriel man, was a captain in the squadron. The library was opened with full solemnity in 1603, and in the following year King James granted letters patent naming the library after its founder. That was an honour most richly deserved, for Bodley was "the first practically public library in Europe; the second, that of Angelo Rocca at Rome, being opened only in this same year."

To this library, two years later, James, the pedant, who seemed determined to prove that a learned king, too, could be a crowned ass, paid a visit. After making an excessively feeble pun anent the bust of the founder in the large room, which had been sent there by the Earl of Dorset, Chancellor of the University, he looked at the book shelves, and remarked that he had often had proof from the University of the fruits of talent and ability, but had never before seen the garden where those fruits grew, and whence they were gathered. He examined various MSS. and discoursed wisely on them; took up the treatise by Gaguinus entitled "De puritate conceptionis Virginis Mariæ," and remarked that the author had so written about purity, as if he wished that it should only be found on the title of his book. The opportunity of thus displaying his learning was so grateful to the King, that he was moved to an astonishing act of generosity. He offered to present from all the libraries of the royal palaces whatever precious and rare books Sir T. Bodley might choose to carry away. It does not appear that the number or importance of books so granted was in the event very great. Upon leaving the room the King exclaimed, probably with sincerity, that were he not King James he would be a University man; and that were it his fate at any time to be a captive, he would wish to be shut up, could he but have the choice, in this place as his prison, to be bound with its chains, and to consume his days among its books as his fellows in captivity.

To this library came James' ill-starred son, and here, it is said, he was tempted by Lord Falkland to consult the "Sortes Virgilianæ." The passage which first met his eye runs thus in Dryden's translation:

"Let him for succour sue from place to place
Torn from his subjects and his son's embrace.
And when at length the cruel war shall cease
On hard conditions may he buy his peace."

Lord Falkland then opened the Virgil in his turn, hoping that his "lot" might remove the gloomy impression of this bad omen.

But the passage on which he lit dealt with the untimely death of Pallas:

"O curst essay of arms, disastrous doom,
Prelude of bloody deeds and fights to come."

To this library Bacon sent his new book, "The Advancement of Learning," and here Milton, leaving the allegro of Horton or Forest Hill for the penseroso of Oxford's cloisters, made friends with the librarian, and added his own poems to those treasures which were soon to be defended by the "unshaken virtue" of his friend, Fairfax, and increased by the Chancellor, Oliver Cromwell. This is not the place to catalogue the list of those treasures, the wealth of European literature and the MSS. of the nearer and the farther East; the great collections which immortalise the names of the donors, like Laud and Selden, Rawlinson, Gough, Douce and Sutherland; the books which belonged to Queen Elizabeth and Queen Margaret, to Shakespeare, Ben Jonson, Addison and Shelley; the curios and *objets-d'art*, princely gifts, like the Arundel and Selden marbles, coins and portraits, minor curiosities, like stuffed alligators and dried negro boys, or the lantern of Guy Fawkes, which have all found a resting-place in

"this goodly Magazine of witte,
This Storehouse of the choicest furniture
The world doth yeelde, heere in this exquisite
And most rare monument, that doth immure
The glorious reliques of the best of men."[36]

In such a place, with such a history, it would be strange indeed if we did not feel something of the charm that breathes from the very stones of Bodley.

From the hot and noisy street you pass into the peaceful Schools' quadrangle, lying beneath the shade of that curious tower, which, as it were an academic conceit in stone, blends the five orders of classic architecture with Gothic turret and pinnacle. Architecturally the "Schools" are plain and poor, but you remember that Bodley conceived the idea of rebuilding them, and that it was the day after his body had been put to rest in Merton Chapel (29th March 1613) that the first stone was laid. The Bodleian forms the west side of this quadrangle. The east wing of the great library, built (1610-1613) by Bodley when already there was "more need of a library for the books than of books for the library," is panelled like the Divinity School, and stretches over the entrance to it, the Proscholium or "Pig Market," where candidates for degrees were obliged to wait. The west wing extends over Laud's late Gothic Convocation House (1634-1640); the books have usurped the third story of the Schools and the Clarendon building; they are filling the mighty camera beyond and overflowing into the Ashmolean. But the entrance to the heart of this grand collection is a modest portal. It opens on a long winding stair, so long and so wearisome that you seem to have trodden the very path by which true knowledge is gained ere you pass through a simple green baize door and see the panorama of all learning, lit by the glass of the east window, outspread before your eyes.

So to approach it, and passing by the outer library through the yielding wicket, into Duke Humphrey's gallery, there to turn into one of the quiet recesses, and calling for book after book, to summon spirits from the deep of the past, to hold quiet converse with them, while the breeze and sunlight flow gently in across Wren's huge buttresses from the green garden of Exeter, till Bodley's own solemn bell calls them back to their resting-place; this, as has been well said, is the very luxury, or rather the very poetry of study. "What a place," exclaimed Elia, "What a place to be in is an old library! It seems as though all the souls of all the writers, that have bequeathed their labours to these Bodleians, were reposing here, as in some dormitory, or middle state. I do not want to handle, to profane the leaves, their winding-sheets. I could as soon dislodge a shade. I seem to inhale learning, walking amid their foliage; and the odour of their old moth-scented coverings is fragrant as the first bloom of those sciential apples which grew amid the happy orchard."

The growth of the Puritan feeling in Oxford is shown by the formation of the first Baptist society under Vavasour Powell of Jesus College, whom John Bunyan once accompanied to this city. The growth of the Puritan tendency to preach is also indicated by the strange case of Richard Haydock, a physician of New College, who obtained some notoriety about this time by preaching at night in his bed. Sermons, he said, came to him by revelation in his sleep, and he would take a text in his slumbers and preach on it, "and though his auditory were willing to silence him by pulling, haling and pinching, yet would he pertinaciously persist to the end and sleep still." He was not a married fellow evidently. King James sent for him, and he preached to the monarch in his sleep, but James made him confess that he was a fraud, who had adopted this curious means of advertising himself.

The King and Queen and Prince Henry visited Oxford in 1605, and were welcomed very much as Elizabeth had been. The King, we are told, showed himself to be of an admirable wit and judgment. The scholars welcomed him by clapping their hands and humming, which, it was explained to him, signified applause.

The presence of King James' court, however, was responsible, if we may believe Wood, for a serious change in manners. For he traces the rise of that "damnable sin of drunkenness" to this time.

"For wheras in the days of Elizabeth it was little or nothing practiced, sack being then taken rather for a cordial than a usual liquor, sold also for that purpose in apothecaries' shops, and a heinous crime it was to be overtaken with drink, or smoke tobacco, it now became in a manner common, and a laudable fashion."

The vice in fact grew so prevalent in Oxford, as in the rest of England, that a statute was passed forbidding members of the University to visit any tavern and there "sit idly, drink, or use any unlawful play." The use of the Latin tongue, attendance at lectures and the wearing of academical dress was also insisted on by the new Chancellor, Archbishop Bancroft, who added an injunction that long hair was not to be worn: long hair in those days being accounted a sign not of a poet but of a swaggerer and ruffian. A few years later it was provided, as a measure directed against the still increasing vice of drunkenness, that no scholar should lodge without his college or hall, and that no citizen should entertain a scholar in his house.

The Gunpowder Plot led to more stringent measures being taken to root out the Roman Catholics from the University. It is possibly to the deep impression made by that event that the foundation of Wadham College is due. The founder of that college (1609), Nicholas Wadham, is said to have intended to endow a Roman Catholic college at Venice, but to have decided to endow a number of non-clerical and terminable fellowships at Oxford instead. His widow, Dorothy, carried out his plans, and, after Gloucester Hall had refused the benefaction, purchased the site of the suppressed settlement of Augustinian Friars and built the front quadrangle with hall and chapel as, externally, we have them to-day. For the interior of the chapel was dealt with by the Gothic revivalists (1834). The Wadhams were West Country folk, and the majority of workmen engaged were Somersetshire men. It is suggested that the extraordinarily fine Perpendicular character of the chapel choir is due to this fact; and that the masons reproduced, in the seventeenth century, the style of their county churches. The choir is a copy of fifteenth-century work; the ante-chapel and the rest of the quadrangle, so charming in its unadorned simplicity, are beautiful examples of the survival in Oxford of the Gothic tradition. Quadrangles at Merton and

Wadham are the most notable examples of this debased and nondescript style, redeemed by most excellent composition, proportioned like some Elizabethan manor.

James had been inclined at first to favour the Puritans, but when he finally cast in his lot with the High Church party, the University, which he, like Elizabeth, had done his best to conciliate as the educational centre of the national clergy, supported him loyally. In the year of his accession he had granted letters patent to both Universities, empowering them each to choose two grave and learned men, professing the civil law, to serve as burgesses in the House of Parliament; and the Universities were again indebted to him when they were called upon to furnish scholars for the great task of preparing the Authorised Version of the Bible.

Thus Oxford had its share in giving the Book to the people. From this time forward every Englishman was more than ever a theologian, and at the Universities, as at Westminster, theological controversy absorbed all energies. Literature, says Grotius (1613), has little reward. "Theologians rule, lawyers find profit, Casaubon alone has a fair success, but he himself thinks it uncertain, and not even he would have had any place as a literary man—he had to turn theologian."

Oxford, in return, declared itself on the side of passive obedience. The Church embraced the doctrine of the Divine Right of Kings; the University burned the books of Paræus in S. Mary's Churchyard, and solemnly decreed that it was not lawful for the subject to resist his sovereign by force of arms, or to make war against him, either offensive or defensive (1622). Thus it is evident that the influence of Calvin had died away at Oxford, and that the University had adopted, by the end of James' reign, the reactionary creed of Laud, and was ready to support the Stuart claim to absolutism. The Divine Right of Kings and the Divine Right of Bishops, as it was indicated by James' own phrase, "No Bishop, no King," was to be for more than a generation the official creed of Oxford schooled by Laud. For meanwhile one William Laud, B.D. of S. John's College, had filled the office of proctor and had been censured by the Vice-Chancellor for letting fall in a sermon at S. Mary's divers passages savouring of Popery. But he survived the reproof. President of S. John's from 1611-1621, he set himself to reform the discipline of the University and to undo the work of Leicester.

In 1630 he was elected Chancellor in opposition to the younger brother of the late Chancellor, Lord Pembroke, who was supported by the Calvinists. Preaching on the points in dispute between Calvin and Arminius was at once forbidden. This, with Laud as Chancellor, meant that the Puritans, who regarded Laud's "High Church" views as little better than Popery in disguise and as exposing the country to a danger which was too near and too deadly to be trifled with, were muzzled or driven from the country; but their opponents, if they preached against the practices of Geneva, met only with the mildest kind of rebuke. Laud's experience of the University had convinced him of the necessity of revising and codifying the statutes "which had long lain in a confused heap." As Chancellor he at once set about that difficult task. The

Caroline or Laudian Statutes were based on the old statutes and customs as collected, transcribed and drawn up by the antiquarian, Brian Twyne, fellow of C.C.C. Laud rewarded him with the office of Custos Archivorum. It was from the vast and scholarly collections of Brian Twyne that Wood quarried freely, and, it must be said, without due acknowledgment. But Wood succeeded in a task beyond Twyne's powers. He achieved immortality by clothing the dry bones of antiquarian fact or fancy in prose at times so racy and at times so musical.

Already (1629) Laud had been responsible for the introduction of the cycle, which put an end to the riots that had hitherto attended the election of proctors. Free election by the academical democracy had resulted in frequent abuses. The cycle invented by Peter Turner of Merton assigned to each college in turn, and in proportion to its size and dignity, the right of nominating proctors. The system, modified in 1856 and 1887, still obtains. His care for discipline led the Chancellor to make some much-needed reforms in the direction of diminishing the number of ale-houses and enforcing a proper system of licensing in the town. By his own proclamation he named a toll-gatherer for the market; he obtained an order from Council for the destruction of cottages which the townsmen had erected round about the wall and ditch; and, in spite of a protest from the citizens, the Caroline Charter was obtained, confirming the rights of the University over the town.

When the labours of Twyne were finished and the Delegacy had at last succeeded in codifying the laws and customs, the code was placed in the hands of Laud. He corrected the draft, and in 1636 the Corpus Statutorum was promulgated, confirmed by the King and gratefully accepted by the University. The new code was destined to govern it for two hundred years and more. Though to a great extent a digest of statutes already in force, the Laudian Statutes completed and stereotyped the changes which had long been taking place. The old order changes; the academic commonwealth becomes an oligarchy; the University is henceforth to be governed by a "Hebdomadal Board," and all power is definitely concentrated in the hands of the colleges and the Heads of Houses.

The old scholastic disputations were superseded by a system of public examinations; the studies required for a degree were organised and defined; the tutorial system was emphasised by the regulation which required the student to enter under a tutor resident in the same college. The code was received with effusive gratitude. The popularity of Laud was not merely due to the vigour with which he had been enforcing his views of orthodoxy, and compelling all, whether Roman Catholics or Puritans, to recant if ever in their sermons they controverted the Arminian doctrines, which the Stuarts had adopted as the fundamental principles of their policy in Church and State. For apart from his narrow Church policy Laud was, in University matters, both an earnest reformer and a great benefactor. He presented the library with a magnificent collection of Oriental MSS.; he founded and endowed the Professorship of Arabic, and, most valuable of all, he obtained for the University the right of printing Bibles, which is one of the most valuable endowments of that insufficiently endowed institution to-day. Besides his buildings at S. John's

College, the building of the Convocation House, adjoining the Divinity School (1634-1638), with the extension of the Bodleian above it, mark the chancellorship of Laud, and as the seat of Oxford's government fitly recall the age of its great lawgiver. The Botanic Gardens were also founded at this period, and the porch of S. Mary's was erected in 1637 by the Archbishop's chaplain, Dr Owen. The beautiful twisted columns of this, the south-west porch, are surmounted by a fine statue of the Virgin, crowned, with the Child in her arms. This statue gave such offence to the Puritans, that it actually figured in the articles of impeachment against the Archbishop.

Under Laud the University had quite recovered its popularity. There were no less than four thousand students; many men of learning and piety were numbered among its alumni; discipline was to a great extent established. But the coming struggle soon began to upset the new régime. For the Civil War was inevitably approaching. The chancellorship of Laud was crowned by a visit from the King and Queen in 1636. But though the University and town went out, as was their custom, towards Woodstock to meet their royal visitors, and though speeches and ceremonies were performed as usual, Wood notes that in the streets "neither scholars nor citizens made any expressions of joy or uttered as the manner is, Vivat Rex!" The visit lasted three days. The Elector Palatine and Prince Rupert received honorary M.A. degrees. Charles paid special attention to S. John's College, out of compliment to Laud, who entertained the royal party there, and drew attention to the library he had enlarged and the quadrangle he had built, mainly out of the stones obtained from the old Carmelite Convent in Beaumont Palace—once the Palace of Kings. From that time forward S. John's was the most royalist of colleges. One of its most treasured possessions was the portrait of the Royal Martyr, "which has the whole of the book of Psalms written in the lines of the face and the hair of the head." Of this picture, as of other things, the story is told that Charles II. begged it of the college, and promised in return to grant them any request they might make. They gave the picture, and requested His Majesty to give them—the picture back again. Comedies were performed at S. John's and Christ Church. The play at S. John's, "The Hospital of Lovers" was "merry and without offence," but that at Christ Church, by William Strode, the public orator, called the "Floating Island," had more of the moralist than poet in it. The scenery was realistic, but Lord Carnarvon declared the piece to be the worst he ever saw, except one at Cambridge. Another play at Christ Church, "The Royal Slave," by William Cartwright, was more successful. The scenery of the interludes was arranged by Inigo Jones. The Queen was so pleased with this piece, that she borrowed the Persian dresses and the scenery of the piece and had it repeated at Hampton Court, but "by all men's confession, the players came short of the University actors."

Charles, in this matter at least, was more fortunate than his father. For James had suffered much boredom from a play called "Technogamia, or the Marriage of the Arts," in which "there was no point and no sense but non-sense." He was with difficulty induced to stay to the end.

"At Christ Church 'Marriage,' done before the King,
Lest that those mates should want an offering,

The King himself did offer—what, I pray?
He offered twice or thrice to go away."

CHAPTER IX

THE ROYALIST CAPITAL

CHARLES I. had matriculated at Oxford in 1616; his brother Henry had been a student at Magdalen. On his accession to the throne, an outbreak of plague in London led to the meeting of Parliament at Oxford. For the accommodation of members, the colleges and halls "were ordered to be freed from the Fellows, Masters of Arts and students." Christ Church was prepared for the reception of the Privy Council by the same process. The Houses sat in the Divinity Schools. And some said that they caught the theological infection of the place, and that ever after that the Commons thought that the determining of all points and controversies in Divinity belonged to them. Parliament returned the compliment by infecting Oxford with the plague, which they had fled from London to avoid.

The coming struggle was foreshadowed by conflicts between town and gown. Once more the alarm bells of S. Mary's and S. Martin's rang out and summoned the opposing parties to the fray; once more it was true that when Oxford drew knife England would soon be at strife. Nothing, Laud had noted, could be transacted in the State, without its being immediately winnowed in the parliament of scholars. Windows were broken, proctors jostled; books were burnt by order of Parliament; young Puritans from New Inn Hall or Lincoln were forced to eat their words.

Prynne's ears had been cut off, but the Puritans multiplied their conventicles in Oxford. But it was not till after Laud's impeachment, and his short pathetic resignation of his chancellorship, dated from the Tower, 1641, that they grew so bold as to preach and discourse as they listed. Then the Puritan feeling grew rapidly not only among the townsmen but also in the colleges. A maypole set up in Holywell in derision of a certain Puritan musician was pulled down by the scholars of New Inn and Magdalen Hall. The report that the Mitre Inn was a meeting-place for recusants, gave occasion for the enemies of Laud to allege in the House of Commons that through his influence the University was infected with Popery. A certificate was accordingly drawn up by the Heads of Houses to the effect that "they knew not any one member of this University guilty of or addicted to Popery." Parliament, however, requisitioned the records of the University in order to obtain evidence against Laud. Some of his regulations, such as the encouraging of the use of copes and of Latin prayers in Lent, were indeed used to support the charge of high treason against him.

The Puritans, however, remained in the minority at Oxford. The part which she would take in the Civil War was never doubtful. Laud had filled the chief posts of the University with carefully chosen High Churchmen of great ability. Oxford was committed to the doctrines of passive obedience, and fast rooted in the tenets of the Anglican Church. The University pressed upon Parliament the duty of maintaining Episcopacy and the Cathedrals. The contemptuous treatment their arguments met with was contrasted with the reply of Charles, that "he would rather feed on bread and water than mingle any part of God's patrimony with his own revenues." Learning and studies, he maintained, must needs perish if the honours and rewards of learning were destroyed; nor would the monarchy itself stand long if the hierarchy perished. "No Bishop, no King!"

Parliament, it was felt, had shown unfriendly feeling towards the University. The town, headed by Alderman John Nixon, had most unmistakably shown that its sympathies were with the Parliament. It is not surprising therefore to find that in the coming struggle the University is always unreservedly on the side of the King. Royalist colleges like New College and Christ Church took the lead, and Puritan establishments like Lincoln and Magdalen followed unprotestingly.

When (1642) a letter from the King at York, asking for contributions to his necessary defence, was laid before Convocation, it was unanimously resolved that whatever money the University was possessed of, should be lent to the King. The colleges and private persons were equally loyal. University College set an example which was freely followed. The bulk of the college plate was pawned, and the sum advanced on it was immediately dispatched to the King.

The Parliament retorted in vain with prohibitory letters, and demanded the surrender of the chief champions of the King—Prideaux, Rector of Exeter; Fell, Dean of Christ Church; Frewen, President of Magdalen; and Potter, Provost of Queen's.

Since there was a strong report that divers troops of soldiers were constantly passing hard by the city on their march to secure Banbury and Warwick for the Parliament, the University began to put itself in a posture of defence. Masters and scholars rallied together on 18th August to drill in Christ Church Quadrangle, and marched from the Schools up the High Street to the number of three hundred and thirty or more, making ready to defend the city.

"On the Saturday following they met at the Schools again in the forenoon. Thence they marched through Holywell and so through the Manor Yard by the Church where by their commanders they were divided into four squadrons of which two were musketeers, the third pikes, the fourth halberds. After they had been reasonably instructed in the words of command, and in their postures, they were put into battle array, and skirmished together in a very decent manner. They continued there till about two of the clock in the afternoon, and then they returned into the city by S. Giles' Church, and going through the North Gate, went through the market-place at Quatervois, and so down the High Street, that so both the city and country might take notice thereof, it being then full market, to the Schools, from which place they were soon after dismissed and sent to their respective Colleges to their devotions."

Among the array are mentioned some divines and a Doctor of Civil Law from New College, who served with a pike. As for drums and colours, those belonging to the Cooks' Corporation served their turn for the present. Meantime the highway "at the hither end of East Bridge, just at the corner of the Chaplain's Quadrangle of Magdalen College," was blocked up with long timber logs to keep out horsemen, and a timber gate was also erected there and chained at night. Some loads of stones were carried up to the top of Magdalen Tower, to be flung down on the enemy at their entrance. Two posts were set up at Smith Gate, with a chain to run through them to bar the way; a crooked trench in the form of a bow was made across the highway at the end of S. John's College walks; and measures were taken to provide the scholars with barbed arrows. A strict watch was kept at nights.

Charles raised his standard at Nottingham, and on 28th August Sir John Byron rode in at the head of one or two hundred troopers to secure Oxford for the King. The scholars "closed with them and were joyful for their coming. Yet some Puritanical townsmen out of guilt fled to Abingdon, fearing they should be ill-used and imprisoned."

On 1st September twenty-seven senior members of the University, with the Vice-Chancellor, Prideaux, and the proctors, formed themselves into what the scholars nicknamed a Council of War, to arrange with Byron for the safety of the University. Drilling went on steadily in the quadrangles of Christ Church and Corpus Christi, of New College and Magdalen. Attempts were also made to take up Osney Bridge and to substitute a drawbridge. But the townsmen and their train-bands, which had assembled in Broken Hayes, objected, and the scholars and troopers were forced to desist.

But a strong Parliamentary force lay at Aylesbury. It was evident that, with the best will in the world, a few hundred troopers and enthusiastic scholars could not hold the city, which lay at present so far from the King's quarters. The townsmen were by no means eager Royalists. They made fair pretences of joining with the University and King's troops, but they informed Parliament that all they had done for the King was at the instigation of the University. The University accordingly sent to Aylesbury to inform the threatening Parliamentarians there that they would lay down their arms and dismiss the troopers. Dr Pink, however, Warden of New College and Deputy Vice-Chancellor, who had gone to make his peace at Aylesbury, was seized and committed to prison in the gate-house at Westminster. On 10th September Byron rode away.

About a hundred volunteers from the University accompanied him, and most of them made their way to Worcester before the siege.

Two days later Colonel Arthur Goodwin rode into the city with a troop of Parliamentarians. Goodwin was lodged at Merton, and his troopers picketed their horses in Christ Church meadows. The college gates were kept open, and the soldiers wandered in to see the cathedral and painted windows, "and much admired at the idolatry of them." Lord Say, the Parliamentarian Lord Lieutenant of Oxford, a New College man, arrived on 14th September, and immediately ordered that the works and trenches of the scholars should be demolished. The colleges were searched for arms and plate. The Christ Church plate was hidden by the staunch Dr Fell. It was found hidden in the walls behind the wainscot and in the cellar. The plate of University College was found in the house of Mr Thomas Smith. This Say adjudged to be lawful prize, but he told the fellows that as long as they kept their plate in places fit for plate, the treasury or buttery, it should remain untouched.

The city was mustered at Broken Hayes, and the arms of the train-bands were shown to Lord Say, who shortly afterwards left the place with his men, for both sides were now massing their forces. Little damage had been done, but "his Lordship caused divers Popish books and pictures, as he called them, which he had taken out of churches, and especially the houses of Papists here in Oxford and in the country, to be burned in the street, against the Star Inn," where he had lodged. And as they were leaving the town, one of the London troopers, when passing S. Mary's Church, discharged a brace of bullets at the "very scandalous image" of Our Lady over the porch, striking off her head and the head of the Child, which she held in her right arm. Another fired at the image of Our Saviour over All Souls' gate, and would have defaced all the work there, if he had not been remonstrated with by the citizens. He retorted that they had not been so well entertained at Oxford as they expected.

Say made a disastrous miscalculation in thus evacuating Oxford. For within a few weeks it was destined to become and to remain the headquarters of the King.

Many Royalists who had been wounded at Edgehill were brought into Oxford. On 29th October the King, with the Duke of York, Prince Charles and Rupert, rode in with the army at the North Gate. The colours taken from the enemy were carried in triumph; the King was received by the mayor with a present of money at Pennilesse Bench, and the heavy ordnance, twenty-seven pieces in all, were driven into Magdalen College Grove. The princes and many of the court took their degrees. Charles stayed but a short while, for, after having recruited his army and having been presented by the colleges with all the money they had in their treasuries, he presently left the city to make an advance on London. For Reading had surrendered to the Royalists, and Rupert's daring capture of Brentford now threatened the capital. But the junction of the train-bands of London with the army of Essex forced Charles to fall back on his old quarters at Oxford. There the fortification of the town was giving him a firm hold on the Midland counties.

A plan of fortifications had been prepared by one Rallingson, a B.A. of Queen's College. A series of earthworks, with sharp angles flanking each other, was to be thrown up outside the town. On 5th December 1642 the University bellman had gone about the city warning all privileged persons that were householders to send some of their families next day to dig at the works. The citizens, however, who were set to work north of S. Giles', were not enthusiastic. The King found only twelve of them working where there should have been one hundred and twenty-two, "of which neglect his majesty took notice and told them in the field."

The trench and rampart thus begun by the privileged men and workmen paid by the colleges, ran from the Cherwell at Holywell Mill, passing by Wadham and S. John's gardens and S. Giles' Church up to the branch of the Thames at Walton Bridge. Next, similar earthworks were made to cover S. Clement's, the east suburb. As time was pressing, and the city and county were not eager workers, the King called upon the University to help in February. The members of the various colleges were set to work on the line which ran from Folly Bridge across Christ Church meadow in front of Merton. (The bastion traceable in Merton Gardens dates from this time.) In the following June every person resident in a college or hall between sixteen and sixty was required to give a day's work a week with pick and spade, or to pay for a substitute, if unable or unwilling to anticipate the labours of Mr Ruskin. Finally (January 1644), the colleges were commanded to raise the sum of forty pounds a week for twenty weeks to complete the works.

Before leaving for Reading, the King had reviewed the regiment of scholars in Christ Church meadows. They were armed with helmets and back and breast pieces. The regiment, which consisted at first of four companies only, soon grew, as enthusiasm waxed, to eight or nine companies. The gown was exchanged for the military coat, and square caps for the helmet. Meanwhile arms and provisions had been accumulated, and ammunition, "the want wherof all men looked upon with great horror," had been thrown into the town.

The New College cloister and tower were converted into a magazine for muskets, bullets and gunpowder; corn was stored in the Law and Logic School, and victuals in the Guildhall. Clothes for the army were stowed in the Music and Astronomy Schools. The mill at Osney was used as a powder factory.

The King now established his court at Christ Church. Never perhaps has there existed so curious a spectacle as Oxford presented in these days. A city unique in itself, so the author of "John Inglesant" has described it, became the resort of a court under unique circumstances, and of an innumerable throng of people of every rank, disposition and taste, under circumstances the most extraordinary and romantic.

The ancient colleges and halls were thronged with ladies and gentlemen of the court, some of whom found themselves like fishes out of water (as one of them expressed it), when they were obliged to be content with "a very bad bed in a garret of a baker's house in an obscure street, and one dish of meat a day, and that not the best ordered, no money and no clothes." Soldiers were quartered in the college gates and the kitchens. Yet, amidst all this confusion, there was maintained both something of a courtly pomp and something of a learned and religious society. The King dined and supped in public, and walked in state in Christ Church meadow and Merton Gardens and the Grove of Trinity, which the wits called Daphne. A parliament sat from day to day. For (1644) the members of both Houses who had withdrawn from Westminster were summoned to meet at Oxford. The King received them very graciously in Christ Church Hall, made them a speech, and asked them to consult together in the Divinity Schools and to advise him for the good of the kingdom. About three hundred commons and sixty peers thus sat at Oxford, and a hundred commons and ten or a dozen peers at Westminster, so that the country enjoyed the felicity of two parliaments at once, each denying the right of the other to exist. The branch at Westminster rejected overtures of peace from the branch at Oxford. The latter devoted themselves to finding funds for the war. Contributions were called for, and the members themselves headed the list. A mint was established at New Inn Hall, and all plate that was brought in was coined.[37] At Westminster, on the other hand, the system of an excise upon beer, wine and spirits was invented.

And whilst Parliament sat in the Divinity Schools, service was sung daily in all the chapels; books both of learning and poetry were printed in the city, and the distinctions which the colleges had to offer were conferred with pomp on the royal followers, as almost the only rewards the King had to bestow. Men of every opinion flocked to Oxford, and many foreigners came to visit the King. Christmas interludes were enacted in hall, and Shakespeare's plays performed; the groves and walks of the colleges, and especially Christ Church meadow and the Grove at Trinity, were the resort of a brilliant throng of gay courtiers and gayer ladies; the woods were vocal with song and music; love and gallantry sported themselves along the pleasant river banks.

"Many times," Aubrey of Trinity tells us, "my lady Isabella Thynne would make her entry into our grove with a lute or theorbo played before her. I have heard her play on it in the grove myself; for which Mr Edmund Waller hath in his poems for ever made her famous." But old Dr Kettell of Trinity had no feeling for this sort of thing. He lectured Lady Isabella and her friend Mrs Fanshawe in no mincing terms when they attended chapel one morning "half dressed, like angels." "Madam," he cried by way of peroration, "get you gone for a very woman!" The poets and wits vied with each other in classic conceits and parodies, wherein the events of the day and every individual incident were portrayed and satirised. Wit, learning and religion, joined hand in hand, as in some grotesque and brilliant masque. The most admired poets and players and the most profound mathematicians became "Romancists" and monks, and exhausted all their wit and poetry and learning in furthering their divine mission, and finally, as the last scenes of this strange drama came on, fell fighting on some hardly-contested grassy slope, and were buried on the spot, or in the next village churchyard, in the dress in which they played Philaster, or the court garb in which they wooed their mistress, or the doctor's gown in which they preached before the King, or read Greek in the schools.

This gaiety was much increased when the Queen joined Charles on 14th July 1643. Two thousand foot, one thousand horse, six pieces of cannon and two mortars, which formed her escort, proved a welcome addition to the cause. The Queen, who had entered the city in great state and had been loyally welcomed, held her court at Merton, where, ever since, the room over the archway into the Fellows' Quadrangle has been known as the Queen's Chamber. From it a passage was constructed through Merton Hall and its vestibule, crossing the archway over Patey's Quadrangle, and descending to the sacristy, thence by a door into the chapel, and so to the grove and the gardens of Corpus. Hence a door, still traceable, was opened in the garden wall, and the private way was continued till it reached the royal apartments in Christ Church.

Well might the classic wits compare the scene to the marriage of Jupiter and Juno of old, for here indeed wisdom and folly, vice and piety, learning and gaiety, terrible earnest even unto death and light frivolity jostled each other in the stately precincts of Parnassus and Olympus.

Meantime, the war was going more and more in favour of the King. Parliament redoubled its endeavours. Essex, whose army had been freshly equipped, was ordered to advance upon Oxford. But he did not care to risk his raw forces, and contented himself with recapturing Reading. The King was ready to "give him battle about Oxford if he advanced; and in the meantime, encamped his foot upon the downs, about a mile from Abingdon, which was the head-quarters for his horse." At Westminster it was believed that Charles could not withstand a resolute attack on Oxford. Disease, however, thinned the ranks of Essex, and his inaction gave the Queen an opportunity of dispatching to Oxford a much-needed convoy of arms and ammunition. Charles now felt that he could resist any attack, and even afford to send part of his small force from Oxford to aid the rising in the west. At last, to quiet his supporters in London, Essex advanced towards Thame. His presence there, and the information given him by Colonel Hurry, a Scottish deserter, provided Rupert with an opportunity for making one of those daring raids which have immortalised the name of that dashing cavalry leader. Essex had made a futile endeavour to capture Islip. The same afternoon, with a force of about a thousand men, Rupert sallied out, hoping to cut off a convoy which was bringing £21,000 from London to Essex's army. An hour after midnight the tramp of his band was heard by the sentinels at Tetsworth; two hours later, as the sky was whitening before the dawn, he surprised a party of the enemy at Postcombe. He then proceeded to Chinnor, within two miles of Thame, and again successfully surprised a force of the enemy. It was now time to look out for the convoy. The alarm, however, had been given. The drivers were warned by a countryman, and they turned the heads of their team into the woods, which clothed the sides of the Chiltern Hills. Rupert could not venture to follow. Laden with prisoners and booty the Royalists were returning to Oxford, when, about eight o'clock in the morning, they found themselves cut off by the cavalry who had been dispatched by Essex. Rupert had just passed Chalgrove Field and was entering the lane which led to Chiselhampton Bridge, where a regiment of foot had been ordered to come out to support his return, when the enemy's horse was found to be overtaking him. He immediately ordered the guard with the prisoners to make their way to the bridge, whilst he with his tired troopers drew up on Chalgrove Field. The Parliamentarians hoped to hold him till succour arrived from headquarters. It was a dangerous game to play with Rupert. "This insolence," he cried, "is not to be borne." He was the first to leap the hedge behind which the enemy was drawn up. The Roundheads fought that day as they had never fought before. They were put to flight at last, but not before Hampden himself, who had slept that night at Wallington and had ridden out as a volunteer at the sound of the alarm, had been seen "to ride off the field before the action was done, which he never used to do, with his head hanging down, and resting his hands upon the neck of his horse." He was indeed mortally wounded, and his death seemed an omen of the ruin of the cause he loved. Disaster followed disaster. Essex fell back towards London; Bristol was surrendered into Rupert's hands, and the flight of six of the few peers who remained at Westminster to the camp at Oxford proved the general despair of the Parliament's success.

But the discontent and jealousy which were always rife among the soldiers and courtiers in Charles' camp, broke out afresh when the King returned to Oxford after his failure to take Gloucester. From this moment, indeed, the firmness of Parliament and the factiousness and foolishness of the King's party began slowly to reverse the fortunes of the war. Parliament obtained the assistance of Scotland, and Charles negotiated with the Irish Catholics. The alliance was fatal to his cause. Many of Charles' supporters left him; the six peers fled back to Westminster. The covenant was concluded. A Scotch army crossed the border and co-operated with Fairfax and Leven in the north; Essex watched the King at Oxford, and was presently supported by Waller, who had been holding Prince Maurice in check in the west. The Queen, who was *enceinte*, and afraid of being besieged, now insisted on leaving Oxford (April 1644). She made her way safely to Exeter.

The Royalists abandoned Reading and fell back on Oxford, where measures were being taken for defence. Regiments were enlisted; trees were felled in Magdalen walks, and means were provided for flooding the meadows beyond. Batteries were erected at suitable points. One of these, at the north-east corner of the walks, was called Dover Pier (Dover's Peer?), probably after the Earl of Dover, who commanded the new University Regiment. This regiment mustered for the first time on 14th May 1644 in Magdalen College Grove, and, along with the City Regiment, was reviewed on Bullingdon Green a few days later. The rise in the ground at the end of Addison's Walk, which is still noticeable, is probably due to the high and strong causeway which we know led from the walks to the battery in the river.

The Parliamentarians advanced, Abingdon was evacuated by the Royalist army under Wilmot, and occupied by Essex. Charles was forced to withdraw all his forces to the north of Oxford. The King's position was now so serious, that it was confidently reported in London that Oxford was taken and the King a prisoner. Another rumour ran that the King had decided to come to

London, or what Parliament chiefly feared, to surrender himself to Essex. Presently, indeed, his own supporters advised this course, but His Majesty indignantly rejected the suggestion, saying that possibly he might be found in the hands of Essex, but he would be dead first.

As no help could be looked for from north or west, he determined to stay in Oxford and watch for an opportunity of fighting Waller or Essex separately. With this object in view he disposed his army so as to prevent the rebels from crossing the Cherwell or Isis, the foot holding the former and the horse and dragoons the latter. A series of smart skirmishes ensued. Some of Waller's forces attempted to pass the Isis at Newbridge, but were repulsed. The next day (29th May), however, Essex crossed the Thames at Sandford Ferry with his whole army and quartered himself at Islip. On his way thither he halted on Bullingdon Green, "that the city might take a full view of his army and he of it." He himself rode up within cannon shot, whilst parties of his horse skirmished about the gates, and gave the scholars and citizens an opportunity of trying their prowess. "It gave some terror to Oxon," says Wood, "and therefore two prayers by his Majesty's appointment were made and published, one for the safety of his Majesty's person and the other for the preservation of the University and City, to be used in all the churches." But there was no intention of making an assault upon the town. Essex was merely covering the passage of his baggage train. Whilst he was thus occupied and the scholars were making a sortie, Charles and Rupert ascended Magdalen Tower and watched the movements of the enemy. Next morning a determined effort was made by Essex to pass over the Cherwell at Gosworth Bridge, but he was repulsed by the musketeers with considerable loss. Essex being now on the east side of the river and cut off from communication with Waller, the King strove to avail himself of the opportunity of retaking Abingdon and engaging Waller singly.

But after an unsuccessful move against Abingdon, the design was abandoned, and the Royalist forces were once more concentrated on the north side of Oxford. Sir Jacob Ashley, Major-General of the Foot, himself took command at Gosworth Bridge, where, he perceived, Essex intended to force a passage. There he threw up breastworks and a redoubt, and succeeded in repulsing the enemy, who renewed their attacks from day to day and even brought up cannon to their support without avail. Meanwhile, however, Waller effected the passage of the Isis at Newbridge, quartered his van at Eynsham, and threatened the rear of the King's army. Ashley was compelled to retire. Essex immediately threw his men across the Cherwell, and quartered them that night at Bletchington. His horse advanced to Woodstock. The King seemed to be enveloped by the opposing armies. But after making a demonstration against Abingdon, Charles slipped out of Oxford on the night of 3rd June. Marching out with six thousand men by S. John's Road, he made his way along a rough crooked lane and got clear away to the north of the city. He left the Duke of York in the town, and promised, if the place was besieged, to do all he could to relieve it before it was reduced to extremity. But the town had scarcely enough provisions to stand a month's siege.

A series of brilliant successes rewarded the perseverance of the King, for he now waited till Essex marched to attack Prince Maurice at Lyme, then turning on Waller, crushed his army at Copredy Bridge on the Cherwell, fourteen miles north of Oxford. After two days' rest at Oxford, he followed up his success by pursuing Essex into Cornwall and gaining a complete victory over him there. But in the midst of these successes came the news of the disaster in the north. The star of Cromwell had risen where Rupert's had begun to set, at Marston Moor. The battle of Newbury checked the King's advance on London, and he withdrew once more to winter at Oxford (27th October 1644). He was much pleased with the progress that had been made with the fortifications. In order to carry on his operations against Waller and Essex, he had been obliged to denude Oxford of troops. But before leaving it he had provided for its safety. For Parliament had a strong garrison at Reading and another at Abingdon, and the danger of a siege seemed imminent. The inhabitants were therefore commanded to provide themselves with corn and victuals for three months, or to leave the town "as persons insensible of their own dangers and the safety of the place." The safety of the place having been secured, the garrison had felt themselves strong enough to send out a force to the relief of Basing-House. The objections of the governor, Sir Arthur Aston, who had succeeded Sir William Pennyman in that office, were overruled. Colonel Gage made a dash from Oxford, relieved the Marquis of Winchester and returned safely to Oxford after having performed one of the most brilliant of the minor feats of arms that occurred during the war. Charles, on his return, appointed him Governor of Oxford, in place of Sir Arthur Aston, who had broken his leg. Gage, who is buried in the Cathedral, was killed shortly afterwards at Culham Bridge in an attempt to surprise Abingdon.

In the spring of 1645 Oliver Cromwell appeared in the parts about Oxford. He was in command of some cavalry, and the object of his movements, in conjunction with those of Sir Thomas Fairfax, was to prevent Prince Maurice from removing heavy guns from Oxford to Hereford, and thereby to disarrange Charles' plan for an early campaign. Cromwell routed Northampton at Islip. A party of the defeated Cavaliers took refuge at Bletchington House. Cromwell called upon the governor, Windebanke, to surrender. Deceived by the sheer audacity of the demand, and moved, it is said, by the timorous entreaties of a party of ladies from Oxford whom he was entertaining at Bletchington, he yielded. Windebanke paid dearly for his weakness. He was shot in the Castle garden on his return to Oxford. Cromwell swept round the city and defeated Sir Henry Vaughan at Bampton. The Parliamentarians had now achieved their object. They moved away from Oxford. In a few weeks they were back again, and the new fortifications of the city were at length put to the test. The siege was heralded by the appearance of some scattered horse near Cowley on 19th May. Thence they, with other horse and foot, passed over Bullingdon Green to Marston, and showed themselves on Headington Hill. On the 22nd Fairfax sat down before Oxford. He threw up a breastwork on the east side of Cherwell, and constructed a bridge near Marston, across which he passed some regiments. Cromwell was commanding at Wytham and Major Browne at Wolvercote. The most considerable incident that occurred during the fifteen days' siege was a successful sortie in the direction of Headington Hill, which was made by Colonel William Legge, the governor of the town. Then Fairfax raised the siege and moved north; a few weeks later the fateful battle of Naseby was fought. Thereafter the King finally made his way to Oxford from Newark. Here for a while he was safe; but in the spring Fairfax marched upon Oxford. The King was driven from his last refuge. At three in the morning of 27th April, disguised as a servant, with his beard and hair closely trimmed, he passed over Magdalen Bridge in apparent attendance upon John Ashburnham and a scholar, one Hudson, "who understood the byeways as well as the common, and was indeed a very skilful guide." "Farewell, Harry," Glenham called out to his sovereign, as he performed the governor's duty of closing the gates behind him. Charles' departure was kept so secret that Fairfax, who arrived before Oxford on the fifth day after, sat down before the city, and made his circumvallation before he knew of it.

The Duke of York and all the King's Council remained shut up in Oxford. Fairfax found the city well prepared for a siege.

"The rising ground to the north was protected by many strong bulwarks flanking one another. Round about the line, both upon the bulwarks and the curtain, was strongly set with storm poles. Outside the ditch was a strong palisade beyond which were many pits dug so that a single footman could not without difficulty approach to the trench. Within the city were 5000 foot, and the place was well supplied with stores. All this strength being apprehended and considered by Sir Thomas Fairfax, he concluded that this was no place to be taken at a running pull, but likely rather to prove a business of time, hazard and industry."

Accordingly he proceeded to make a fortified camp on Headington Hill, to make a bridge over the Cherwell near Marston, and establish a post between the Cherwell and Isis on the north for the main body of his troops. Lines were drawn from Headington to S. Bartholomew's common road, and from thence to Campus pits. A memento of the siege, a cannon shot which is said to have struck the gateway tower of S. John's College, is preserved in the library of that college.

Little progress, however, had been made with the siege, though the defence was for a lost cause, when Charles, who had been handed over by the Scots to a Committee of the House, sent orders to the governor to make conditions and surrender the place to Fairfax.

Honourable terms were granted. Fairfax had expressed his earnest desire to preserve a place "so famous for learning from ruin." His first act, for he was a scholar as well as a soldier, was to protect the Bodleian. A clause to the effect that all churches, colleges and schools should be preserved from harm was inserted in the Articles of Surrender. The liberties and privileges of the city and the University were guaranteed, and on 24th June the garrison, some three thousand strong, marched out in drenching rain over Magdalen Bridge, colours flying and drums beating, between files of Roundhead infantry.

So ended the Great Rebellion. And the history of it remained to be written by Edward Hyde, the Earl of Clarendon, who came to the task equipped with a wisdom that is born of a large experience of men and affairs. A moderate but faithful adherent of the Royalist cause, he could say of himself that he wrote of events "quorum pars magna fui." He had been one of the King's most trusted advisers at Oxford. There he lived in All Souls' College, and the King wished to make him Secretary of State. "I must make Ned Hyde Secretary of State, for the truth is I can trust nobody else," wrote the harassed monarch to his Queen. In his great history, so lively yet dignified in style, so moderate in tone and penetrating in its portrayal of character, he built for himself a monument more durable than brass. A monument not less noble has been raised for him in Oxford out of the proceeds of that very book. For the copyright of the history was presented to the University by his son, and partly out of the funds thus arising the handsome building north-east of the Sheldonian Theatre was erected, from designs by Sir John Vanbrugh (1713). Here the University Press was transferred from the Sheldonian Theatre, where it had found its first permanent and official home. The "Clarendon" Press was removed in 1830 to the present building in Walton Street, when it had outgrown the accommodation of the Clarendon building.

Like Sir Harry Vane, Clarendon had been educated at Magdalen Hall. The chair in which he wrote his history is preserved at the Bodleian, and there too may be seen many of the notes which his royal master used to throw him across the table at a Council meeting.

There had been another inhabitant of Oxford in these stirring days much affected by these events, a youth endowed with unbounded antiquarian enthusiasm and an excellent gift of observation. This "chiel amang them taking notes" was Anthony Wood, to whose work every writer on Oxford owes a debt unpayable. Born in the Portionists' Hall, the old house opposite Merton and next door to that fine old house, Beam Hall, where, he says, the first University press was established, Wood was carried at the age of four to see the entry of Charles and Rupert, and was a Royalist ever after. Educated first at a small Grammar School near S. Peter le Bailey and then at New College School, he became familiar with the aspect of old Oxford as it was before the changes wrought by the siege, and he was able to transcribe into his notebooks many old inscriptions and memorials just before a period of wanton destruction. When the war broke out there was much ado to prevent his eldest brother, a student at Christ Church, from donning the armour with which his father decked out the manservant. The New College boys grew soldier-struck as they gazed from their school in the cloister upon the train-bands drilling in the quadrangle. They were presently turned out of their school to make room for the munitions of war.

But I have no space to write of the vicissitudes of "A. W.'s" life; of the fate which befell his biographies of Oxford writers; of his quarrels with Dean Fell, that staunch Royalist and stern disciplinarian of whom every child learns to lisp in numbers:

"I do not like thee, Dr Fell;
The reason why I cannot tell.
But only this I know full well,
I do not like thee, Dr Fell."

The first step taken for the "reformation" of Oxford was a Parliamentary order (July 1646) suspending elections in the University and colleges, and forbidding the granting or renewing of leases. The University petitioned Fairfax to obtain the recall of this order, on the ground that it was contrary to the Articles of Surrender. The prohibition was not enforced. But the condition of the University was deplorable. The quadrangles were empty, the courts overgrown with grass. Scholars ceased to come up, and those who were in residence were utterly demoralised by the war. Before the changes and chances of war and religion, learning shrank in dismay and discipline disappeared.

Six Presbyterian preachers were now sent down to supersede the Royalist preachers, to beat the pulpit, drum ecclesiastic, and convince the University. All they succeeded in doing was to rouse the Independents among the garrison who had already been practising in the schools and lecture-rooms. The Military Saints now set themselves, "with wry mouths, squint eyes, screwed faces, antic behaviours, squeaking voices and puling tones," to out-preach the proselytising Presbyterians. Royalist Oxford rocked with laughter and congratulated itself prematurely that the revolution had begun to devour its own children.

But a commission was appointed to visit the University in May 1647. Sir Nathaniel Brent, Warden of Merton, was chairman, and Prynne a member. Their proceedings were delayed by an absurd trick. The University had been summoned to appear before them in the Schools between nine and eleven. But the preliminary sermon in S. Mary's was of such length that eleven had struck and the University had dispersed before the commissioners could get to work. The University appointed a delegacy to act on its behalf, which drew up a very able and moderate series of reasons for not submitting to the tests that were to be proposed. The authority of the Visitors was challenged. Time was thus gained, and the struggle that was going on between the Presbyterians and the Independents paralysed the Visitors. A committee of the Lords and Commons, however, presently armed them with fresh powers. After three hours of preliminary prayer, "a way" says Wood, "by which they were wont to commence their actions for all sorts of wickednesses," they proceeded to inquire "into the behaviour of all Governors, Professors, Officers and members." Dr Fell and the majority of the University offered a firm resistance.

Fell was seized and imprisoned. The action of the Visitors, however, was still paralysed by the lack of constitutional authority. They were once more strengthened by the London Committee. The business of deprivation began. Sentence was passed upon half a dozen Heads of Houses, "but not a man stirred from his place." The University, in fact, continued to ignore the proceedings of the Visitors. Even after the arrival of the Chancellor, Lord Pembroke, and of

Fairfax's troops, whom the Visitors were empowered to use, the expelled Heads refused to leave their colleges. Mrs Fell held the deanery of Christ Church valiantly. When the Chancellor, with some soldiers, appeared there and desired Mrs Fell to quit her quarters, "she refused that kind proposal, had very ill language given to her by him, and then she was carried into the quadrangle in a chair by soldiers," and her children on boards. The buttery book was then sent for and Fell's name dashed out. Passive resistance of this kind and the use of every legal device to delay the action of the Visitors were adopted everywhere.

The University fought every inch of the ground, standing firmly on the vantage ground of constitutional right. But the gown usually has to yield to arms. New Heads were appointed, new M.A.'s created, and the Visitors proceeded to purge the colleges. Every fellow, student and servant was asked, "Do you submit to the authority of Parliament in this present Visitation?" Those who did not submit were turned out. Presently the Negative Oath was tendered, and subscription to "the Engagement" was required. Rather than submit to these tests over four hundred fellows preferred to be ejected. Puritans, men for the most part of real learning and piety, were substituted, though those who suffered described "the new plantation of saints" as an illiterate rabble, "swept up from the plough-tail and scraped out of Cambridge."

At New College a very large proportion of the fellows were expelled: fifty at the lowest computation. The inquisition even extended its investigations to the college servants. The organist, sexton, under-butler, manciple, porter, groom and basket bearer were all outed, when they could not in conscience submit. At Merton Wood refused to answer, but by the goodwill of the warden and Arch Visitor, a friend of his mother, "A. W. was connived at and kept in his place, otherwise he had infallibly gone to the pot."

The Visitors acted, on the whole, in the spirit of genuine reformers. Apart from imposing a system of Puritan morals, they worked with a sincere desire to make the colleges fruitful nurseries of learning. What they did, and still more what they wished to do, with regard to the discipline of the place was on the right lines of educational advance.

In July an attempt was made to recapture the guard and magazine in New College. The conspiracy was revealed by a boozing and boastful conspirator. Two years later a mutiny of the garrison, in protest against excise, tithes and lawyers, was checked by the vigilance of Colonel Ingoldsby, the governor.

Fairfax and Cromwell visited Oxford to see how the reformation was progressing (17th May 1649), and lodged at All Souls'. They dined at Magdalen, where they had "good cheer and bad speeches, and afterwards played at bowls in the College Green." They both received a D.C.L. degree, and Cromwell assured the University that he meant to encourage learning. Next year he became Chancellor, and besides presenting some MSS. he resisted the proposal to reduce the academical endowments which Milton supported.

Learning and discipline were never popular; long sermons, compulsory attendance at innumerable religious exercises, and catechisms in the tutors' rooms were not more so. As the sands of the Commonwealth ran out the approaching Restoration found a welcome at Oxford. It was a sign of the times that, when Richard Cromwell was proclaimed Protector, the mayor and the troopers were pelted with turnip-tops by the scholars in front of S. Mary's. Without waiting for a formal proclamation of the new order, men reverted to it by a kind of spontaneous instinct. Six weeks or more before the Restoration, a bold man read the Common Prayer in S. Mary Magdalen Church in surplice and hood, and that church was always "full of young people purposely to hear and see the novelty."

At the news of the Restoration all England "went mad with joy"; at Oxford the rejoicing "lasted till the morning." And when Coronation Day came, "Conduit ran a hogshead of wine." Common Prayer was restored and surplices; Puritan preaching went out of fashion; the organs of Magdalen, New College and Christ Church sounded once more; plays were performed and the Solemn League and Covenant was burnt.

Yet the prejudice against surplice and organ was deep. Many still denounced organ-music as the whining of pigs. At Magdalen men clad in surplices, with hands and faces blackened, paraded the cloisters at twilight to encourage the story that Satan himself had appeared and adopted the surplice. Filthy insults and ribald abuse were heaped upon the innocent garment.

A Royal Commission visited the University to eject the intruders and restore those whom Parliament had expelled. The Presbyterians took the Oath of Allegiance and Supremacy, and were allowed to hold their places unless some ejected fellow or scholar appeared to claim them. But at Lincoln, where the Independent faction was strong, several fellows were turned out, George Hitchcock among them. He defied the bedel who was sent to arrest him when he refused to go. With a drawn sword and a sported oak Hitchcock remained master of the situation until the arrival of the military who, undaunted, stormed the Independent's castle and marched him off to jail.

Life at Oxford resolved itself at last to peace and quiet study.

"The tumult and the shouting dies,
The Captains and the Kings depart"—

and the groves and quadrangles that had echoed with the clash of arms, the loud laugh of roystering Cavaliers, or the gentle rustle of sweeping trains, or the whining of a Puritan, now resounded with the noise of the bowling-green and tennis-court, or the chamber music of such scholarly enthusiasts as Anthony Wood with his fiddle, and Edmund Gregory with his bass viol.

With the Restoration a new kind of student came into prominence. Very different from his mediæval brother was the new type of rich "young gentleman" so wittily satirised by Dr Earle, as one who came to Oxford to wear a gown and to say hereafter that he had been at the University. "His father sent him thither because he heard that there were the best fencing and dancing schools.... Of all things he endures not to be mistaken for a scholar." For it was now the fashion for students to live like men of the world, to keep dogs and horses, to swash it in apparel, to wear long periwigs. They discussed public affairs and read the newsletters in the coffee-houses. For Canopus, the Cretan, had set the example of drinking coffee, and in 1651 Jacob the Jew opened a coffee-house at the Angel. Four years later Arthur Tillyard, "an apothecary and great Royalist, sold coffee publicly in his house against All Souls' College. He was encouraged to do so," says Wood, "by some royalists and by the company of 'Vertuosi,' chiefly All Souls' men, amongst whom was numbered Christopher Wren."

With the Restoration, too, the study of mere Divinity began to go out of fashion, and a humane interest in letters began to manifest itself. Plays, poems and drollery, the old-fashioned scholars complained, were in request. Science, too, suddenly became fashionable. Charles and the Duke of Buckingham took a keen interest in chemistry; Prince Rupert solaced his old age with the glass drops which are called after his name. At Oxford many scholars already had private laboratories. Robert Boyle and Peter Sthael had for some time been lecturing on chemistry at the Ram Inn (113 High Street) to the curious, John Locke included. The King now gave its title to the Royal Society, which had its origin in the inquiries of a little group of scientific students in London before the end of the Civil War. It was now divided into two by the removal of its foremost members, Dr Wilkins, Warden of Wadham, and Dr Wallis, Savilian Professor of Geometry, to Oxford. The Oxford branch of the society was strengthened by such men as Sir William Petty, the first of English economists, Dr Ward, the mathematician, Robert Boyle and Christopher Wren. In the lodgings of Wilkins or Petty they would meet and discuss the circulation of the blood or the shape of Saturn, the Copernican hypothesis, the improvement of telescopes or Nature's abhorrence of a vacuum—any subject, in fact, which did not lead them into the bogs of theology or politics.

"That miracle of a youth," Dr Christopher Wren, was one of those deputed by the University (1667) to take a letter of thanks to Henry Howard, heir to the Duke of Norfolk, for his princely gift of the Arundel Marbles to the University. This gift the University owed to the kindly offices of John Evelyn, the diarist. The marbles were laid in the Proscholium till the Sheldonian Theatre was finished. Ingeniously designed by Wren to accommodate the University at the "Act" or "Encænia," this theatre was consecrated by Archbishop Sheldon (1669), at whose cost it was erected. Sheldon was a warden of All Souls', put out under the Commonwealth and afterwards restored, before being promoted to the Primacy.

Wren left many other marks of his genius upon Oxford. The chapel of B.N.C. is said to be from his design, and may be, for it reveals the struggle that was going on (1656) between the Oxford

Gothic, as the beautiful fan-tracery of the ceiling and the windows bear witness, and the Italian style of the rest of the building. Wren migrated from Wadham to All Souls', presenting on his departure a clock (now in the ante-chapel) to the college where he had been a fellow-commoner. In the college of which he, with Sydenham, was made a fellow under the Commonwealth, he made the great and accurate sun-dial, with its motto "Pereunt et Imputantur," that adorns the back quadrangle. His pupil Hawksmoor it was who designed the twin towers of All Souls' and the quadrangle at Queen's, whilst Wren himself designed the chapel, which he reckoned one of his best works. At Trinity he gave advice to Dean Aldrich, made suggestions which were not taken, and actually designed the north wing of the garden quadrangle, one of the first Italian buildings in Oxford. At Christ Church he added, as we have seen, the octagonal cupola to Wolsey's Tower. The buttresses in Exeter Garden which support the Bodleian are also the result of his advice. The beautifully proportioned building close to the Sheldonian was presently built (1683, Wood, architect) by the University to house the valuable collection of curiosities presented to it by Elias Ashmole.

When the plague broke out in London, Charles and his court fled to Oxford (September 1665), where, since July, a watch had been set to keep out infected persons flying from London. The King and Duke of York lodged at Christ Church; whilst, all under the rank of master at Merton having been sent to their homes, the Queen took up her abode there till the following February. Once more courtiers filled the college instead of scholars; the loose manners of the court were introduced into the college precincts; the King's mistress, Lady Castlemaine, bore him a bastard in December, and libels were pinned up on the doors of Merton concerning that event. It is sadly recorded that founders' prayers had to be recited in English, because there were more women than scholars in the chapel. And as for the courtiers, though they were neat and gay in their apparel, yet were they, so says the offended scholar, "very nasty and beastly; rude, rough, whoremongers; vain, empty and careless."

The House of Lords sat in the Geometry School, the House of Commons in the Convocation House, whilst the Divinity School and the Greek School were employed as a committee room and the Star Chamber. After sitting for a month and passing the Act which prohibited dissenting ministers from coming within five miles of any city, Parliament broke up in October. When this Act was suspended in 1672 and Nonconformists were allowed to meet in towns, provided they took out a licence, the Independents and Baptists set up meeting-houses in Oxford, the Baptists meeting first in Magdalen Street and then in S. Ebbe's Parish. The Nonconformist chapels were destroyed in the Jacobite riot of 1715, but in 1720 a new chapel was built behind the present chapel in the New Road by the Baptists and Presbyterians in common.

The *Oxford Gazette* made its first appearance during Charles' visit, the first number coming out on 7th November 1665.

Again, in 1681, Parliament was summoned by Charles II. to meet at Oxford on 21st March. He had written in January choosing Merton, Corpus and Christ Church to house him, his Queen, his Court[38] and his Parliament. The scholars as usual departed, but in a week the King dissolved the wicked, or week-ed, Parliament, and the collegians returned to their quarters and the use of their silver plate, which they had wisely hidden from their guests.

"We scholars were expelled awhile to let the Senators in,
But they behaved themselves so ill that we returned again,"

sang the poet of the day. For the rest of his reign the monarch was nearly absolute. "Now I am King of England, and was not before," he remarked; and he signalised his victory over the Exclusionist Party, who wished to guard against the danger of a Catholic king, by procuring, at Oxford, the condemnation of Stephen College, a Protestant joiner, who was forthwith hung in the Castle-yard.

The sudden influx of so many persons into the town was calculated to send up the price of provisions. The Vice-Chancellor accordingly took the precaution of fixing a limit to the market prices. A pound of butter, for instance, sweet and new, the best in the market, was not to cost more than 6d.; six eggs 2d.; or a fat pig, the best in the market, 2s. 6d.; whilst not more than 2s. 8d. was to be charged in every inn for a bushel of the best oats.

Meantime the University was not in too flourishing a state. "All those we call Whigs," Wood complains, "will not send their sons for fear of their turning Tories, and because the Universities are suspected of being Popish." And Stephen Penton, the Principal who built the chapel and library of S. Edmund's Hall (1680), thought it expedient to write that charming little book, "The Guardian's Instruction," in answer to the "rash and uncharitable censure of the idle, ignorant, debauched, Popish University." But the manners of the place are indicated by such facts as these: "The Act was put off because 'twas said the Vice-Chancellor was sickish from bibbing and smoking and drinking claret a whole afternoon." In 1685 the mayor and aldermen, who had been splendidly entertained by the Earl of Abingdon in return for their election of his brother to represent them in Parliament, "came home most of them drunk and fell off their horses." About the same time three masters of All Souls' came drunk to the Mitre in the middle of the night, and because the landlady refused to get up and prepare them some food, they called her "strange names and told her she deserved to have her throat cut, whereupon being extremely frighted, she fell into fits and died." The masters were examined by the Vice-Chancellor and compelled to "recant in the Convocation." A few months later a debauched Master of Arts of New Inn was expelled for biting a piece off the nose of a B.N.C. B.A.

At Balliol the buildings were literally falling to pieces, and it was the solace of Dr Bathurst's old age to sit on his garden wall—he was President of Trinity—and throw stones at the few windows that still contained any glass, "as if happy to contribute his share in completing the appearance of its ruin." This was the same Dr Bathurst, who as Vice-Chancellor, according to Prideaux' story, had already done his best to encourage the "men of Belial" to deserve the nickname bestowed upon them by Nicholas Amherst.[39]

"There is," wrote Prideaux, "over against Balliol a dingy, horrid, scandalous ale-house, fit for none but draymen and tinkers. Here the Balliol men continually lie and by perpetual bubbing add art to their natural stupidity to make themselves perfect sots."

The master (Dr Goode, a good, honest old toast, and sometime a Puritan) remonstrated with them and

"informed them of the mischiefs of that hellish liquor called ale. But one of them, not willing to be preached so tamely out of his beloved liquor, made reply that the Vice-Chancellor's men drank ale at the Split Crow and why should they not too? The old man, being nonplussed with this reply, immediately packeth away to the Vice-Chancellor, formerly an old lover of ale himself,"

who informed him that there was no hurt in ale. Accordingly the master told his men that since the Vice-Chancellor said there was no hurt in ale, though truly he thought there was, he would give them leave to drink it. "So now," Prideaux concludes, "they may be sots by authority."

In 1682, Wood notes, "fighting occasioned by drunkenness fell out in S. John's common chamber." Common rooms, it may be observed, which were regarded as a luxurious innovation, had been introduced into Oxford in 1661 by Merton, where the room over the kitchen, with the cock-loft over it, was turned into a room "for the common use of the Fellows." Other colleges quickly followed an example which had been set eleven years before in the Combination Room of Trinity at Cambridge.

The accession of James II. was hailed at Oxford with many expressions of loyalty. A large bonfire was lit at Carfax and five barrels of beer broached in the Town Hall, to be drunk by all comers. There were bonfires in all the colleges, where the respective societies drank a health, kneeling, to the King and Royal Family. At Merton, Wood tells us, "the gravest and greatest seniors of the house were mellow that night, as at other Colleges." And the coronation was celebrated by a sermon and bonfire at S. Mary's and "great extraordinaries in eating and drinking in each College." But there were many townsmen who had been ready (1683) to shout for "a Monmouth! a Monmouth! no York!" and after Monmouth's Rebellion, when the University raised a regiment, whose uniforms at any rate were gallant, several of the citizens were arrested as rebels. It was not long before the bigotry and tyranny of James drove the University itself into that resistance to the royal authority which was so alien to its teaching and tradition. For James set himself to convert the training-place of the English clergy into a Roman Catholic seminary.

The accession of a sovereign attached to the Roman Church had been the signal for many who had hitherto concealed their opinions to avow their devotion to that communion. The Master of University College was one of those who had conformed to the rites of the Anglican Church whilst supporting so far as he dared, in the pulpit and the press, the doctrines of Rome. He now openly avowed his conversion and did his utmost to promote the Roman Catholic cause. Ave Maria Obadiah, as he was nicknamed from an academic catch of the time, was authorised by the King to appropriate some college rooms for a chapel under the Roman ritual. He had already been absolved by a royal dispensation from the duty of attending the services of the Church of England, and from taking the Oaths of Allegiance and Supremacy. Walker's doings were at first received with ridicule and then with indignation. But secure of the King's favour, he continued on his Romanising way. He erected a press at the back of the college, and published, under royal licence, a series of controversial books maintaining Romish doctrines. The University was disgusted and alarmed at this deliberate attempt to undermine the National Church in the very centre of its chief stronghold. A pamphlet war ensued, but it was a war in which the King made it evident on the occasion of a visit to Oxford in 1687 that he was on the side of Obadiah. A statue of the monarch was set up over the gateway of the large quadrangle of University College to commemorate the visit of the royal "reformer of heresy."

At Christ Church, meanwhile, Massey, a convert and creature of Walker, had been appointed dean by the Crown and installed without protest by the Chapter. The old refectory of Canterbury College was fitted up as a private chapel for the dean's use, and James attended mass there. At All Souls', too, the fellows had admitted as warden the nominee planted on them by the royal prerogative. But James was not to have it all his own way with the colleges. Men had stiffer backs at Magdalen.

The office of President was vacant. The King recommended for election Anthony Farmer, a disreputable Cantab of notoriously bad character, who had migrated to Oxford, and who, never having been fellow either of Magdalen or New College, had no qualification for the presidentship. But he was reputed to be inclined to Romanism. This virtue was apparently sufficient in James' eyes; he ignored the objections stated by the fellows. The fellows in turn ignored the mandate of James and elected Dr Hough, a man to whom there could be no objection. Cited to appear before the Ecclesiastical Commission on complaint that they had disregarded the King's mandate, the Vice-President and fellows, through their delegates, justified their action by reference to their statutes and the character of Farmer. Jefferies, who presided, had to admit that Farmer was proved to the court to be "a very bad man." The college was commanded to elect another tool of the King's, Parker, Bishop of Oxford. The college held that the place of President was already filled. To enforce obedience, James now came over from Woodstock (3rd September) in person.

The King wore a scarlet coat, and an old beaver hat edged with a little lace, not worth a groat, as some of the people shouted. He proceeded very slowly to the North Gate, where he found eight poor women all clad in white, some of whom strewed the way before the King with herbs,

"which made a very great smell in all the street, continuing so all the night till the rain came. When he came to Quatervois he was entertained with the wind music or waits belonging to the city and University, who stood over the Penniless Bench—all which time and after the Conduit ran claret for the vulgar."

The fellows of Magdalen were summoned to the royal presence in Christ Church Hall, where they were rudely reprimanded and bidden to go to their chapel and elect the bishop forthwith or they should know what it was to feel the weight of a king's hand. "Is this your Church of England loyalty?" James cried. "Get you gone. I am King. I will be obeyed!" Curious to think that William Penn, who had formerly been sent down from Christ Church for Nonconformity, was present at this scene; and a servitor of Exeter, the father of the Wesleys, quitted it, "resolved to give the tyrant no kind of support." The fellows protested their loyalty, but declared that it was not in their power to do what the King required. Penn, the courtly Quaker, endeavoured to bring about a compromise, but seems to have been convinced at last that an agreement was impossible. Hough's comment on these negotiations was, "It is resolved that the Papists must have our College. All that we can do is, to let the world see that they take it from us, and that we do not give it up." A commission was appointed. Hough, who refused to surrender his lodgings, was declared contumacious, and his name was struck off the books. His lodgings were broken open; Parker was introduced. Twenty-five of the fellows were expelled, and were declared incapable of ecclesiastical preferment. The demies, who refused to recognise Parker, were not interfered with by the commission; they remained in the college holding chapel services and disputations among themselves and ignoring the Papist fellows who were being introduced. When they refused to obey the officers nominated by the King, eighteen of them were expelled. Parker died, and Gifford, a Papist of the Sorbonne, was appointed. All but two of the original fellows were now ejected, and their places were being filled up with Roman Catholics when it was brought home to James that he had been going too fast. He began to bid desperately for the support he had alienated. He restored the ejected fellows, but they had scarcely returned when William's supporters, under Lord Lovelace, entered Oxford in force. They were received at the East Gate by the mayor and magistrates in their black gowns, who went with them up the High Street amid the shouts and congratulations of the people.

Meantime the Master of University had fled to London with his nominee, the Dean of Christ. He was captured by the mob and thrown into the Tower on a charge of high treason. And at Oxford "trade," to use the judicious metaphor of an Oxford priest, "declined." The Jesuits, who had been "in a very hopeful way and had three public shops (chapels) open" there, found all their schemes frustrated. The intrigue and plotting of years were brought to nought.

The Coronation of William and Mary was observed by a special Act ceremony, in which one of the pieces recited was "Magdalena Ridens," Magdalen smiling in triumph at the flight of her oppressor. October 25, 1688, was the day on which James had restored the ejected fellows. Ever since the college has observed that day, and yearly the members pledge each other in a loving-cup, *Jus suum cuique*.

CHAPTER X

JACOBITE OXFORD—AND AFTER

AMONG the demies elected at Magdalen the year after the expelled fellows returned was Joseph Addison, whose name is traditionally connected with the northern part of the Magdalen walks, where the kingfisher "flashes adown the river, a flame of blue," and Henry Sacheverell, his friend and chamber-fellow. The former outlined the pacific policy of the Hanoverians in the Freeholder; for the latter, when he hung out his "bloody flag and banner of defiance" against the existing order, as for Atterbury, Oxford was loud with the cheers of "honest" men. For during the first half of the eighteenth century Oxford was violently Jacobite.

John Locke, who had been suspected of complicity in Shaftesbury's design against the succession, and had been removed (1684) from his student's place at Christ Church in accordance with the directions of a royal mandate, had warned William that the good effects of the revolution would be lost if no care was taken to regulate the Universities. But the Hanoverians avoided oppressive measures. The Tory Wine Club, under the cabalistic name of High Borlace, to which no member of a Whig college like Wadham, Christ Church, Exeter or Merton might belong, was allowed to meet annually at the King's Head Tavern on 18th August to toast the King across the water and drink confusion to the rival Constitution Club. But the triumph of the Whigs at the accession of George I. and the disappointment of "honest" men, led to a great riot on the first anniversary of the birthday of the new sovereign.

"Mobs paraded the streets, shouting for the Pretender and putting a stop to every kind of rejoicing. The Constitution Club had gathered to commemorate the day at the King's Head. The windows were illuminated and preparations made for a bonfire. Tossing up their caps and scattering money among the rabble that flocked to the front of the hotel, the Jacobite gownsmen egged them on with shouts of 'No George,' 'James for ever,' 'Ormond,' or 'Bolingbroke!' The faggots were torn to pieces, showers of brickbats were thrown into the clubroom. The Constitutioners were glad to escape with their lives by a back-door. Thus baffled the mob rolled on to attack all illuminated houses. Every Whig window was smashed. The meeting house was entered and gutted.... At last the mob dispersed for the night, publicly giving out that 'the glorious work' was left unfinished till to-morrow. The twenty-ninth of May was associated with too significant reminiscences to be allowed to pass in quiet. Sunday though it was, the streets were filled with people running up and down with oak-boughs in their hats, shouting, 'King James, the true King. No usurper! The Good Duke of Ormond.' The streets were brilliantly illuminated, and wherever disregard was shown to the mob's fiat, the windows were broken.... The crowds grew thicker and noisier towards even. A rumour had got abroad that Oriel had given shelter to some of the Constitutionalists. The mob rushed to the attack and threatened to break open the closely-barred gates. At this moment a shot from a window wounded one of the ringleaders, a gownsman of Brasenose, and the crowd fled in confusion to break fresh windows, gut the houses of dissenters, and pull down the chapels of Anabaptists and Quakers" (Green).

The omission of rejoicings on the birthday of the Prince of Wales led to further disturbance. The major of a recruiting party then in Oxford drew out his regiment to celebrate the day. They were attacked by the crowd, and were obliged to have resource to blank cartridges. The matter was made the occasion of a grand debate in the House of Lords. But in the meantime the Government had shown its appreciation of the dangerous disloyalty of Oxford by dispatching Major-General Pepper thither with a number of dragoons, on the outbreak of Mar's Rebellion. Martial law was at once proclaimed, and suitable measures were taken "to overawe the University." The Crown had recently purchased Bishop Moore's magnificent library and presented it to Cambridge. The difference in the treatment of the two Universities inspired Dr Trapp, the first Professor of Poetry, to write the famous epigram:

"The King, observing with judicious eyes
The wants of his two Universities,
To Oxford sent a troop of horse; and why?
That learned body wanted loyalty.
To Cambridge books he sent, as well discerning
How much that loyal body wanted learning."

To which the Cambridge wit, Sir Thomas Browne, retorted with still greater neatness and point:

"The King to Oxford sent a troop of horse
For Tories own no argument but force;
With equal care to Cambridge books he sent,
For Whigs admit no force but argument."

The famous county election of 1754, when the Jacobite rioters held the approach to Broad Street, but the Whigs managed to slip through Exeter College and so gain the polling booths, shows that Oxford had not changed its sentiments, but when Tory principles mounted the throne with George III., Jacobitism disappeared like a dream. The reign of Toryism did little to promote the cause of learning or conduct. During the eighteenth century examinations for a degree were little better than a farce;

"E'en Balaam's ass
If he could pay the fee, would pass,"

sang the poet. Lecturers ceased to lecture; Readers did not read. In many colleges scholars succeeded to fellowships almost as a matter of course, and tutors were as slow to enforce, as "Gentlemen Commoners" would have been swift to resent, any study or discipline as part of the education of a Beau or Buck. Though Oriel produced Bishop Butler, for Oxford was still the home of genius as well as of abuses, the observance of religion dwindled down to a roll-call. And corrupt resignations of fellowships, by which the resigning fellow nominated his successor, in return for a fee, were paralleled in the city by wholesale corruption at elections. The mayor and aldermen in 1768 even had the effrontery to propose to re-elect their representatives in Parliament for £7500, the amount of the municipal debt! This bargain, in spite of a reprimand from the Speaker and a committal to Newgate for five days, they succeeded in striking with the Duke of Marlborough and Lord Abingdon.

For the rest, it was the age of periwigs and patches, of coffee-houses and ale, of wine and common rooms, of pipes and newsletters, of a University aping the manners of London and Bath in Merton College Gardens or the race-course of Woodstock.

Bucks and Bloods were succeeded by the Smarts, whose beautiful existences Terræ Filius has described for us. Called by the servitor at six, they tumbled out of bed, their heads reeling with the last night's debauch, to attend a chapel service. For the habit of early rising was still in vogue, and though a Smart might rise late, his lateness seems early to us. For it was held disgraceful to be in bed after seven, though carried there over-night drunk but not disgraced. But the Smart's breakfast was scarce over by ten; a few notes on the flute, a glance at the last French comedy, and in academic undress he is strolling to Lyne's coffee-house. There he indites a stanza or a billet-doux to the reigning Sylvia of the town; then saunters for a turn in the park or under Merton wall, while the dull regulars, as Amherst has it, are at dinner in hall according to statute. Dinner in his rooms and an hour devoted to the elaborate business of dress, and the Smart is ready to sally forth in silk-lined coat with laced ruffles at breast and wrist, red stockings and red-topped Spanish leather shoes, and laced hat or square cap most rakishly cocked. So emerging from his rooms, with tripping gait and jaunty dangle of his clouded amber-headed cane, he is about to pay a visit to the coffee-house or parade before the windows of a Toast when he stops to jeer at some ragged servitor of Pembroke, a Samuel Johnson perhaps, going round shamefacedly in worn-out shoes to obtain second-hand the lectures of a famous Christ Church tutor, or a George Whitefield, wrestling with the devil in Christ Church walks, or hesitating to join the little band of Methodists who, with Charles and John Wesley of Christ Church and

Lincoln at their head, are making their way through a mocking crowd to receive the Sacrament at S. Aldate's, S. George's in the Castle or S. Mary's.

But the Smart cares for none of these things. Sublimely confident in his own superiority he passes on; drinks a dram of citron at Hamilton's, and saunters off at last to chapel to show how genteelly he dresses and how well he can chaunt. Next he takes a dish of tea with some fair charmer, with whom he discusses, with an infinite nicety of phrase, whether any wears finer lace or handsomer tie-wigs than Jack Flutter, cuts a bolder bosh than Tom Paroquet, or plays ombre better than Valentine Frippery. Thereafter he escorts her to Magdalen walks, to Merton or Paradise gardens; sups and ends the night, loud in song, deep in puns, put or cards, at the Mitre. Whence, having toasted his mistress in the spiced cup with the brown toast bobbing in it, he staggers home to his college, "a toper all night as he trifles all day."

Meantime certain improvements were taking place in the city. Under the Commissioners Act (1771) the streets were widened and paved, and most of the walls and gates removed—Bocardo along with them. Turnpike Roads and the Enclosures Acts led to the disappearance of the highwaymen, by whom coaches, ere railways took the place of the "flying coach," which first went to London in one day "with A. W. in the same coach" (1669), had so frequently been held up near Oxford. Curiously enough highwaymen were most popular with the fair sex, and the cowardly ruffians occasionally returned the compliment so far as to allow them to ransom their jewels with a kiss. Dumas, the prince of highwaymen, after capturing a coachful of ladies, was satisfied with dancing a coranto with each in turn upon the green. He was executed at Oxford. He had maintained his nonchalance to the end; played "Macheath" in the prison, and threw himself off at the gallows without troubling the hangman. It was not death, he declared, but being anatomised that he feared. And, lest their hero should be put to so useful a purpose, a large body of bargemen surrounded the scaffold, carried off the body in triumph to the parish church and buried it in lime forthwith.

At length, after the Age of Reason and Materialism, came the Age of Revival and Romance. The spirit of mediævalism summoned up by Sir Walter, was typified in Oxford architecture by Sir Gilbert Scott and Pugin. In the University the beginning of a new order of things, which was to end in throwing open the Universities to the whole Empire and rendering them on every side efficient places of education, was begun in 1800 by the system of Honours Lists, long advocated by reformers like John Eveleigh of Oriel and brought into being by the energy of Cyril Jackson, Dean of Christ Church, and Parsons, Master of Balliol. The work of nationalising the Universities was developed by the two University Commissions and by that "Extension" movement, of which the pioneer was William Sewell, a remarkable tutor of Exeter, who, in 1850, urged that "It may be impossible to bring the masses to the University, but may it not be possible to carry the University to the masses?" This development of the University, which must ever be closely connected with the name of Dr Jowett, Master of Balliol, and has received a further significance from the last testament of Cecil Rhodes, of Oriel, is illustrated on every side by new buildings; by the Indian Institute, the Nonconformist colleges, Mansfield and Manchester, the Women's Halls, the Science Buildings and the new foundation of Hertford College, grafted on that of old Hart Hall and Magdalen Hall by Mr Baring. Intellectually the spirit of revolt produced by the French Revolution at the beginning of this period, is illustrated by the careers of Shelley and Landor, and the musical lyrics of Swinburne; the deep questionings prompted by the Tractarian Movement are voiced in the poems of Clough, Keble and Arnold. For in the first half of the nineteenth century there was a revival of spirituality, and men followed the lead, not of a Wycliffe, an Erasmus or a Wesley, but of Keble, Pusey and Newman. Oriel College, whose fellowships were confined neither to members of the college nor, in most cases, to candidates from certain places, was the centre whence men like Hurrell Froude, Keble's pupil, preached their doctrine of reaction; men who, finding the Church of England in a very parlous state, counselled a return to what was best in mediævalism, and, protesting against the Protestantism of the English Church, taught Newman to look with admiration towards the Church of Rome. The name of Keble and the impulse which he gave to Anglicanism are commemorated in Keble College; the prominence of the chapel, which contains Holman Hunt's "Light of the World," and the arrangement of the buildings emphasise the fact that it was founded to provide the poorer members of the Church of England with higher education on Church lines.

The revival of mediævalism in Religion was echoed by a revival of mediævalism in Art. John Ruskin, who had matriculated at Christ Church in 1836, lectured intermittently as Slade Professor of Art from 1870 till 1884. William Morris, "poet, artist, paper-hanger and socialist," came up to Exeter in 1853 and there, in intimate friendship with Sir Edward Burne-Jones, looked out upon "the vision of grey-roofed houses and a long winding street and the sound of many bells," which was, for him, Oxford. The two friends have left behind them signs of their genius in the famous tapestry at Exeter Chapel and in the windows of the Cathedral; whilst at Corpus and in the Schools the great teacher gathered round him a circle of enthusiastic young men, and like an Abelard, Wycliffe, Wesley or Newman in the religious world, so advised and inspired them with his social and artistic gospel, that when, in pursuance of the old monastic principle "laborare est orare," he called upon them to mend a farmer's road at Hincksey, they laid aside their bats and oars, and marched, with the professor at their head, to dig with spade and shovel. Out of such inspiration grew the various University Settlements in the East End of London, inaugurated by Arnold Toynbee.

Oxford owes much to the stimulating if incoherent teaching and the generosity of John Ruskin, [40] but architecturally his influence was responsible for several bad buildings in the would-be Venetian style—the Christ Church New Buildings and the Natural History Museum in the parks, for instance, proving deplorably enough that the critic was no creator.

Last, but not least, it is good to be able to record that City and University have gradually settled their differences. The new Municipal Buildings and the Town Hall in S. Aldate's would seem, by their deliberate variety of styles, to give municipal sanction to every style of architecture that can be found in the University, and to look back upon the history of the town, and of the learned institution with which for good and evil it has been so closely connected, with no ungracious feeling.

FOOTNOTES:

[1] *Cornhill Magazine.*

[2] Pie-Powder Court—a Summary Court of Justice held at fairs, when the suitors were usually country clowns with dusty feet—(*pied poudré*).

[3] The earliest mention of Oxford occurs in the Anglo-Saxon Chronicle under the year 912. It is there spelt Oxnaforda and Oxanforda, and in Domesday Book it is spelt Oxeneford. Coins from Eadward's day onwards show that Ox at least was regarded as an essential element in the word, and it is most easy to assume that the place was called after the Ford of the Oxen in the river here. But the easiest explanation is seldom the best. And a rival theory explains the name as a corruption of Ouse-ford, or Ousen-ford, *i.e.*, the Ford over the River. For the evidence is strongly in favour of the probability that the name Ouse was at one time applied to the Thames, which indeed has one of the dialectic forms of the word Ouse retained in it, viz. Tam-*ese*, though the theory that the junction of the Isis or Ouse and Thame made Tamisis = Thames, is fanciful. The other form of the word is retained in the Oseneye of Osney Abbey, and a tributary stream retains the hardened form Ock. Therefore Ousen-ford or Oxen-ford may mean the River-ford. There is no certainty in these matters, but the latter derivation commends itself

most. [See Parker's "Early Oxford" (O.H.S.), to which I have been frequently indebted in the first part of this chapter.]

[4] The manor took its name from a well that lay to the north side of the Church of S. Cross. The manor-house, itself (near the racquet courts) was recently used as a public-house, called the Cock-pit, because there was a pit where the citizens of Oxford fought their mains. It was afterwards converted into a Penitentiary, a home for fallen women. Traces of the Holy Well have recently been discovered beneath the new chapel.

[5] The wall is clearly traceable between 57 and 58 High Street. The passage by No. 57 is a piece of the old Royal Way under the walls. This way can be traced in King's Street from its western edge to the gardens of the small houses facing the New Examination Schools. It occurs again in Ship Street, from Jesus College stables to the rear of the houses facing them, and again between the Divinity School and the west front of the Theatre. (See Hurst, "Topography.")

[6] The crypt, which had been beneath the apse of the chapel, was afterwards replaced approximately in its position, north-east of the tower. The capitals of the four dwarf pillars which support the groining are interesting, and should be compared and contrasted with those in S. Peter's in the East.

[7] The original crypt is preserved and a Norman arcade, east of the north aisle.

[8] Aldrich was a man of remarkable and versatile talents. The author of admirable hand-books on logic, heraldry and architecture, he was equally skilled in chemistry and theology. In music he earned both popularity and the admiration of musicians by his catches, services and anthems; and as an architect he has left his mark on Oxford, in Peckwater Quadrangle (Ch. Ch.) and All Saint's Church. As a man of sense he loved his pipe, and wrote an amusing catch to tobacco; as a wit he gave five good reasons for not abstaining from wine:

"A	friend,	good	wine,	because	you're	dry
Because	you	may	be,	by	and	bye;—

Or any other reason why."

It was under Aldrich that the Battle of the Books arose, the great literary controversy, which began with the immature work of a Christ Church student and ended with the masterpieces of Swift and Bentley.

[9] It was probably built for him. Some of the original Tudor work remains, but the greater part of the visible portions are rough Jacobean imitation, of the year 1628.

[10] During the restoration of the Cathedral in 1856 a remarkable crypt was discovered beneath the paving of the choir. It was but seven feet long by five and a half, and contained lockers at each end. It has been most reasonably supposed that this was a secret chamber, where the University Chest was deposited. This crypt, situated between the north and south piers of the tower, was covered up after investigation. The site of it recalls the time when charitable people were founding "chests" to help the education of the poor. Grossetete in 1240 issued an ordinance regulating S. Frideswide's Chest, which received the fines paid by the citizens. From this and other charitable funds loans might be made to poor scholars on security of books and so forth, no interest being charged. Charity thus entered into competition with the usury of the Jews, who had to be restrained by law from charging *over 43 per cent.* on loans to scholars (1244).

[11] The Vintnery, the quarter of taverns and wine cellars, which was at the north end of S. Aldate's, flourished mightily. The students, for all their lust of knowledge, were ever good samplers of what Rabelais calls the holy water of the cellar. You might deduce that from the magnificent cellars of the Mitre Inn or Bulkley Hall (corner of S. Edward's Street) and above all from those of the old Vintnery. For the houses north of the Town Hall have some splendid cellars, which connect with another under the street, and so with others under the first house on the west side of S. Aldgate's, the famous old Swindlestock (Siren or Mermaid Inn). These are good specimens of early fifteenth century vaults. It is supposed that when these cellars were

dug, the earth was thrown out into the street and there remained in the usual mediæval way. This, it is maintained, accounts for the hill at Carfax. Certainly the earliest roadway at Carfax is traceable at the unexpected depth of eleven feet seven inches below the present high road, which is some three and a half feet below what it should be according to the average one foot per hundred years observed by most mediæval towns as their rate of deposit.

[12] Wycliffe, we know, appeared before Parliament, and there is a writ of Edward I. requiring the Chancellor to send "quattuor vel quinque de discretioribus et in jure scripto magis expertes Universitatis" to Parliament.

[13] "Universitas est plurium corporum collectio inter se distantium uno nomine specialiter eis deputata" is the well-known definition of Hugolinus. The term "studium generale" or "studium universale" came into use, so far as documents are any guide, in the middle of the thirteenth century (Denifle). Earlier, and more usually however, the word "studium" was used to describe a place where a collection of schools had been established. The epithet "generale" was used, apparently, to distinguish the merely local schools of Charlemagne from those where foreign students were permitted and even encouraged to come, as they were, for instance, at Naples by Frederick II. So that a University or seat of General study was a place whither students came from every quarter for every kind of knowledge.

[14] This term faculty, which originally signified the capacity (facultas) to teach a particular subject, came to be applied technically to the subject itself or to the authorised teachers of it viewed collectively. A University might include one or all of the "Faculties" of Theology, Law, Medicine and the Liberal Arts, although naturally enough each of the chief Universities had its own particular department of excellence. A complete course of instruction in the seven liberal arts, enumerated in the old line "Lingua, tropus, ratio, numerus, tonus, angulus, astra," was intended as a preparation for the study of theology—the main business of Oxford as of Paris University. The Arts were divided into two parts, the first including the three easier or "trivial" subjects—Grammar, Rhetoric and Logic; the second the remaining four—Arithmetic, Geometry, Music and Astronomy.

[15] The example of William of Durham as the first Englishman to bequeath funds to enable the secular clergy to study theology was soon followed by others. William Hoyland, one of the Bedels of the University, left his estate to the University, and (1255) Walter Gray, Archbishop of York, also bequeathed his property to it.

[16] A portrait of Dr Radcliffe, by Sir Godfrey Kneller, hangs over the doorway. The building was used at first to house works on Natural History, Physical Science and Medicine, for it was Radcliffe's object to encourage these studies. The Library was therefore known as the Physic Library. This has been removed to the University Museum, and the Camera, or "the Radcliffe" as it is familiarly called, is now used as a reading-room in connection with the Bodleian. It is open for the use of students daily from ten to ten. Visitors to Oxford are recommended to climb to the roof and obtain the magnificent panoramic view of the city and neighbourhood which it commands.

[17] Worcester Street—Stockwell Street (Stoke-Well, the Well which afterwards rejoiced in the name of Plato's, as opposed to Aristotle's Well, half a mile off). East of the Well was the rough land known till quite recently as Broken Hayes.

[18] It was enacted (1302) that the Regents in two Faculties, with a majority of the Non-Regents, should have the power to make a permanent statute binding on the whole University. This system was calculated to drown the friars. It was confirmed by the arbitrators (1313), who ordered, however, that the majority should consist of three Faculties instead of two, of which the Faculty of Arts must be one.

[19] Founded in 1361 by Simon Islip, Archbishop of Canterbury, to be a nursery for "that famous College of Christ Church in Canterbury." The Doric Gateway—Canterbury Gate—which leads from Merton Street into the Canterbury Quad. of Christ Church, in which Mr Gladstone once had rooms, recalls the name of this Benedictine foundation. The old buildings were removed in 1770; the present gateway was designed by Wyatt, chiefly at the expense of Dr Robinson, Archbishop of Armagh.

[20] "Wycliffe, and movements for Reform." Poole.

[21] Called after the "famous postern gate" (Twirl-gate), pulled down in 1722.

[22] Pennilesse Bench. This was a row of stalls and seats erected outside the church for the convenience of the market folk. A church, in mediæval days, was always the centre of commerce; stalls and even dwellings were frequently built on to the outside walls of a famous fane. Visitors to Nuremberg will remember the Bratwurstglöcklein there. ("Story of Nuremberg," p. 198.)

[23] Vid. *Quarterly Review*, Jan. 1892.

[24] Two M.A.'s who were taking part in the final exercise for their degree were chosen, one by each proctor, to make a Latin speech, one on the Saturday of the Act, the other on the Monday. These speeches were supposed to be humorous and were more often merely exhibitions of scurrilous buffoonery.

[25] See Professor Case's admirable "Enquiry concerning the Pinnacled Steeple of the University Church."

[26] The present ones (1895) are a compromise, and repeat the fault.

[27] "When that is done," Hearne adds, "they knock at all the Middle Chambers where most of the Seniors lodge, of whom they demand crowns apiece, which is readily given, then they go with twenty or thirty torches upon the leads of the College, where they sing their song as

before. This ended they go into their Common Rooms and make themselves merry with what wine every one has a mind to."

According to tradition, a mallard was found in a drain when the foundations of the college were laid, and Prof. Burrows has ingeniously explained the origin of this tradition as arising from the discovery of a seal with the impression of a griffin, *Malardi Clerici*, when a drain was being dug.

[28] Old Dr Kettell of Trinity used to carry a pair of scissors in his muff, and snip off the long locks of his scholars with these, or with a bread knife on the buttery hatch.

[29] His pastoral staff of silver gilt, adorned with fine enamels, survives, and is carried before the Bishop of Winchester whenever he comes to visit the college. A good portrait of the founder hangs in the warden's lodgings.

[30] This is the old name (cattorum vicus) of the street which has now been made over to S. Catherine. A similar instance of the "genteel" tendency to eschew monosyllables and not to call things by their proper names is afforded by the attempts to call Hell Passage, S. Helen's. This is not due to a love of Saints, but to the "refinement" of the middle classes, who prefer white sugar to brown. In the Middle Ages men called a spade a spade. The names of the old streets in London or Paris would set a modern reader's hair on end. But they described the streets. At Oxford the Quakers (1654) first settled in New Inn Hall Street, but it was then known as the Lane of the Seven Deadly Sins.

[31] It was after this patroness of learning that Lady Margaret's Hall was called. It was founded at the same time as Somerville Hall (opened 1879, Woodstock Road) as a seminary for the higher education of women. Lady Margaret's Hall and S. Hugh's Hall are in Norham Gardens. The latter, like S. Hilda's (the other side of Magdalen Bridge), is also for female

students, who have been granted the privilege of attending University lectures and of being examined by the University examiners.

[32] *Cf.* "Magdalen College." H. A. Wilson.

[33] Among the accounts of the Vice-Chancellor is found the following item: "In wine & marmalade at the great disputations Xd." & again, "In wine to the Doctors of Cambridge 11s."

[34] In 1875 stakes and ashes, however, were found also immediately opposite the tower gateway of Balliol, and this spot was marked in the eighteenth century as the site of the martyrdom. Another view is that the site was, as indicated by Wood, rather on the brink of the ditch, near the Bishop's Bastion, behind the houses south of Broad Street. There were possibly two sites. I do not think that there is anything to show that Latimer and Ridley were burned on exactly the same spot as Cranmer. If Cranmer died opposite the college gateway, the site marked, but more probably the third suggested site, near the Bishop's Bastion, may be that where Ridley and Latimer perished.

[35] The door of the Bishops' Hole is preserved in S. Mary Magdalen Church.

[36] Most of the pictures and works of art have been transferred to the University Galleries, opposite the Randolph Hotel (Beaumont Street); the natural science collections, including the great anthropological collection of General Pitt Rivers, to the Science Museum in the parks (1860).

[37] "The crown piece struck at Oxford in 1642 has on the reverse, RELIG. PROT. LEG. ANG. or ANG. LIBER. PAR, in conformity with Charles' declaration that he would 'preserve the Protestant religion, the known laws of the land, and the just privileges and freedom of

Parliament.' But the coin peculiarly called the Oxford crown, beautifully executed by Rawlins in 1644, has underneath the King's horse a view of Oxford" (Boase).

[38] On this occasion Lady Castlemaine lodged in the rooms of Dr Gardiner, who built the fountain afterwards known as Mercury in Tom Quad, from the statue set up there by Dr Radcliffe.

[39] Terræ Filius, 1733.

[40] See the Ruskin Art School in the Art Museum with the collection of Turner's drawings and water colours.

Printed in Great Britain
by Amazon

27982639R00123